THE AWAKENING OF REGGIE

Dr. Felton Earls
BTW Classmate and
life long friend.
Ernest Jones

Seaburn
New York

Seaburn Publishing Group
P.O. Box 2085
Long Island City NY 11102
www.seaburnbooks.com

Jones, E.
The Awakening of Reggie
p. cm.
ISBN: 1-59232-383-9 Paperback
STM1203H13 2012
912'.24_NY12 12-11933
CIP
Printed in the United States of America
10 9 8 7 6 5 4 3 2 1

THE AWAKENING OF REGGIE

Ernest Jones

ACKNOWLEDGEMENT

As I reflect on the journey to completing this novel, I am reminded of the good Samaritans that extended a hand along the way. They expanded the knowledge I needed to tell the story; guided my path as I told the story and encouraged me at moments of need. A world of thanks to Aldore Collier, Lawrence Oliver, Jr, Esq., and my very large loving biological and extended families.

A FLASH OF LIGHTNING, CHASED BY ROARING thunder, invaded the dark, silent room which was only lit by the two-thirty glaring from the digital clock resting on the night stand. Reggie Morton sprang up in the bed, wiped his eyes and placed his hand over his racing heart. He was in a daze for a moment struggling to grasp reality, then realized the thunder had brought him out of that dream that kept coming back haunting him. It was his graduation day from college and he was standing in line ready to cross the stage to receive his degree. He looked out over the auditorium, filled with white faces, searching for his mother. When the professor called his name and he started toward the podium, the professor and what sounded like everyone in the auditorium broke out in loud laughter. He spotted his mother. Her face was buried in a handkerchief. Reggie shook his head in frustration, wondering what it all meant and why the dream always ended before he found out why everyone was laughing. Maybe I should go to a fortune-teller and have her analyze it but wouldn't that be typical of some ignorant, superstitious Black person, he concluded.

He looked at the clock, disappointed that he had not slept longer, and then turned on his side leaving the glare of the clock behind him. As he listened to the sound of rain pelting the window, he pulled the sheet up over his shoulders and began to let go thoughts of the dream and focus on the present. Tomorrow, he declared, would be the beginning of a new phase in his life and he wanted to get off to a good start. He especially wanted to feel rested and fresh. God forbid the weather should delay the flight and hopefully those demonstrators down at Grant Park-members of the National Mobilization Committee to End the War in Viet Nam and the Youth International Party-would not obstruct traffic. Their clashes with the nervous Chicago police had resulted in riots. As a result, there was no telling what impact continuing conflict would have on the flow of traffic. Maybe the rain would have cooled things down and maybe the delegates to this raucous Democratic convention had resolved their differences about whom to nominate for president- Eugene McCarthy, seen as the anti-war candidate or Vice President Hubert Humphrey, seen as continuing President Lyndon Johnson's war policies. Reggie pondered.

If the nominee turned out to be Humphrey, he would probably carry on Johnson's liberal civil rights policies, Reggie concluded. However, he wondered, since the country seemed to have grown weary of civil rights struggles and had become obsessed with the war during this presidential campaign. Reggie's most prominent thought about the war was that you could always be certain the first words out of CBS news anchor Walter Cronkite's mouth during the evening news would be what was going on in View Nam and how many American soldiers died that day. Many of Reggie's friends of draft age were graduates of Ivy League schools and worked as tutor/counselors in a job training center. They found ways to describe their work to meet the government's definition of teachers and applied for and received the deferment that draft boards awarded to teachers and students. The strategy had also worked for Reggie who had had some part time experience managing training programs for entry level employees on his job. One of Reggie's white friend's draft board didn't buy the strategy, so he decided to move to Canada to avoid the draft. There were two Black guys Reggie heard about who also lost their deferment and were drafted. One went to Viet Nam and was wounded in a fire fight with the Viet Cong. He didn't know what happened to the other one.

Reggie remembered Dr. Martin Luther King coming out against the war. In the middle of a vigorous civil right movement, he wasn't sure that was the right move. However, he had great admiration for Dr. King. He motivated both Black and white people to support the movement and the white people around Reggie had nothing but praise for him. His leadership had resulted in the passage of Title VII of the Civil Rights Act of 1964 outlawing discrimination in employment and Title VIII of the Civil Rights Act of 1968 outlawing discrimination in housing, both of which, to Reggie's surprise, President Johnson, the Texan, pushed through Congress.

Reggie shared the shock and outrage throughout the world about Dr. King's assassination. He couldn't imagine anyone on the horizon who would be able to bring together Black and white people to support civil rights for Blacks and other minorities. He openly expressed his feelings with his white friends because they were outspoken about their outrage. However, he was more restrained, in the company of those same friends, in speaking about how awed he was about the work of the very boisterous, grass roots worker Fannie Lou Hamer whose leadership resulted in the seating of the Black Mississippi Freedom Democratic Party at the convention in spite of opposition from the white democratic delegation. It was hard for him to believe her efforts could ever succeed in a fight with a state like Mississippi, the poster state for segregation. It was commonly believed her success was probably one of the factors that turned the entire South into Republican territory. Reggie often felt he should be an active participant in some demonstration promoting civil rights; however, his circle of white friends and associates were not people interested in demonstrating in the streets, so there was no immediate pressure surrounding him to ride his conscience. Also, he wasn't sure what impact such actions would have on his career. He didn't want to be mistaken as a member of the militant Black Panther Party or a cousin of Fannie Lou Hamer.

Reggie decided, at this hour, it was not likely he would recapture the sleep he had been chasing; however, he kept his eyes closed just in case it crept upon him. He turned on his side and rested his head on his hands. His mind began to wander. He was both excited and apprehensive about moving to New York. The job in advertising was fulfilling a goal he had harbored for some time. He remembered how excited he was the day he got the call from the always fashionably dressed Mr. Johnson, president of the Jacob Johnson Employment Agency, the most prominent Black employment agency in the country. They had met at Reggie's company's Christmas party the previous year, when he asked Reggie to send him a resume. He called Reggie two months later and told him he was an ideal candidate for a management position with Benton, Barnes and Fowler advertising agency in New York. He said they were seriously looking for minorities to head-off mounting pressure from some groups about the scarcity of minorities in advertising. Mr. Johnson assured Reggie that his experience as a summer intern in advertising when he was in college made him a shoo-in. A week later, Mr. Johnson called Reggie and asked if he could go to New York for an interview. Reggie was stunned and happy. Now he was on the verge of getting a job in the industry he had bragged so enthusiastically about to his family and friends back home in Smoky Mountain when he was a management intern during the summers while at Davis University. He felt this was an opportunity to redeem himself after he was not offered a position at that agency after graduation.

Reggie's feeling of euphoria was briefly interrupted by thoughts of leaving his Chicago family. His best friend from college, Harry Dubinski's mother, Mrs. Sanders, who was married to a light- skin Black man, had gotten Reggie his first job out of college as an entry- level manager in a company that was once owned by her parents. The family had been a great source of support and had counseled Reggie to be patient when he was passed over for a promotion three times during the last four years. As much as he wanted to appease them, he could not reconcile how fast the time had come for those who got the promotions each time he felt it was his turn. He was going to miss them, but declared it was time to move on, especially since he was recruited for the job in New York. Maybe, he thought, fate was moving in his direction. However, he felt some apprehension thinking the only people he knew in New York were his new boss, Mr. Walsh and Susan, the real estate agent who worked with him in finding an apartment. It seemed at that moment out of nowhere the advice the preacher gave to his class at their high school baccalaureate ceremony came to mind- "If you can take it, you can make it." And Lord knows, Reggie declared, I have taken plenty and have the scars to show for it all and I'm still on my feet and climbing tall. New York is a testament to that. I guess the old preacher was truly a man of wisdom, he concluded as his apprehensions began to dissipate.

Thoughts of New York also brought some feelings of sadness. That is the place where the love of his life was stolen from him. He decided, at his first opportunity, he would walk the grounds of Barnard College where she fell prey to some ego- maniac looking to add another notch to his roster of sexual conquests. Reggie wanted to envision how it could have happened, even though he felt certain his feelings for her were securely in his past. But the search for love still churned in him. Maybe, he thought, New York with its eight million people, would present him with the one who would march down the aisle, say "I do" and commit herself to him for eternity. He could imagine returning to his high school class reunion and informing everyone that he was an account executive at Benton, Barnes and Flower advertising agency and then introduce everyone to his beautiful blond wife. He wondered if they would give him the title of "Most Successful," especially when they met his wife.

Sunlight began to creep through the blinds. Reggie turned toward the clock. It read 5:45. His flight was not until nine. He lay back in the bed. There was no longer the sound of rain pelting against his window, a good sign, he decided. His bags had been packed and the apartment cleared of the second- hand furniture and the makeshift bookcase/entertainment stand made of milk crates, bricks and boards. He had arranged with the superintendent to get rid of everything that had not been discarded.

Reggie decided to get up and start preparing to leave. He thought he might as well get a head start in case his taxi ran into bad traffic conditions resulting from morning congestion or more demonstrations. He could have some breakfast at the airport or on the plane. He rolled out of bed and headed to the small bathroom with the dark green shower curtains that were there when he moved in and a medicine cabinet with a door that could not close completely. He had shaved the night before using Magic Shave which had the smell of rotten eggs, but it did a great job of giving him a clean shave without creating in-grown hairs that caused bumps in the skin. Using it was always a solitary experience because you didn't want anyone to think you had exploded with gas. He showered and dressed in a pair of Khaki bell bottom pants, a white short sleeve shirt and a blue blazer-appropriate dress for flying, he decided.

Before leaving the apartment, he needed to make one call. He checked to see if the phone had already been disconnected. It had not. He dialed the number and Mrs. Sanders picked up. She had arranged a farewell dinner the night before. All of his mentors and friends were there – his buddy Harry and his wife, Dr. and Mrs. Hunt, Mr. Sanders. Consuela, the Sanders' maid, had prepared the dinner of Cornish Hens stuffed with fruit, wild rice, asparagus and a green salad-the kind of food Reggie had gotten used to. He again thanked Mrs. Sanders for the dinner and all her help, support and counseling and asked her to express his thanks to the Hunts who were responsible for getting him the summer intern job. He and Harry had been best friend since college. He remembered when he went off to Davis University which had just been forced to desegregate. He had a lot of doubts about his ability to develop relationships with white people although he was anxious for the opportunity. His relationship with Harry, the Sanders and Hunts had erased many of those doubts.

Mrs. Sanders said she looked forward to hearing from him and to his next trip to visit them. Reggie told her she could count on him keeping in touch.

Reggie went searching all the corners and closets to see if he had overlooked something. He then stood in the middle of the living room thinking this was his first home away from home. It was where he really began to realize what it was like to be independent. There had been nobody to check to see if he cleaned up after dinner or what he had for dinner and most of all he had to pay those monthly bills or suffer the consequences. He felt he would always have some fond memory of this place. He walked out of the apartment onto the street where the taxi he had called was waiting.

As the taxi headed for the airport, Reggie sat back in his seat, crossing then uncrossing his legs and shifting his hips searching for the most comfortable position. He folded his arms and glanced at the husky, bearded taxi driver with one hand on the steering wheel and the other flipping a cigarette out the window, seemingly unperturbed by the congested traffic ahead. Reggie exhaled and finally slumped downed in his seat and began to take note of the tall buildings, attached houses and congested streets that had been his Chicago home for four years-his first adventure living up north.

"Sir, you did say American Airlines didn't you?" the driver asked.

"Yes, it's a nine o'clock flight."

"Well, don't worry I'll get you there. We have plenty time."

"Sure, sure," Reggie said. As he leaned back in his seat a surge of doubts that seemed to always be lurking in the back of his mind no matter how rosy things seems, pushed forward. He remembered when he was an intern; the only other Afro-American in the agency told him that you really had to be careful in the advertising industry because there could be sinister motives behind a smile. He didn't think that turned out to be true. However, he wondered, if in an environment as competitive as New York could that be true and if it were, how long it would take him to be able to discern the difference.

Reggie stepped out of the taxi, reached for his latest designer Samsonite luggage, handed the taxi driver a ten dollar bill and said, "keep the change," then strolled up to the check-in counter.

"Good morning, sir. Do you have bags to check?" Reggie proudly presented his luggage. "Your flight to LaGuardia will leave from Gate 24 and will begin boarding at eight -thirty." The attendant looked up at him with a broad smile and said, "Have a safe trip and enjoy your visit to New York."

Reggie returned the smile and said proudly. "It's not a visit. I'm moving there."

"Well, I look forward to your next visit to Chicago," the attendant said.

Feeling relaxed, Reggie marched toward Gate 24. The waiting area was filled with a large group of chatting people who seemed to be heading for a pleasure trip to the Big Apple. Reggie found a seat next to a woman that was reading a book. Although her solitude was the initial attraction, he continued to glance at her out of the side of his eyes. He could tell she was blond, beautiful breast, nice legs. He didn't want to be caught staring, but Lord knows he wanted to. She seemed to be engrossed in the book and made no attempt to acknowledge him. Beads of sweat began to discharge in his armpits while a feeling of restlessness rumbled in his crotch. His mouth went dry and his mind flashed to Mona, his high school sweetheart who betrayed his love and married the white guy who got her pregnant while she was a freshman to Barnard; and Betty, the beautiful blue- eyed blond who abandoned him for a boy of her own race while Reggie was in college. He dropped his head in a moment of self-pity and took a deep breath trying to wish away the restlessness in his crotch. He raised his head and tilted it slightly to bring the beautiful blond into clear view. The pace of his heartbeat began to increase and a feeling of anxiety traveled through his body. The sound of a heated conversation spreading across the waiting area distracted him. A young Black man who looked to be in his twenties, sporting a head full of bushy hair, was pointing a finger in the face of a Black man obviously at least twice his age.

"There is no such thing as the right time. The time is now. Should we wait another hundred years? That's what I always said, once an Uncle Tom, always an Uncle Tom," the young man said while looking away from the old man.

"You brats have a lot to learn from us old folks. You are too quick to condemn without understanding what it took to get you to the point where we could have such a conversation," the older man said. The young man threw up both hands and stood up facing away from the old man. The dialogue made Reggie a bit uncomfortable. Whenever he heard the term, Uncle Tom, he wondered if people were looking at him. He swallowed, took a deep breath and looked across the waiting area trying to focus away from the two men.

"Flight 240 to LaGuardia is now boarding," the voice over the address system announced. Reggie wondered how long this beautiful "chick" was going to be in New York.

"Good morning sir," the stewardess said as Reggie entered the cabin. "Seat number 12C is straight ahead on your right."

"Thanks you," Reggie said with a grin covering his face. As he placed his bag in the overhead compartment just above his aisle seat, a voice from behind said "excuse me, I'm in seat 'B'." Reggie's heart missed a beat. He couldn't believe he had been given a chance to get to know the beautiful "chick." He stepped out into the aisle and extended his hand toward seat B. The woman asked if he would place her bag in the overhead compartment. He couldn't contain himself. "With pleasure," he said with a huge smile plastered over his face. "I'm Reggie Morton," he said extending his hand for a shake.

"Oh, I'm Carol McKay."

"Heading to New York for some revitalization?" Reggie asked.

"No, I'm going home. I was in Chicago on business."

My stars, is this fate speaking this morning, Reggie was thinking.

"And you?" she asked.

"I'm starting a new job Monday."

"Well congratulations, you are going to love New York. Where are you working?"

"Benton, Barnes and Fowler Advertising Agency on Madison Avenue near 52nd Street."

"Sounds interesting."

"I'm looking forward to it."

"That's not far from my office. I'm at Bitterman Management Consulting on Park and 54th Street. We should have lunch sometimes."

"If you will give me your number, I'll surely remind you of that suggestion."

"Sure, here is my card."

"Ladies and gentlemen welcome to American Airlines Flight 240 to LaGuardia. If I can have your attention for a moment, we will go over the flight instructions for passengers." The stewardess' greeting focused Reggie's attention to the front of the cabin as she spelled out all the precautions. Carol returned to reading her book and Reggie rested his head on the back of his seat and closed his eyes trying to determine if he should disturb her with more conversation or just sit quietly. He wanted to appear cool and calm and hide his anxiety which he felt might give her the wrong impression, so quietly seemed the better choice. The stewardess' serving cart came rolling down the aisle with offers of cereal, fruit or eggs, bacon, hash brown potatoes, toast, coffee and orange juice. Carol nodded "no" to the stewardess' offer. Reggie opted for the eggs and bacon tray with coffee and juice. Besides being hungry, he wanted to avoid any embarrassing growl from an empty stomach. When he finished eating, he lay back in his seat with his eyes closed pretending to be sleeping while he fantasized about making love to Carol.

"Ladies and gentlemen please fasten your seat belts and return your seats to the upright position for our landing in New York." Reggie realized he was running out of time to do something to keep this encounter going. He began searching for his next move but couldn't come up with anything.

"Welcome to New York," the stewardess said as the plane came to a halt at the terminal. Reggie swung from his seat and reached for Carol's bag. "I think this is yours," he said with as warm a smile as he could muster without bursting into a full grin.

"That's me," she said with a smile that Reggie thought might have been seductive. They entered the terminal walking side by side in the direction of the baggage claim area. However, just as they approached the area, Carol turned left toward the sign noting ground transportation. Reggie immediately responded. "Is that your only bag?"

"This is it," she said.

"Well, look for my call for lunch," he shouted as Carol waved him good-bye. He bit his bottom lip and balled his right hand into a fist and slammed it into his left hand thinking maybe he should have let go and showed his anxiety. Maybe it would have impressed her. Now, he was left wondering exactly what kind of impression did he give. Well, he decided, he would show some boldness by making good on his promise to call. He still wanted to kick himself for missing that opportunity to connect with her.

While standing next to the carousel waiting for his luggage, he told himself that his top priority for now should be his new job and what he would do to make the best impression, not Carol. He grabbed that handsome piece of luggage he was proud of as it rolled in front of him and walked out to the taxi stand. A driver sporting a neatly shaped full beard and wearing a turban took Reggie's luggage, placed it in the trunk and open the door for him. Reggie sat back in the seat thinking he is earning his tip as long as he doesn't get lost and try to charge me for his mistake.

"What is your destination, sir?" the driver asked in a British accent.

" 5560 Vales Ave. in Riverdale," Reggie proudly announced. When he mentioned to his boss back in Chicago that he had found an apartment in Riverdale, New York, the man looked surprised. He told Reggie he was familiar with the area and that it was a really nice neighborhood. There were some beautiful detached homes there and some mansions hidden behind clusters of trees. His voice then lowered and he said it had a large Jewish population. Reggie wasn't sure what that meant, but decided not to probe. He remembered Susan, the real estate agent, never mentioned anything about the racial make-up of the neighborhood and didn't seem to have any reservations about showing him the apartment. As a matter of fact it was her recommendation. She told him it was cheaper than Manhattan and was close enough to enjoy all its advantages. It may take you a little longer to get to work, but it's worth it with the money you'll save. Reggie was sold on her promotion and he liked what he saw.

The driver sped down Grand Central Parkway toward the Triborough Bridge and onto the Major Deegan Expressway. Reggie looked to his left across the river and recognized Harlem, the world renowned Black community. He felt a bit of tension as he remembered the real estate agent asking him if he wanted to look there for an apartment and he quickly responded, "no." He turned his head to the right and recalled the agent drove through this area known as the South Bronx which was heavily populated by poor Spanish people. He thought about those street gang wars in Chicago and wondered if things were the same in the South Bronx. Reggie then closed his eyes until the taxi veered off the Major Deegan and headed toward Vales Avenue. The route was lined with lush trees and fresh green grass. Reggie smiled and sat back in his seat. The taxi came to a stop in front of the apartment building which stood in between private homes. It was the only apartment building on the street. Reggie declared this neighborhood was a huge step above his living conditions in Chicago. He collected his suitcase and headed for his apartment which was a large one bedroom on the first floor with a view of a cluster of trees separating the building from the Henry Hudson Parkway which led into Manhattan.

Reggie had four days before reporting to work. He decided he needed to do something about finding a piece of furniture that would permit him to unpack. The apartment only had a bed, an empty refrigerator, a stove and a working telephone which reminded him he needed to call his mother and let her know he had arrived safely in New York and, so far, had not been mugged or beaten to a pulp.

" Hello mom, I'm here in New York snug as a bug in a rug."

"Well, that's good to hear, son. I'm praying that things turn out in a good way for you. I know the Lord will take care of you and I need to leave it in his hands and stop worrying so much. I guess New York can't be any worse than Chicago. It's just about twice the distance from home."

"New York is going to be fine. You have to be willing to move around if you want to succeed in this world, mom, and New York is the place of great opportunities and I am going to grab my share. Don't worry about me. How are dad, Doug and my nephew?"

"They are all doing fair to middling. Your father and I have our days with this old arthritis. There are signs Douglas is drinking too much and poor Doug Junior is as smart as a whip, but there isn't much encouragement he is getting from his parents. But the Lord is taking care of us. Now don't you go worrying."

"Well, mom, I'm going to let you go. Give my regards to all."

"Okay, son."

CHAPTER 2

Reggie spent the weekend scouting the neighborhood. He was impressed that in a city as crowded as New York he could be in a community where there were mostly two- story detached houses and a few apartment buildings stacked between them. The apartment buildings were in the style of pre war construction with ornate facades adorned with crawling ivy, spacious rooms and high ceilings and only ten floors high. He discovered a Safeway grocery store about fine blocks from his building in a small shopping center that also had a movie theater, a bank and a McDonalds. He also found a Salvation Army store in the neighborhood. It had a piece of furniture that looked like the old credenza in his mother's house and a chest of drawers with five drawers that would be perfect for some of his clothes. He purchased both pieces and arranged to have them delivered. As he walked back to his building on this sunny warm day with clear skies, he felt optimistic about what lies ahead and very comfortable in the neighborhood. He noticed he had come in contact with very few Black people in the neighborhood or in his building. He remembered his old boss' comment about Jews living in the neighborhood. He wasn't sure how you could tell if a person was a Jew. Back in his hometown, on one corner was a grocery owned by Mr. Bob and he was a Jew and on the other corner was a store owned by Mr. Salvo and he was Italian and the both looked the same to him. Nobody in the neighborhood tried to distinguish them. They were just white people.

The only drawback, Reggie concluded, to living in the neighborhood was the public transportation. From where he lived he would have to take a fifteen minute bus ride to the subway or walk about a mile to the Metro North commuter train that would bring him about ten blocks from the office. Susan, the real estate agent, told him there was an express bus about five blocks from his apartment that stopped just a few blocks from his office. He decided that was his best bet.

By Sunday, Reggie had settled into the apartment and found himself with nothing to do except wait for Monday. After reading the New York Times that he had purchased the night before at a local newsstand and watching the secondhand television which he also purchased at the Salvation Army and brought home with him, he became restless. He felt he had had enough news about the upcoming election battle between Richard Nixon and Hubert Humphrey and the endless commercials and dull movies. He decided to go for a walk. The day was warm with overcast skies. It was comfortable but not a spirit booster, he thought. He walked along busy Broadway and into the expansive Van Courtland Park where a group of young kids were playing a game of baseball and a few adults were walking their dogs that were controlled by a leash. The size of the park and the small number of people there helped Reggie appreciate its beauty-fields of fresh green grass, clusters of healthy trees and high hills. He felt a stroke of optimism and began to wonder what it would be like walking with Carol McKay through the park holding her hand and smiling as they looked into each other's faces. With a smile on his face, he stretched his hands behind his head as he walked. He wished he knew how to call her then, but decided, as soon as he was able to detect how things were going in the office, he would call and invite her to lunch.

When the alarm went off, Reggie had already been awake for an hour. The navy blue suit, white shirt and blue and white striped tie had been laid out the night before. He felt excited and anxious. He tried to remember everything he had done at the advertising agency during his summer internship. He wanted to get off to a good start by flaunting his knowledge of the business. He reminded himself that he had to succeed at this job, if for no other reason than to assure his mentors back in Chicago that everything they thought of him was true. He began to feel anxious. He jumped into the shower and stood under the pulsating water piercing his body and giving some relaxation to the muscles in his back that had begun to tighten. He closed his eyes to enhance the relaxation, but the memory of his first shower in the dormitory at Davis University where the white boys paraded around the stall to see if he had a tail, crept in his mind. The muscles in his back tightened again. He took a deep breath, stepped out of the shower, and wrapped himself in the soft, terry cloth robe that hung from the rack on the door. As he stood before the mirror applying deodorant and hair tonic, without realizing what he was doing, he began to whistle Nancy Wilson's version of "Our Day Will Come." A smile crept across his face as he brushed his hair. He stepped out of the bathroom and made himself a cup of coffee to drink while he dressed. He decided the butterflies were not ready to admit sold food into his stomach. He took his time dressing. The shirt was carefully folded on both sides in the military tuck and the knot in the tie was carefully positioned against his shirt. He twisted and turned a couple of times before the mirror, took a deep breath and bolted out of the apartment as if it were his regular routine.

As Reggie stepped out of the building he looked up and noticed the bright sun beaming down unobstructed by clouds, hinting that the day would be more than just warm. As he walked to the bus stop, he wanted to shed his jacket to head off sweat, but he wasn't sure how that would look to his white neighbors. When they saw him, he wanted them to think of him as a successful executive capable of enduring, so he endured by walking slowly to keep from sweating.

He noticed there were three white women and one white man waiting in line for the bus. The man was reading the Wall Street Journal and the women were looking straight ahead. No one abandoned their position to acknowledge him so he stood there looking in the direction of the bus. The seven-thirty was right on schedule. Reggie entered the bus behind the four people ahead of him. There was an empty row of seats in the middle of the bus. He headed to that row and took the seat next to the window. The fabric covered adjustable seat was comfortable and the bus was air conditioned. He sat back and relaxed as the bus pulled into the traffic. At the second stop after Reggie got on, a young Black guy in a well- tailored beige suit and wearing dark sun glasses and carrying a New York Times got on. He looked toward the empty seat next to Reggie then took a seat in the front of the bus next to a white woman and began reading his paper. Reggie noticed he was not sporting the recently stylish, bushy Afro hair cut. Their hair lengths were about the same so maybe he could tell him where to get his hair cut, Reggie decided. He had noticed only one barber shop in the neighborhood and it was filled with white barbers and he wasn't about to go into one of those shops and ask for a hair cut. He now saw a way of overcoming that obstacle so he sat back in his seat a bit more relaxed as the bus maneuvered through the traffic heading south to Manhattan.

The bus stopped on Fifth Avenue and 52nd Street. Reggie stepped off into the bustling traffic of smartly dressed pedestrians exuding confidence by their gait and a countenance unperturbed by its surroundings. He felt energized. He was now a part of the most famous city in the world and working for one of the most influential businesses in the world. He unconsciously raised his shoulders, extended his chest, and placed his right hand in his pocket while the left hand swung freely along his side just like the guy in front of him. After walking the one block between Fifth Avenue and Madison, he remembered he had not had breakfast.

Checking his watch, he realized it was only eight fifteen and he wasn't due in the office until nine. He stepped into a coffee shop and took a seat and began to go over the menu. He was in New York now and ready to blend in. A white waitress in a faded yellow uniform came to his table and plopped down a napkin, knife, fork and spoon and a glass of water and, without looking at him directly, asked if she could take his order. He decided on what seemed to be a popular New York breakfast- that oversized donut without sugar, with cream cheese oozing out of it, called a bagel, and a cup of coffee. The waitress returned quickly with his order and his bill, still without any eye contact. He wondered if he had done something that made her angry, but quickly concluded, he was witnessing part of New York culture- rudeness, something to get used to. He wondered what kind of tip the waitress was expecting with that kind of behavior. The bill came to $3. 85. He left a quarter tip and never looked back to see the look on her face.

Reggie walked out of the coffee shop into the warm morning sun that was somewhat obstructed by the tall buildings and strolled the few blocks to the office, feeling anxious. He took the elevator up to the tenth floor. He stepped out and walked through the glass doors and was greeted by a Black receptionist with dark brown skin and sporting a neatly cut Afro. She looked up and with a wide smile said, "Good morning brother. What can I do for you?"

"I'm Reggie Morton and I am here to see Mr. Walsh," Reggie answered.

"Oh, yes, he's expecting you. I'll tell him you are here," the receptionist said as she dialed the phone and announced Reggie. "He said he will be right out to get you. How are you doing brother? It's good to see you. I'm Harriett," she said as she extended her hand and looked at him with a flirtatious smile. "Let me know if there is anyway I can help you get settled," she said as her left eye winked at him.

"Thanks for the offer," Reggie said as he reached for her hand. All the time he was wondering if she was a Black Nationalist and what that would mean if he got hooked -up with her. He tried to return her smile with a smile, but he could only muster up a forced one.

"Good morning, Reggie," Mr. Walsh said with a glowing smile as he grabbed Reggie's hand and patted him on the back. "Are you all settled in your apartment? Have you mastered our public transportation system yet?" Reggie started to answer, but Mr. Walsh cut him off and said, "Come with me. I'll take you around to personnel. After they complete your orientation, they will bring you back to me and I will get you started. Good to have you on board, buddy."

As the two began walking away from the receptionist station, Reggie looked back over his left shoulder to acknowledge Harriett and saw that she was still sporting a seductive smile. As he sat before the personnel manager whose hand grasped a cup of steaming black coffee and whose eyes seemed to be striving to stay open as they traveled from the papers on her desk and up at Reggie, his mind drifted. He was certain Harriett was flirting with him, but he wasn't attracted to her, but she was Black and it might help to have her friendship since she was probably an encyclopedia of information of how to maneuver this place. He figured his challenge was how to cultivate her friendship without becoming romantically involved. The personnel manager ended their meeting by asking him if he had any questions, then handing him a large brown envelope and saying come back to her if there was something he doesn't understand. For the first time, she smiled. She didn't offer to escort him to Mr. Walsh, but that didn't matter since he knew exactly where to go. He decided to take the route around the hall that would not pass the receptionist desk because he had not decided how he wanted to react to Harriett.

"Are you all set now?" Mr. Walsh asked smiling as Reggie stepped into his office faking a smile trying to hide his nervousness about this new beginning. A discomforting thought flashed in his mind. He remembered that conversation he had with Walter, a Black colleague who befriended him when he started his college intern program at Rodman Advertising in Chicago. Walter told him he had to stay alert because the white people at the firm could not be trusted. Their smiles often cover up sinister motives. Reggie wondered what was on Mr. Walsh's mind as he continued to smile during their conversation. He took a deep breath and said,

"I'm all set and ready to go. What do we have today?"

"Why don't you get settled in your office and I will come by in about a half hour to pick you up. We are going to a meeting with the client, Texas Oil, to present our strategy for their campaign on social responsibility."

When Reggie walked out of Mr. Walsh's office he was greeted by Barbara, the secretary he would shared with Mr. Walsh. "Welcome Mr. Morton. Are you finding your way around the Big Apple yet?" Barbara's dirty blond hair reached the middle of her back. She was carrying a little more weight than her body frame required, but she exuded warmth that made Reggie comfortable.

"I'm getting the feel of it and so far it feels good," Reggie said.

"Well, let me know if I can guide you in any way."

"Thanks, I know I'm going to have to take you up on that offer soon."

"I hope you find things in your office okay. I have left some supplies you might need. Feel free to make any changes in the way I have arranged things. Your comfort is the guide. You are scheduled to attend a client meeting with Mr. Walsh. He will be ready to leave in fifteen minutes."

"Yes, he told me. By the way, call me Reggie."

"Okay Reggie," she said with that warm smile spreading over her face.

Reggie closed the door behind him, shed his jacket and sat down on the leather couch across from his desk, crossed his legs and rested his hands behind his head. The only thing he could accomplish in fifteen minutes, he decided, was to calm himself before meeting with clients. He wanted them to see him as someone secure and comfortable in their presence and he wanted to be rested enough to fake it. He tried to visualize how he would react to various situations, but ideas were coming to mind faster than he could sort them. There was a knock on the door. He jumped up grabbed his jacket and opened the door.

"It's that time," Mr. Walsh said with a look of stress covered with forced pleasantness. His six foot frame draped in a charcoal gray Brooks Brothers suits stepped ahead of Reggie. As they waited for the elevator, he said, "We will hail a taxi. They are only ten blocks away."

"Would you prefer to walk?" Reggie asked.

"No sir, that's what taxis are for."

When the elevator landed in the lobby, Mr. Walsh rushed out looking back for Reggie who was now trying to maneuver through the crowd separating them without constantly saying, "excuse me." He wondered why the rush since they were leaving at exactly the time he had been told. He began to wonder what the meeting would be like or what would be expected of him since they had had no discussion to prepare him. Surely they didn't expect him to know anything about Texas Oil except those times he filled up his father's car with their oil. As he sat in the taxi he couldn't decide if he should try to make conversation or keep quiet since Mr. Walsh looked like he was in deep concentration and might not be interested in a distraction. He decided to leave it to Mr. Walsh to strike up conversation, but sitting there looking out the window was a bit disconcerting. The unusually smooth flow of traffic caused the trip to last only ten minutes. Mr. Walsh handed the driver a bill that Reggie could not see and said keep the change.

"Reggie you are going to be working with me on this account for a while. I will introduce you as the new account executive who has been assigned to work with me. They may ask you some questions about yourself, but otherwise I will make the presentation."

"Good enough," Reggie said, somewhat relieved as the elevator traveled to the fifteenth floor. They stepped out into an unpretentious lobby with an artificial potted plant next to the receptionist's desk. The receptionist was an elderly white woman whose movements seem to coincide with her age. She recognized Mr. Walsh and greeted him in what seemed like a white southern accent.

"How are you today, Sara? Are you keeping these guys in their place?"

"Good to see you again, Gordon. I'm doing my best."

"Sara, I want you to meet Reggie Morton. He will be working with me on your account."

Sara slowly extended her hand to Reggie and said unemotionally, "It's a pleasure to meet you, Mr. Morton."

Reggie shook her hand and with a half smile said, "The pleasure is mine."

"You gentlemen have a seat and I will let Mr. Howard know you are here," Sara said as she turned her head away from the two men and stared at the telephone as if she had forgotten the number she was about to dial. After a brief pause she pressed the intercom button and said, "Mr. Walsh and Mr. Morton are here." She paused again then repeated, "Morton."

Mr. Walsh sat with his legs crossed staring at the painting of three horses grazing, which hung on the wall behind the reception desk. Reggie felt there was some tension in the air and figured it probably had something to do with him, but he had no idea what to do except to watch and see how things developed.

"Morning Gordon. How have you been, fellow?" Mr. Howard, a short stocky guy with a receding hair line, said as he extended his hand to shake Mr. Walsh's. "Still managing to survive in sin city? Who is this you have with you?"

"Morning Jerry. I've got the Big Apple under my thumb. You should let me show it to you sometime. Oh, excuse me, this is Reggie Morton. He just joined the firm and will be working with me on the account."

"Oh, yes, I remember. Well, welcome Mr. Morton. Why don't you all come on in? Can Sara get you gentlemen anything?"

"No, no," each responded.

As they entered the conference room with bare walls and a view of the wall of another building, Reggie took note of the three elderly men seated at the far end of a long conference table. All had flat top hair cuts and wore short sleeves white shirts with ties designed without imagination. Reggie wondered if they had just shed their white robes with KKK embroidered on them before he entered the room. He then began to think, Good Lord, I hope cultivating a working relationship with these men is not my only job. My hair could grow gray in one week. I think I had better find a quick way to schmooze up to Harriett. She is probably the only one at the agency able to understand the challenge, but doing that might exact a price I am not willing to pay. She might be looking for something more than a buddy and that's all I can handle.

Maybe if it takes a long time for me to score with someone else, I might be able to take her on for one night, but then there is still the morning after, the week after, the month after. If she concluded I was just trying to get a nut off, I'm likely to lose her friendship and acquire an enemy and then I would be doomed. In any event, if I tried and it turned out the way it did the last time I was trying to make love with a sister when it took quite a while to get into it and how unsatisfying it turned out to be, I would not only be doomed, but too embarrassed to show my face around her again. But mom, those sisters at her church and all the neighbors would be tickled to death to see me hooked up with someone like Harriett, except for her Afro hair- do. Dad and my brother Doug would probably give me the green light with a hearty, "Right On!" But they would probably say the same thing if I walked in with Carol McKay.

"You all know Gordon," Mr. Howard said to his colleagues.

"Hello Gordon. Good to see you again. You look like you are in good health. So the fast pace of the high life of New York hasn't gotten you down yet," one of the men said.

"No, this is my kind of life. Always ready to go."

"This is Reggie Morton. He just started with us today and he'll be working with me on your account," Gordon said.

Each of the three men nodded their heads and said, "Good morning Mr. Morton, nice to meet you," as they turned their heads toward Gordon.

"It's a real pleasure for me to meet you all," Reggie said in a contrived, forceful voice trying to hide his anxiety. He wondered if he should have just said, "nice meeting you all."

That might have been more business like. Christ, am I being intimidated and screwing-up the first day? he thought.

"Why don't we all take a seat and see what Gordon has for us today," Mr. Howard said.

Reggie followed Gordon to the opposite end of the table from the men. Gordon handed each of them a folder and began to explain each graphic showing how the agency would implement a campaign that would show individuals who have benefited from the company's charitable contributions. Each of those interviewed would tell their story extolling the company for their charity and service programs. Statistics of the dollar amounts of the company's annual charitable contributions and a listing of the company's research projects to protect the environment were also presented. After a round of questions regarding the logistics of such a campaign and Gordon pouring on a barrage of compliments about the company's social conscience initiatives, the three men looked at each other and nodded.

"Let's go with it, Gordon," Mr. Howard said.

"Thank you. I will take the news back to our creative team and we will get right on it. Anyone interested in lunch on me?" Gordon asked.

"Thanks, but we have a few things to clean up here and my colleagues have a two o'clock flight back to Houston," Mr. Howard said.

Gordon walked over to the men and shook each of their hands and said, "I look forward to seeing you all next time. Have a safe trip." Reggie followed with hand shakes and also said, "Have a safe trip."

"Take care of yourself, Sara," Gordon said as he and Reggie entered the elevator.

"Thank God that's over," Gordon said as the muscles in his face seem to relax. "Those oil guys from the South make me nervous. It's hard for me to read their body language. A lot of the times, I don't know if they are laughing at me or with me. I guess I should be satisfied that they realize we are one of the best agencies in the business and they are getting their money's worth out of us." Gordon said as he looked out of the sides of his eyes at Reggie hoping to get his reactions to the meeting. Reggie turned his head toward Gordon and with a very serious look on his face asked, "How long have you been on the account?"

"We just won the account two years ago and I have been the executive from the beginning, but the company representatives changed a couple of months ago. Thank God for old Howard, he has been around all along and he is from New York, which makes him easier to understand."

"Yes, he seems like a nice guy," Reggie said still looking serious and concerned.

"Why don't we get some lunch? I need a drink," Gordon said.

"I can handle that," Reggie said with a relaxed smile on his face.

" How about a juicy steak?" Gordon asked as he rested his hand on Reggie's shoulder and released a big smile of relief. "I know just the place that will not disappoint us. It's called The

Cattlemen Club. With that name you know it won't let us down."

"Sounds like a winner to me," Reggie answered.

"Taxi, taxi," Gordon yelled as he waved his hand toward an oncoming yellow cab. "Cattlemen Club," Gordon ordered as he and Reggie scooted into the cab. "You know where that is don't you?" Gordon asked.

"Yes sir," the cab driver, a Black woman sporting a big Afro, said as she turned on the fare meter. Gordon showed no emotional reaction to the woman. Reggie was very much surprised, but said not a word, but was thinking New York is definitely another world where mostly anything goes.

Gordon pulled out a folder from his briefcase and began to write what seemed like notes on the meeting. Reggie alternated between staring out the window and at the driver. He thought she definitely seemed like she knew what she was doing as she maneuvered from lane to lane, dodging traffic and blowing her horn at drivers or pedestrians who got in her way. The streets were very congested and everybody seemed to be competing for space and impatient with anyone demanding the same thing. The only thing guiding pedestrians when they wanted to cross an intersection was whether or not the oncoming traffic was close enough to beat their pace of crossing. Whether the traffic light was red, green or yellow was of no significance in their decisions. It seemed like there was a war between cars and pedestrians. He imagined it must be chaos on a rainy day when visibility was not good. New York was fascinating, he concluded.

The taxi pulled up in front of the restaurant where a crowd of white men dressed in dark suits and conservative ties and a few white women in two piece suits were entering. Reggie and Gordon hauled out of the taxi and joined the crowd, Reggie feeling a bit self- conscious. He reminded himself that he had to fit in to be successful in this very competitive business so he had to pretend that he was not intimidated by his environment in spite of the fact that he often was. The thought, however, curbed his appetite which caused him to think about what he would order. A steak might be a bit much, so he considered maybe a tuna sandwich and some ice tea. As he remembered the name of the restaurant, he wondered if they had such a sandwich. Then he remembered someone once said when you are eating lunch with your boss, don't embarrass him by ordering something light while he orders a steak. Anyway, he remembered he had already agreed that a steak was a good idea.

"A table for two," Gordon said as they reached the front of the line.

"Right this way, sir," the Maitre D' said as he led them to a table in the center of the restaurant and placed two menus in front of their seats. "Your waiter will be right with you," he announced. Gordon did not pick up the menu. He looked around the restaurant as if he were looking for someone in particular. Reggie picked up the menu and pretended he was trying to determine what he wanted when the waiter approached and asked if they were having drinks. Gordon immediately ordered a scotch on the rocks. Reggie was caught off guard. He wasn't ready for alcohol in the middle of the day, but suddenly remembered Gordon had said he needed a drink.

Reggie couldn't think of any alcohol he could handle at that time of day except a beer, so he decided to assert a bit of independence and ordered one. Gordon never blinked or showed any kind of reaction when he heard Reggie's order. Reggie felt relieved. However, he thought he would not push his luck regarding the steak. When the waiter brought the drinks and asked for their orders, Gordon ordered a sirloin and baked potato. When the waiter asked what kind of dressing he wanted on his salad, Gordon replied, "blue cheese." The waiter then turned to Reggie and he said, "I'll take the same." Gordon didn't seem to be listening to Reggie. He was downing the second gulps of scotch from the glass he had not permitted to touch the table since it was handed to him.

"Well, Reggie how did you get interested in advertising? Did you study marketing in college?"

"No, I was in Liberal Arts with a major in Social Science. I had summer intern jobs in advertising while in school, but landed a job at Woodland Foods in management after graduation. Luckily, I was recruited for this job and leaped at the opportunity because I liked working in advertising."

"Well, it's a great business. I can't complain. I came here right out of Yale. My father was a senior vice president at the Wells Agency before he passed away. He thought advertising was the business for me. I wasn't so sure, but he insisted. I decided I would go for it if I didn't have to work under him. He bought my terms and got me the job here." Gordon downed the last drop of scotch' and finally rested the glass on the table. He sat back in his chair and looked from side to side asking out loud, "Where is that waiter?" He spotted the waiter and beckoned him over. He pointed to his glass and said, "Another one. What about you Reggie?"

"I'm okay", Reggie said pointing to his half filled glass.

The waiter brought Gordon's drink and he took a sip and this time rested the glass on the table.

"During my sophomore year at Yale my roommate was a Black guy from Charlotte. He was sharp as a nail, good-looking and smooth with the girls. We had some great times. He used to go to church every Sunday as if he were a devoted Christian, but he would tell me some of the horniest women were in church on Sunday and he would charm them into inviting him over to their homes. Just about every time he would score and the next Sunday he would go to a different church and start over again. He could down a six pack of beer and still walk a straight line. He was so smart he didn't have to study that much and still got good grades. Every now and then I hear from him. After graduation, he went on to law school then went back to Charlotte, started practicing law, married and had two children."

"I envy guys like that. They seem to have all the luck," Reggie said.

Gordon took another sip of his drink and seemed to become more relaxed.

"I think you are going to do well here, Reggie, with me at your side. I was glad when they decided to assign you to work with me. I have some good accounts that you are going to enjoy. They are not all like Texas Oil, although I think they are manageable. We just have to get used to them. There is a great creative staff to work with. I want you to meet Henry. He is an art director, great guy."

"Thanks, Gordon. I appreciate any guidance or help you can throw my way. You can be honest with me if you see that I am on the wrong track any time. That would mean a lot."

"Don't worry buddy, you are in good hands. You should also feel free to ask me any questions about anything or anybody, especially the bigots you are likely to run into."

"That would be a huge help," Reggie said, feeling a sense of relief and hoping he had truly found his first friend in New York.

The waiter arrived with the orders and Gordon ordered another scotch. Reggie continued to sip his now warm beer. The restaurant had gotten crowded. It seemed every table was occupied with people in animated conversation with a glass of something close to their hands. This is New York, Reggie was thinking. He glanced at his watch and noticed it was one-thirty and wondered if Gordon had lost track of time and if someone would be trying to contact them back at the office. Gordon didn't seem to be the least concerned, so Reggie continued to enjoy his Sirloin.

"Will there be anything else?" the waiter asked. "I'm done," Gordon replied. "Would you like anything else, Reggie?" Gordon asked.

"No, I'm okay," Reggie answered.

The waiter handed Gordon the check and Reggie reached for his wallet. Gordon shook his head and said, "business expense."

Gordon stood up and walked out of the restaurant without one stumble although he did seem more relaxed than when he walked in. His hand shot up, his finger snapped and a taxi rolled up and he and Reggie were off to the office. Reggie also felt more relaxed than he had all day. The buzz he felt from his beer disappeared with the digestion of that steak, but he was beginning to feel relaxed with Gordon, but he felt those guys from Texas Oil might take some getting used to. He wasn't sure what Gordon had said about them was to cover what he perceived as their reaction to his race or his newness. Any- way, he thought, just about all the agency's clients would probably be white, but hopefully not all of them would be from the South. He felt that some day he and Gordon would probably be able to discuss the impact of race on what he encountered.

Reggie spent the afternoon going over the package personnel had given him about the agency and their various benefits and getting used to his office. It had a view of another office building about twenty feet away where he could see office workers busy at work. His desk was facing the wall so he could turn his head at any moment and see what was going on next door. He wondered if he should wave at them in the morning when he arrived. The leather couch across from his desk, he concluded, would be a good place to take a nap, but it would be in full view of his neighbors. Maybe, he thought, if the time ever comes where a nap might be needed, he would sit on the couch and pretend he was thinking through a problem and close his eyes.

As he sat going over his various office supplies, Gordon walked through the opened door and said, "Have you had enough for one day? If you have, why not join me for a drink before you head up north to Riverdale." Reggie's first thought was how much can this guy drink in one day or maybe this is what people do in New York advertising. He really didn't want a drink, but thought this was not the time to appear antisocial. "I've had enough and a drink might just be the thing I need to end my first day," Reggie said.

Gordon led him into a bar a few blocks from the office. It was filled with mostly white men his age. The mood was jovial.

There were groups sitting at the bar engaged in loud conversation and laughter. Others sat in booths lined along the wall, leaning across the table with serious looks on their faces and speaking in low tones.

"Hey fellows, let me introduce you to Reggie Morton. He just started today and will be working with me on my accounts for a while," Gordon said as they approached one of the groups at the bar. All conversation stopped and each of them nervously shook Reggie's hand and said, "welcome aboard." Then turned to Gordon and asked," How did things go with Texas Oil today? Are they on board with the new campaign?"

"It went fine and yes, they are onboard."

"Congratulations!" the group said in unison.

"What would you like to drink Reggie?" Gordon asked.

"I don't know," Reggie responded. "What are you having?"

"My usual, scotch," Gordon said.

"I'll have the same, but I think I'll have mine with some ginger ale," Reggie said.

"If you want to spoil some good scotch with ginger ale be my guest," Gordon said.

"Bartender, one scotch on the rocks and one scotch with ginger ale," Gordon ordered.

The group returned to their conversation and Gordon joined in while Reggie sipped his one drink and listened. Each member of the group seemed to be able to down as many drinks as

Gordon did at lunch without any signs of out of control behavior. Gordon looked at his watch after his third drink and said with a look of surprise, "Hey guys, I have a dinner date on the other side of town so I will see you tomorrow. Reggie are you okay?"

"I'm going to head out too. Nice meeting you guys," Reggie said.

"We'll see you around," one of them said.

Reggie took off his jacket and walked the few blocks to the stop for the express bus to Riverdale. Rush hour had passed and the streets were less crowded than when he left the office. He felt the scotch and ginger ale kicking in which seemed to make his steps seem lighter. As he walked, the first day tensions began to dissipate. He began to think that Gordon was going to be a good guy to observe to learn how to maneuver the system. He thought Gordon's comment about not being able to read the body language of the men from Texas Oil gave him an opening to ask some probing questions about the best tactics to use with them if he ever had to work with them without Gordon. He thought Gordon was comfortable with him before and after a drink. He opened up a bit about his life. Reggie concluded.

Reggie boarded the bus that was half empty and leaned back in the cloth covered high back seat. As the bus driver confronted the traffic leading out of Manhattan, Reggie's thoughts drifted back to his days at Davis University where, as one of the first Blacks to enroll there, he was subjected to daunting racism for four years, but was helped in enduring by an angel of a white professor and a white friend and his family. He remembered that first bus ride into Danville on his way to college and how excited and apprehensive he was. He remembered those bus rides out of Danville which were godsend escapes. Now, here he was in the Big Apple working in advertising. Such is life, he thought.

Reggie stopped off at the pizza shop on his way home and picked up dinner. The shop was filled with noisy teenagers-one Black and the rest white, he noticed.

CHAPTER 3

As Reggie approached the door to his apartment, he heard the phone ringing. He felt excited because he couldn't imagine who would be calling him. He quickly reached in his pocket for the key and shoved it into the keyhole and dashed to the phone. "Hello, hello," he said.

"It's your mother," he heard.

"Hey mom."

"Where have you been? I've been trying to get you for the last hour. Are those people working you to death already?"

"I stopped off after work and had drinks with some of the guys from the office."

"I hope your education taught you not to start drinking. You see what it has done to your brother, Doug. He doesn't come around much anymore, but Doris tells me he's usually drunk every weekend. Lord knows she's probably driving him to drink, such a hussy. I heard a rumor someone saw her in a café up on Butler Street with that no good hoodlum Olden who is known to be a home breaker. I knew time would prove you couldn't wash those Jezebel ways out of her. Of course she is always complaining to me that Doug is in the bed with every woman he can dream of. What does she expect with her behavior? Poor Doug Junior caught up between a drunken father and a hussy of a mother. I wish they would let me keep him. He is such a gifted child, reminds me of you. He's always asking about you. Don't forget you promised to call him sometime to encourage him. Lord knows he's probably doesn't get much of that at home."

"I've been intending to call him, but I knew I would also have to talk to Doug and I would dread that conversation because he doesn't want to hear anything I have to say anymore. But, I promise I will figure out something and make the call."

"Don't forget. He needs to know someone in this family is worthwhile."

" By the way, mom, I assure you I am not becoming an alcoholic. I was just being sociable and I need to do that to do my job."

"What kind of job is that that requires you to drink? Isn't it enough to be good at your work? That drinking can slip up on you and before you know it you will be drinking all the time. Lord knows I don't want that to happen to you."

"You don't have to worry about that, mom. It ain't going to happen to me. How is dad?"

"I didn't want to worry you, but he had what the doctors call a light stroke. I don't know how light it was. His speech is slurred and he has problems moving anything on his right side. He's being given therapy, but he gives the therapist a hard time whenever something hurts him. The doctors say he should regain his speech and the ability to move his hand and leg. So, things could be much worse. I'm praying for him. It's in the Lord's hand."

"Are you going to be all right, mom?

"Oh yes, son. The Lord is my anchor in the time of need. I trust Him. He never gives me more than I can bear."

"Well I will pray for you and dad. Tell him I said hello and I'm rooting for him to have a speedy recovery."

"I certainly will. Have you found a church yet? How far are you from Harlem? I know there are plenty of churches of God in Christ there. I want you to go there and find yourself one if you haven't already. There will be plenty of saints there and a lot of good women anxious to make you a good wife. I want you to promise me."

"I am not far from Harlem. I promise I will go there and check it out."

"I know you just got there, but have you given any thought to when you will be coming home for a visit?"

"No mom, but as soon as I get a chance I will see what I can do."

"All right son, I won't keep you. By the way what are you eating for dinner?"

"I picked up some pizza on my way home."

"That doesn't sound like a meal to me. Boy, you had better start cooking yourself some food at home. That's another reason you need to find yourself a good wife. I'm worried about you."

"I'm doing fine, mom. I haven't lost a pound since arriving here, but I plan to cook some meals as soon as I get a chance."

"You know you need to eat, so you make time, boy. Too bad I can't mail you some of my collard greens, fried chicken, potato salad and macaroni and cheese."

"I wish I could taste them, but I will be all right."

"All right, son. I'm going to let you go. Mother loves you."

"Bye mom, I love you, too."

Reggie laid down the phone, threw his jacket on the bed and breathed a sigh of relief. He walked back to the dining area and sat down in one of the two chairs at his adjustable table that was now accommodating his dining needs, and opened the pizza box. The pizza was no longer hot and not as enticing. He took a bite and a sip of the Pepsi Cola that was no longer cold. Somehow, his feeling of disappointment with the food made him conscious of how quiet it was in the apartment.

With no distraction, his mind began to wonder. He tried to recount some positive thoughts-working with Gordon, working in advertising in the Big Apple, an apartment in Riverdale; but those thoughts would slide away and the conversation he had with his mother would work its way back to his conscience. All the things she spoke about were things he didn't want to worry about, but he was unable to escape. He felt being in New York put a healthy distance between him and those problems much more than Chicago did and that sending home money whenever requested would free him, but tonight he realized that neither distance nor a few dollars were a shield. At least, he thought, he could use his demanding job and the expense of traveling to Smoky Mountain from New York as rationale for infrequent trips home. The thought made him feel guilty.

He remembered the pride his mother felt when she came to his graduation from the prestigious Davis University and saw him get his degree, standing among all those white professors and white students. He remembered how upset she was when he telephoned her from Chicago the day after graduation telling her he had decided to take the job offer in Chicago instead of the teaching position with the Smoky Mountain school system-the job she had prayed so hard he would take. He imagined she must have thought the Lord had let her down by permitting that to happen and leaving him in the hands of a group of misdirected white liberals and Blacks full of self- hatred who were responsible for his being in Chicago. He thought about his first trip home after a year in Chicago and how happy she was to see him and how the neighbors greeted him in spite of their disappointment about him not being the first Black to teach in an integrated school in their community. He took another bite of the cold pizza then shoved the box aside and took a napkin and covered his eyes to halt some tears that were trying to break loose.

He got up from the table and shed his business clothes for more comfortable Bermuda shorts and T- shirt and turned on the television and watched the hit show, "I Spy," with Bill Cosby and Robert Culp. It was a comforting distraction watching positive interactions between a white and Black man on national television. He lay back on the couch with his hands clasped behind his head and began to feel tension slowly ebbing away. The show went off and a commercial came on with an elderly grey-haired woman in her kitchen serving her grandson oatmeal and claiming its greatness. She reminded him of his grade school teacher, the grey-haired Miss Wright. He had gone to visit her on one of his trips back home. He shared with her his work in Chicago. She listened intensively and asked him how he felt about what he was doing. He answered with exaggerations of his satisfaction with management responsibilities. She looked at him and nodded her head and said, "You keep at it, young man." He was hoping for a word of congratulations. He was haunted by that response. He shook his head from right to left several times and went to brush his teeth before going to bed.

CHAPTER 4

The sound of Aretha Franklin's voice from the radio next to Reggie's bed blasting, *".Each morning I wake up, before I put on my make-up, I say a little prayer for you. Before combing my hair now, I say a little prayer for you......forever, forever.....to live without you would only mean heart break for me,"* alerted Reggie that his night of rest had come to an end. After coaching his eyes open, he shoved aside the sheet covering him, stretched out his arms, yawned and began to hum along with Aretha. The rising sun shone through the frosty glass window in the bathroom. Reggie smiled into the mirror as he washed his face. The weather forecast was for a warm, sunny day with temperatures in the mid eighties. It was going to be a good day, Reggie declared as he dressed and headed out the door. As the bus snaked through the traffic en route to midtown, Reggie wondered what Gordon had in mind for the day. He decided he was going to quiz him on some details of exactly what the plan was for him. He wanted to prepare himself for that opportunity to impress someone with his knowledge and abilities. He wanted to develop a strategy for dealing with those guys from Texas Oil that would not make him look like he was a cousin of "Uncle Tom."

"Good morning, Mr. Morton," Harriett said through a bright seductive smile as Reggie entered the reception area.

"Good Morning, Harriett," Reggie responded with a slight smile as he continued to walk toward his office.

"Have a good day," Harriett said looking at Reggie's back.

Reggie turned around and waved at Harriett who winked back at him.

"Good morning, Barbara. How are you doing today?" Reggie asked as he approached the door to his office.

"I'm doing fine. How are you doing Reggie?"

"Couldn't be better. Is Gordon in yet?"

"No, he won't be in until around ten. You all have a meeting with the creative team for the Texas Oil account at 10:30."

"Thanks," Reggie said as he closed the door to his office. His "raring to go" energy had to be put on hold for the next hour, he thought. As he sat consuming the bagel over stuffed with cream cheese and the cream colored sweet coffee he purchased at the lobby snack bar, he wondered if Gordon would brief him or develop strategy with him before the meeting. If Gordon didn't, he didn't think there would be anything he could offer, except that he was at the meeting with Gordon and that he didn't think the company representatives were comfortable with him, but of course he wasn't about to expose those feelings at this point on the job. He decided if Gordon didn't give him a role he would make a concerted effort, without seeming pretentious, to show the team that he was comfortable with them and the job and that he looked forward to working with them.

He decided the best way to approach that was to work up his best smile as he gave each member of the team a hearty handshake and say something like, "I'm really glad to be joining the team. I hope you will allow me to pick your brain as I get adjusted to the agency." Comfortable he had a plan for the meeting, Reggie again picked up and began to thumb through the package the seemingly sleep- deprived personnel manager had given him. He turned to the section on leave time. Two weeks vacation-never enough, two personal leave days. What does that mean? Unlimited sick leave. What's behind that? he wondered. He looked at his watch. It was ten o'clock. He figured Gordon would knock on his door any minute, but that didn't happen until 10:25 so he knew his plan B had to be put in place.

"How are you doing, Reggie?" Barbara said she informed you about the meeting. You ready?"

"Yes sir, I'm ready to march," Reggie said in a teasing manner and with a forced smile.

"Okay soldier, let's march," Gordon said as he smiled and placed his hand on Reggie's shoulder.

Gordon led the way into the small conference room with a table and ten chairs. The walls were bare and a blackboard was on the wall in the far end. There were three men seated at the far end reminiscing about the days of the Brooklyn Dodgers and making jokes about the struggling Mets. One was Black.

"Hey you guys, I want you to meet Reggie Morton. He came aboard yesterday and will be working with me on the Texas Oil account. Reggie this is Rick, Donald and Jeff."

"Welcome aboard, Reggie," they all said in a matter-of fact tone, except, Jeff, the Black one. His face lit up. Before Reggie could execute his plan B, Gordon sat down and began announcing the client had agreed on the new campaign. Reggie felt it was a bit awkward to walk to the other end of the table and shake hands at this point. So he waved his hand and said, "Thanks guys," and sat down.

Gordon went into a discussion of the time frame for casting and shooting the commercial. At the end of the meeting, the two white guys walked out with Gordon, but Jeff came up to Reggie extended his hand and said assertively, "Welcome aboard, brother." Jeff was sporting a thick, well groomed Afro hair cut. His skin was very dark and he had a baritone voice. His face implied he had been on this earth no longer than Reggie. Like the other guys in the room, he wore a sports shirt and trousers. Reggie felt somewhat intimidated by Jeff's look of racial pride and his reference to him as "brother" which had become a common reference used by Black nationalists. He became conscious of and uncomfortable that both Harriett and Jeff had Afros and he did not.

"Hey man," Reggie said, trying to portray an identity with Black pride. But he immediately felt guilty that he had not said, "brother." Jeff's expression did not seem to change, so Reggie's blood pressure lowered a notch. "Glad to meet you. How are things going?" Reggie asked trying to force a smile through his discomfort.

"Why don't we get together for lunch sometime? Are you free today?" Jeff asked. Reggie felt the muscles in his back tightening. He didn't know what Gordon would think if he headed out to lunch his second day on the job with one of the few Black people at the agency. He didn't want Jeff to think he didn't appreciate the invitation by saying he had plans and then have Jeff walk by his office and discover him there at lunch time. So he said, "Let me see if Gordon has plans."

"Gordon is having lunch today with some of the other vice presidents. They have this gathering once at month. They are supposed to be exchanging ideas about better management, but I think it's just an excuse to drink all afternoon at the agency's expense."

"Well, that settles it. I'm free," Reggie said as he felt sweat begin to roll down his back. He prayed Jeff could not detect his reservations.

"Okay, I'll drop by your office around twelve- thirty," Jeff said.

"I'll see you then," Reggie responded as he started toward his office. He took a deep breath, exhaled and began to wonder what he should say to Gordon about his plans or if he should say anything at all. While he sat in his office pondering his options, Gordon walked in and announced he would be out of the office the rest of the day and handed Reggie a folder with a document entitled U.S. Navy and said, "You might want to look this over. We are going to go after that account. It's going to be a pretty big one if we get it. I'm out of here. I'll see you tomorrow."

"Okay," Reggie said as he slumped back in his chair thinking that clears the way for me not saying anything about my plans unless he asks- and if he does, it would seem perfectly normal to accept a lunch invitation from someone if you had no plans. Well, the first crisis is behind me, he decided, smiling at himself and thinking that was a mole hill made into a mountain.

"Well, what are you up to today besides looking gorgeous?" Jeff asked Barbara as he walked up to her desk.

"Only the usual stuff, Mr. Cool," Barbara said in a very jovial tone. "And why am I rewarded with your presence this afternoon?"

"First of all, I wanted to see your face to brighten my day and second, I'm here to take the new employee to lunch."

"Well, your day has been brightened, now go and have a shining lunch. Reggie is in his office," Barbara said, still jovial.

Reggie could hear the conversation between Barbara and Jeff and it made him comfortable thinking Jeff must be well-respected. He thought maybe I'll have a drink during lunch.

"Hey man, you ready to go?" Jeff asked as he stood in the door of Reggie's office.

"Yes sir," Reggie said with confidence as he reached for his jacket.

"I've got this great place I would like to introduce you to. It's called Jezebel's. Sounds wicked doesn't it? Well, in a sense it is. The food is to die for. I understand it is owned by a Jew and a Black woman and the woman is the chef. She puts out some of the best ribs and collard greens in New York. When you enter the place you get the feeling you are walking down Bourbon Street in New Orleans. One of the tables has a swing instead of chairs around it. I think you are going to like it," Jeff said with excitement in his voice and, for the first time, a big smile on his face.

"Sounds like a winner to me," Reggie said as he thought maybe the place and the food will dominate discussion during lunch and the conversation will not turn to something that will embarrass him because his hair was not like Jeff's.

Jeff hailed a taxi, ushered Reggie in and announced his destination. The taxi headed for the Westside of Manhattan, maneuvering through the congested traffic and dodging secure pedestrians moving at will without any regard for traffic lights. The taxi's fare meter seemed to change continuously without any pauses for distance. After about twenty minutes, the taxi rolled up in front of a building with an entrance that looked like a storage room. Jeff paid the driver and headed toward the door to the building. Reggie thought this can't be the place he has been bragging about until he walked in. This place is nothing like the building. It indeed reminded him of pictures he had seen of the relaxed and jovial life on Bourbon Street. He felt relaxed and began to anticipate having a meal that reminded him of sitting around his mother's table on Sunday afternoons after church.

When the waiter came over to take their orders, he asked if they were having drinks. Reggie sat silently while Jeff pondered without looking at him. "I'll have iced tea." Jeff said. The waiter looked at Reggie and he said "I think I will have the same," thinking when you are in Rome you do as the Romans and concluding that everyone in advertising doesn't drink at lunch.

"Check out that menu. What you think?" Jeff asked.

"I think I'm about to have a real down home meal," Reggie answered.

"By the way, where is your home?" Jeff asked.

"I'm from Smoky Mountain, Tennessee, but I haven't lived there since going to college. I came here from Chicago where I worked after college." Reggie answered.

"Where did you go to college?" Jeff asked.

"I went to Davis University, a state university in Danville, Tennessee."

"Isn't that a white school?"

"Yes, it was before the Brown Decision. I was one of the first Blacks to enroll."

"Wow! What was that like?"

"It was tough."

"Did you ever get beat up by those hillbillies?"

"No, but there were times when I felt like I had been. Some of the professors were real bigots. Most of the students just had nothing to do with you, but there were a few who were friendly and there were some professors who were fair."

"What did the experience do to you?"

"Well. I got the degree I went there for. I'm sure it wasn't as much fun as going to Tennessee State, but what can I tell you."

"My hat is off to you, brother. I think they would have kicked me out of that school. I probably would have ended up going up against some of those bigots' heads if they thought they could get away with treating me unfairly, especially concerning my work.

What was your social life like? How many other Blacks were there?"

"There were about ten other Blacks and there wasn't much of a social life. I was the only Black living in the dormitory. The other Blacks lived in town."

"I would have gone out of my mind there," Jeff said.

"May I take your orders gentlemen?" the waiter asked.

"I'm having the fried chicken with macaroni and cheese and tomatoes and okra," Jeff said.

"Give me the ribs, potato salad and collard greens," Reggie answered.

While they waited for their orders to come, Jeff gave Reggie an overview of all the desserts. His favorite was the peach cobbler, but he said you couldn't beat the sweet potato pie with pecans or the coconut cake. "You will only need a light dinner after this."

The waiter arrived with their orders and, for a while, the only sounds coming from their table were wows. Reggie began to look at his watch. When he did it for the second time, Jeff said, "Don't worry about the time, everybody takes long lunches in advertising, usually a minimum of two hours." With that news, Reggie reached for another rib and checked out his fingers which he was tempted to lick, but squashed the idea, determining that might be a bit too much in this restaurant with mostly white customers surrounding his table.

After succumbing to the tempting coconut cake for Reggie and the pecan pie for Jeff, they looked at each other, leaned back in their seats and Jeff said, "Well done, my brother. Now let's get out of here before we go to sleep at this table." Reggie reached in his pocket to pay the bill, but Jeff said, "next time." Reggie bounced from the table feeling energized. It had been a great meal, but more importantly the conversation had been comfortable without any reference to his short, flat wavy hair.

When Reggie returned to his office he picked up the Navy folder and began to thumb through it. Most of the background information about its history and mission were some- what familiar and then there were a bunch of statistics that needed to be studied to determine which were significant for a campaign strategy. Reggie noticed the scarcity of Blacks in the different photos. He had not thought much about the Navy over the years but he suddenly remembered when he was growing up, there was one guy from the neighborhood who joined and the rumor had it that he was a dishwasher.

Reggie wondered if the Navy was looking to recruit more Blacks and if the agency was looking to him for ideas. The thought was exciting and, at the same time, frightening. He wondered what would be expected of him and whether he could live up to those expectations. However, this could be his chance to prove his worth, he thought, and he would find a way to rise to the job. Reggie closed the folder, leaned back in his chair with his hands in lock behind his head, looked out the window thinking, this is going to work. He reached for his coat and walked out of the office with the folder clearly apparent to impress Barbara that he was taking work home.

"Good night, Barbara," Reggie said with a big smile on his face.

"I'll see you tomorrow," Barbara said, smiling back at him.

Reggie stepped out of the building into a fresh, cool breeze that had swept across the city after a late summer shower. He felt relaxed and a bit energized. It was early and there was no reason to rush home, so he made his way to the bar he and Gordon had gone to the day before. He walked in and took over an empty stool at the entrance end of the bar and ordered a scotch and ginger ale. He was immediately recognized by Rick, the guy from the creative team at the agency. He was with a group of guys at the far end of the bar.

"Hey Reggie, come join us down here."

Reggie waved at him, picked up his drink and joined them.

"This is John, Leo and David." Reggie extended his hand and said, "Glad to meet you guys." They were all white.

John and Leo were dressed casually in slacks and an open shirt which made Reggie feel they were in the creative department. David wore a lightweight grey suit, a white shirt and a blue tie. He was probably from management, possibly an account executive.

"How's it going Reggie?' Rick asked.

"Fine, man, I'm doing just fine," Reggie answered feeling happily surprised by this unexpected extension of friendship.

"What's Gordon doing to lead you in the wrong direction?" Rick asked.

Reggie looked perplexed. "I'm kidding. Gordon is a great guy. He really knows the business. You couldn't be working with a better guy," Rick quickly explained himself.

"Yes, I agree. He's really a great guy. We are beginning to look at going for the Navy account," Reggie said in an attempt to appear a valued member of the team.

"Oh, is that so?" Rick said with a bit of sarcasms. "That would be a real catch for the agency. That could be a multimillion dollar account," Rick added still with a smirk on his face.

David, who had been quiet and looking like he was feeling no pain until now, laid down his glass on the counter and looked in Reggie's direction and asked in as friendly a tone as he could muster, "Where were you before you came to the agency?"

"Woodland Foods in Chicago."

"Chicago!" John said jumping into the conversation. "Are you a Cubs or White Sox fan? What do the folks in Chicago think about their teams this year?"

"Well, I guess you could say this wasn't the teams' best year; however, it looks like the Cubs might make it to the playoffs. The White Socks will not do that well. But folks in Chicago are loyal fans. They stick with their teams through good times and bad times. I guess you could say it's like having an ugly child and dreaming that one day there is going to be some discovery that will transform the child into the envy of the neighborhood," Reggie said with a grim on his face.

John and Rick broke out in laughter. David smiled.

"Now tell me what it feels like supporting the Mets with their record," Reggie asked, laughing.

Before John or Rick had a chance to answer, David broke in and asked, "have you had any previous experience in advertising?"

"Not really, I was a student intern in college," Reggie answered still smiling.

"Well, welcome to the business. It might be a little different from life at Woodland. Let me know if I can be helpful with anything you might run into," he said in a very casual tone while patting Reggie on the shoulder.

"Thanks David, I'll keep your offer in mind."

"I've got to go guys. My wife will kill me if I make us late for some concert at Carnegie Hall," David said.

"Yeah, I've got to go too," John and Rick said. They all shook Reggie's hand and said, "We will see you around."

"Okay," Reggie said as he finished his drink and then walked out of the bar.

As he walked toward the bus stop, he felt like taking a few dance steps but just smiled, thinking how people might react if he gave in to those feelings in spite of his perception that there were a lot of free- spirited people in New York. Of course he had not noticed any in advertising, so far. Instead of dancing, he began to pop his fingers and humming Gloria Lynn's "Our Day Will Come." He turned his head in the direction of downtown and saw the Riverdale bus approaching. After it came to a halt he climbed in and sat in the comfortable high- back seat feeling the cool air conditioning brushing his face.

He began to think about how he could gain some respect with the creative team for Texas Oil. Maybe, he thought, if Texas Oil isn't already under pressure from the community or government to recruit Blacks, they probably will be. So why don't we get some famous Black people to be part of those featured in the campaign we are working on. Surely something they do has a positive impact on the Black community and seeing Blacks speaking favorably about the impact of those efforts could indicate some willingness to employ Blacks. In today's climate, it could give them some sand to throw on any raging fire about their discriminatory hiring practices, which surely exist somewhere. Maybe we could get someone like Jackie Robinson or Bill Russell or Wilt Chamberlain. That just might do it. At least, he thought, he had a good idea to add to the discussion and wouldn't have to sit in a meeting silently. He sat back in his seat and folded his arms feeling he had accomplished something.

The bus rolled into its last stop to pickup passengers before heading for the expressway. Reggie noticed there were only two seats left. One next to him and one next to a white man with his head buried in the morning edition of the Wall Street Journal. Reggie looked toward the door to see who was boarding. Much to his pleasant surprise, the only person entering was the Black guy who boarded the other morning. Reggie remembered he thought he might ask him where to get a haircut. Anticipating the guy would sit next to him, Reggie felt this was a good chance to get to know somebody in the neighborhood and most of all to find out the location of a good barber.

The guy walked past Reggie and sat next to the white man as if he knew him. Reggie felt the blood flush from his face. So much for that idea. Anyway, what would he know about a black barber, even though his skin is brown and he has those defining Negroid features of thick lips and wide nose, his hair is straight, must have some American Indian blood in him, Reggie concluded. No problem, he thought, I can ask Jeff to recommend a barber, but he immediately concluded that could be embarrassing since it was clear Jeff was not a faithful customer of a barber and he might be wondering why he still was. Reggie concluded he was not up to answering that question if it ever came up.

On his way home, Reggie stopped at the McDonald's and picked up a cheeseburger, French fries and a Pepsi. He turned on the television while getting out of his suit and into some Bermuda shorts. After getting comfortable, he nibbled on the burger and fries and began to concentrate on the news. Walter Cronkite was following his usual pattern, opening by reporting on the causalities in Viet Nam for that day. It occurred to Reggie that since the riots after the assassination of Dr. King, civil rights struggles got very little attention of the news media. Everything was about the Viet Nam war, especially after the confrontations at the Democratic convention and the ongoing campaigns of Hubert Humphrey and Richard Nixon. Both were being measured by their strategy for ending the war.

Reggie couldn't see any good coming out of Nixon. First, he was a Republican and the country had just experienced eight years of the Democrats dismantling the impact of slavery and Jim Crow laws, a legacy the Republicans could not claim. Now that we have come this far, it would be a shame to bring this progress to a halt which is what would happen if Nixon won the election, Reggie thought. Things were bad enough with the vacuum in civil rights leadership created by the assassination of Dr. King. At least, Hubert Humphrey had a civil rights record. Reggie wondered if Nixon won what would happen to his job if there were no pressures to employ Blacks. Could he be forced to return to Smoky Mountain and take a job teaching? The thought was enough to scratch the spirit he felt leaving work. He wandered off to sleep and woke up hearing a local reporter announcing the eleven o'clock news. "Not for me," Reggie said as he prepared for bed.

The next morning Reggie woke up feeling he had slept for a week. He was anxious to get to the office and share his idea for the ad campaign. He couldn't remember when the next meeting with the creative team was scheduled, but was praying it was that day. When he arrived in the office, Barbara informed him that Gordon had been called overnight to go to Ft. Wayne to meet with clients for Capitol Records and would not be back for the rest of the week. He had left Reggie a folder with a list of tasks to follow up on. Reggie was disappointed to discover there was no mention of any contact with the creative team; however, he decided if he got a chance to see Rick, Donald or Jeff he would try out his idea on them.

The rest of the week seemed to rush by and Friday seemed to have leaped over the other days. When he was on his way to lunch, he ran into Rick who was rushing to a lunch date. As they rode down the elevator and out of the building, Reggie shared his idea with Rick. Rick's response was it's an idea worth exploring and he thanked Reggie for sharing it with him. That response gave Reggie confidence that he was ending a good week.

When he returned from lunch, Harriett was on the phone busy trying to accommodate a couple of men standing at the reception desk waiting to be announced. When she saw Reggie, her face flashed an unusually wide smile followed by a short wave of her hand. Reggie waved back and headed for his office. Around three o'clock, Jeff stuck his head in Reggie's office and said, "Hey man, its time to reward yourself. It's the weekend. Don't worry about all that paper, it will not forsake you over the weekend. What's on your agenda for the weekend? If you are free Harriett asked me to bring you to a party at her house Saturday night. What you say?"

"I'll say it sounds like a good idea. What are the specifics?"

"Ten o'clock at Lenox Terrace, in Harlem. I'll meet you on the northeast corner of 135th and Lenox Ave at 10:30."

"It's a date," Reggie said but he wondered what Harriett was up to and what kind of people would be there. At least, he decided, it had to be better than spending Saturday night at home watching dull television.

Saturday morning found Reggie feeling life in the Big Apple was beginning to turn out the way he had hoped for- a job worth writing home about and maybe, just maybe, a new friend to hang out with. He was ready for some partying. It would be great to meet some folks outside of work, he decided. He yawned and stretched as he stepped out of bed. His hand hit his head. I need to get my wig chopped (hair cut) he said. Got to look cool tonight. But where do I go to get that done? No indication that it can be done in Riverdale. Never could trust a white man to cut my hair. Maybe I'll just take the subway down to Harlem and walk around until I find what looks like a good shop.

He decided to get off the train at 145th Street and began his walk. He headed east. About a half block after crossing Eighth Avenue he saw the white and red turning cylinder barber sign. There were two barbers in what appeared to be lively conversation as they clipped away at the hair of their customers. There were three men sitting in the line of chairs against the wall leaving two empty. One was shaking his fist into the air as he spoke. The writing on the window read Bob's Barber Shop. It looked like life back home when he was growing up. He walked in and took one of the empty seats. Everyone continued their conversations without acknowledging him.

"The Jews just don't want to give up power to poor Black women in the communities. That's why they are so against community control of the schools. Most of the teachers are Jews. Don't you know that?" the man waving his fist said.

"I hear what you are saying, but Jews have always been at our side in the civil rights struggle. You don't turn your back on that kind of friendship," one of the barbers said.

"But now you are talking about power sharing and that is where the Jews get off. As long as they can use you they are willing to work with you. Its time for Black families to have some say about what goes on in their schools, that's being responsible and we have been accused of not being responsible," the man with the fist said.

The door opened and a man in a dark brown brimmed hat, a green and white flowered shirt carrying a pencil and a small piece of paper approached one of the barbers and spoke quietly to him. The barber reached into his pocket and pulled out some bills and gave them to the man. The man wrote down something and left. The conversation paused during the transactions, but no one acknowledged the incident. The other barber finished cutting his customer's hair, dusted off the seat and invited Reggie to take the seat. Reggie looked around at the other men waiting, but no one seemed concerned. He took the seat and said, "Even it out and a razor lining." The door opened again and another man wearing a light blue jump suit entered and pulled up his sleeve which was lined with gold watches. He walked up to everyone in the shop and asked if they wanted to buy one. No one took him up on the offer. Most shook their heads and fanned him away. Reggie noticed that all the men in the shop were at least fifteen years older than him and all had their hair cut close to their heads. The barber cut Reggie's hair without engaging him directly in conversation. When Reggie paid him, he said, "Thanks young man, see you next time." He then returned to the conversation with the men in the chairs lined against the wall. None of them seemed to be waiting to get their hair cut. As he was walking out the door, a woman with a neat waistline, voluptuous hips and wearing a tight-fitting dress was walking past the window of the shop. He heard one of the men blurt out, "Hey Bob (the barber) what could you do with that?" Bob replied, "Whatever she wants."

Reggie had been watching the clock since returning from the barber shop. When the short hand reached eight and the long hand twelve, he headed for the shower and then to the closet to select that outfit that would impress that crowd he was anticipating connecting with. After he was confident that those chocolate brown pants and the white silk shirt would do the trick, he headed out to the Number 1 train for that long ride from 242nd Street to 96th Street and then a transfer to the Number 2or 3 up town to Lenox Avenue and 135th .

He arrived promptly at ten o'clock. Realizing Jeff was not due to meet him until ten-thirty, Reggie stood in front of Harlem Hospital watching the pace of Harlem on a Saturday night. Ambulances rolled down the street with sirens blasting. The streets were crowded and individual voices occasionally rose above the noise calling someone by name or releasing a litany of profanity. It all reminded him of Saturday nights when he was growing up. There was usually some disturbance at Sam's Bar and the police would end up arresting someone. However, that was nowhere near what he was viewing at the moment. The crowds were larger, the noise louder and the area of the activities much bigger. He felt a bit of nostalgia standing there, but he also felt out of place. It occurred to him that it had been some time since he was in a crowd as Black as that one on that corner of Harlem.

"Hey brother, I see you have learned to maneuver your way around New York or did you take a taxi?" Jeff asked as he walked up behind Reggie.

"No man, I took the iron horse as you New Yorker like to call the subways. It's almost a direct route."

"Yes I know, but I thought since you took the express bus to work you were maybe a little afraid of the subways, like many out –of- towners.

"Well, I'm not one of them."

"Well, I'm glad. Come on my New York brother follow me. We are going to party tonight as Sam Cooke would say."

As they stepped off the elevator, the sound of James Brown's "Say it loud I'm Black and I'm Proud" rolled down the hall. Jeff began to pop his fingers and step to the beat. Reggie, walking a few steps behind, felt the music charge through his body and made him feel like dancing. Jeff never stopped his rhythmic steps as he rang the doorbell. When Harriett opened the door he embraced her and began to swirl her around to the beat of the music. She smiled at Reggie and winked her eye and pulled away from Jeff. The dimly lit L- shaped living/dining room was full of people who extended onto the terrace which faced north overlooking Harlem Hospital. About three quarters of the people were dancing while the others lingered on the terrace.

"Hello Reggie," Harriett said as she pulled away from Jeff who continued to dance alone into the dance area. "Did you have any trouble finding your way here?" She asked as she took his hand and began leading him through the crowd toward the kitchen where drinks were being served.

"No, I took the Number 1 train down to 96th Street and transferred to the Number 3 uptown. No trouble at all, but it did take a while."

"Well, you do live way up in the Bronx, so it might take a little time to come down to visit us in Harlem," she said with a smile.

"Well, it's worth every minute if I end up at a party like this one," Reggie said trying to appear cool and hip.

"I hope when you leave you'll still be saying the same."

"I can't imagine that I won't."

"Reggie, this is Larry. He is handling the bar for me tonight."

"Hey Reggie, what can I fix for you?" Larry, a short, stocky fellow dressed in a multi colored dashiki, asked.

"I'll take a scotch and ginger ale if you have it." Reggie said as he extended his hand to shake Larry's.

"You've got it, my brother." As soon as Larry handed Reggie the drink, he gulped down about half of it, looking for some help in maintaining his cool look.

"What's up my man?" Jeff asked as he approached the bar and reached over to hug Larry.

"You're the man. What can I get for you?" Larry asked.

"How about a screwdriver?" Jeff said as he grabbed Harriett around the waist and began to bump her. Harriett bumped back but danced away and pulled Reggie into the dance area and began to dance as Aretha Franklin pumped out, "Think." Reggie wondered if he was ready since he had not danced like the people at the party for some time. But the drink was beginning to make him feel he was at peace with the world. As Harriett let go of him and began to twist her body to the rhythm of the music, all the old steps came back and he began moving with the music. He closed his eyes, remembering what it was like at those parties they used to have when he was in high school. The music then turned to Percy Sledge's, "When A Man Loves A Woman." Still lingering in the fantasy of those high school days, he pulled Harriett close and began to grind. She rested her head on his shoulder and held him tight. When the music stopped, Harriett kissed Reggie on the neck as another woman pulled her away to help put out food.

Just as Reggie started walking toward Jeff, a plump woman wearing a caftan touched him on the shoulder. When he turned around she began to dance and beckoned him to join her. Ben E. King's "Stand By Me" was blasting and Reggie was still feeling light on his feet, so he joined in. It seemed the record had been played twice. When it was over, Reggie thanked his partner who was standing before him smiling. He then walked toward the terrace where Jeff was engaged in conversation with a woman, but before he got there, Harriett turned up the lights and announced that food was ready. After about a half hour of dancing, Reggie's high was fading and he felt hungry so he did a U turn and headed for the table with the food. There was rice and beans, stewed chicken, fired chicken wings, macaroni and cheese, collard greens, potato salad and a green salad. Reggie loaded his plate then walked out on the terrace where he stood and proceeded to work on cleaning it. Jeff, picking up a piece of chicken from his plate, came and stood beside him.

"How you doing man?" Jeff asked with a little more animation than usual. "Do you see anything you might want to take home?"

"Not yet," Reggie answered, feeling confronted by the question.

"The one you just danced with is hot. She might be a little heavy, but she can make you holler for your mama. She's flexible if you get my drift."

"That's good to know, but let me check out the rest of the flock before settling on one. Tell me, how much grazing of this flock have you done?" Reggie asked in jest trying to direct the conversation away from him.

"Well, Harriett won't let me out of the pasture long enough to do too much grazing. But this old bull breaks the fence enough to keep him tamed," Jeff answered as he slapped Reggie on the shoulder.

Reggie suddenly lost his appetite. He wondered what Jeff might have thought about the way he was holding Harriett when they were dancing and if he saw her kiss on his neck. He put down his plate and picked up his drink and took a sip. Jeff continued chewing without looking directly at Reggie.

Feeling he needed a moment to regroup, Reggie asked, "Where is the rest room?"

"Down the hall to your left," Jeff answered.

As Reggie was making his way through the crowd, he noticed he was the only person without a bushy Afro. As he looked at himself in the bathroom mirror, his mind flashed back to those days in college when he was the only Black in a class. He suddenly felt conspicuous and wondered what the people at the party thought of him. He wondered if Jeff was trying to make a subtle statement by bringing him here. Added to that feeling he wondered if Jeff was a bit ticked off because he thought he was after Harriett. This is no longer a party, he thought. This is a torture chamber and I need to escape, but how without seeming to be ungrateful for the invitation or maybe conveying the impression that he thought he was better than the people around him. He continued to stare at himself in the mirror wondering what he should do now and feeling angry that he had placed himself in the situation. He concluded he was unable to be creative enough to leave the party early without leaving behind some doubts about his decision, so he decided to use the over-used story that he had developed an upset stomach, probably from the liquor he had on an empty stomach. So he needed to leave before embarrassing himself. Maybe tomorrow, he thought, he could come up with a way to do any damage control with Jeff and Harriett, if it appeared necessary.

In somewhat slow deliberate speech, Reggie said to Harriett, "I think I have consumed too much too fast of your good liquor on an empty stomach and I need to get out of here before I embarrass myself. Thanks for inviting me. I really had a good time. I'll see you Monday."

"You just got here," Harriett said.

"Yes, but I guess I was over anxious to have a good time and indulged too much too fast. I'm a cheap drunk."

"Are you going to be able to get home okay?"

"O yes, I'll be okay."

He then walked over to Jeff and whispered, "Man I got to get out of here. That scotch ain't agreeing with me. I'll see you Monday."

"Come on man, you mean you can't handle a little liquor. What did you all do at Davis University?"

"I flunked the course on handling liquor."

"Are you going to be all right?"

"Yes, I'll be ok after a night's rest."

Reggie started to walk down to 125th Street and over to Broadway where he could get the Number 1 train. However, he squashed that idea thinking he had had enough of Harlem for one day and night. Instead, he headed downstairs for the downtown trains for a connection to the Number 1.

On the ride home, Reggie began to count the number of Black people on the train that had an Afro and those with short cut hair like his. He tried to imagine what the person was like with the different hair cuts. Those with hair cuts like his tended to be older than him and he imagined they were aligned with the segment of the Black population that thought the civil rights revolution was moving too fast and all those with Afros were waiting for the day the revolution would come. He didn't feel he fitted comfortably in either group. Neither Martin Luther King, Malcolm X, nor Roy Wilkins had Afros and they were leaders of the movement, he declared. So why should I change my hair? I believe in the civil rights movement. What would they think at the job if I suddenly grew an Afro? Would they be intimidated by me? What kind of assignments would I get? Jeff has an Afro, but he is in the creative department. They are expected to be odd. I am in management and have to meet clients. If I succeed on my job, I am a role model for other Blacks in business, so I'm doing my part for the movement, he declared.

CHAPTER 5

The sound of the telephone ringing awakened Reggie from a dream that he was standing before representative of Texas Oil answering their questions about the ad campaign. Gordon was seated at the other end of the conference table smiling. The company representatives were nodding their heads in approval. Reggie was feeling a shot of euphoria as he was transported back into the real world. As the disturbing sound of the phone rang again, he wondered who could be calling this early. It's Sunday morning, he thought. God knows I hope it ain't Jeff or Harriett calling to check on me. "Hello," he answered in a slow, deep voice, typical of his first utterances in the morning.

"Hello, son, you sound like you are just waking up. Shouldn't you be getting up and getting ready to go to church?"

"Hello mom, I thought I would turn on the radio today and find a good service. I haven't had time to search for a good church yet, but it's on my agenda. How are thing at home?"

"Now, don't you try to fool me, boy. You need the Lord guiding you in New York and you need some good Christians in your life and you are more likely to find that in a church, so I want you to promise me you'll get out there and join a church. You promised me you would go to Harlem and find one."

"I know, mom, and I will. How is dad?"

"He is about the same. There is no improvement in his speech. He sits in that wheelchair looking angry most of the time. When he tries to speak and can't tell you what he wants to say, he tries to cuss. He gives me a hard time when I try to give him his medicine. All that anger causes his blood pressure to go up which could cause another stroke. It's in the Lord's hand. I'm doing the best I can to make him comfortable."

"Mom I know you are doing the best you can. Don't you worry yourself so much that you get sick."

"I pray everyday, son, asking the Lord to take care of us all."

"Did Doug get the job with the police department?"

"Not yet. They say he is way down on the list of qualified applicants to be hired. I'm concerned about your brother. He seems to be heading for destruction. When he comes around, he looks like he's been wearing the same clothes for a week. You know how he was always concerned about how he looked. Well, I think he has lost that. I was so hopeful when he got out of the Army. He was a changed man-very responsible. I know he was disappointed that he had to go to work at the factory with his father because nothing else was available. Now he's probably upset he hasn't been called for a job with the police department after waiting a year. He needs faith and you can't get him to go near a church. I pray the Lord will take care of him. I hate to see him this way. That wife of his, I understand, is up to her old trick- trying to see how many men she can get interested in her. If Doug knows about her behavior, that probably causes some of his problem, too. But I understand he is as guilty as she is-trying to test his power over any hussy that crosses his path. Lord knows I don't know what effect their behavior is having on Doug Junior. He's doing a great job in school. He shows me his report card which has mostly A's and a few B's. I pray he keeps it up. He reminds me of you when you were in school. Maybe you could keep in touch with him and encourage him. He often asks about you."

"I'm going to try to do that, mom."

"I don't mean to worry you. By the way, thanks for the money you sent. It really helped with things around here. The cost of your father's medicine is a real strain on us. Well, I won't keep you and run up this telephone bill. Now make sure you turn on that radio and get some of God's message today. It will help you make it through the week. I've been doing all the talking about us. Are things really okay with you?

"I'm doing fine. I'm getting into the job fairly quickly and beginning to make my mark. Don't worry about me."

"All right I'm praying for you. Good bye now."

"Don't worry, mom. I love you."

Reggie rolled over on his back, placed his hands behind his head and stared at the ceiling. He wondered if his mother would be all right and whether he made the right decision when he decided not to return home and take a teaching job after graduating from college, if he was being selfish thinking only of what he wanted and forgetting sacrifices the family had made for him to get where he was. He couldn't imagine returning home after having the opportunity to work in New York-the dream of many. He closed his eyes tightly trying to squeeze out those thoughts.

Unable to succeed, he rolled out of bed and turned on the television and started switching channels and just happened to run upon a service at a Black Baptist church. He remembered his promise to his mother and decided to leave it on that station although he went about his activities while it was on. While standing in the bathroom looking in the mirror trying to decide if he should shave since he had no scheduled activities where he would want to impress people, the minister's voice reached a crescendo saying, "Your selfish ways will damn you!" Reggie felt a lump rise in his throat. "Why the hell am I listening to this charlatan?" He asked while rushing to the television to change channels.

As he returned to the bathroom, still pondering whether or not to shave, he glanced in the mirror again and stared at his hair. He bit his bottom lip, slammed the mirrored door and walked out of the bathroom. He walked around the apartment a couple of times and decided to put on some clothes and go searching for a newspaper. The sun dominated a clear blue, cloudless sky warming the winds coming out of the northwest. Reggie seemed to have forgotten why he left the apartment and began to walk aimlessly through the quiet and peaceful streets of the neighborhood. Some of the trees lining the streets were showing early signs of fall as they began to shed their leaves. As Reggie walked, taking in the scenery around him, he felt this was the kind of neighborhood he dreamed of living in when he was growing up in the segregated South. He began to feel the tension that had been bubbling in him began to evaporate. He took a deep breath, exhaled and began to step briskly. At the newsstand he picked up a New York Times and headed back to the apartment, declaring that he had been handed a great opportunity to do something that not many other Blacks had and he would pursue it and make a mark that others would be proud of. I will meet any challenges interfering with that goal, he proclaimed, as he brushed his hand over his head feeling the small waves in his short cropped hair.

Reggie stopped at the deli shop and picked up a cinnamon - raisins bagel with cream cheese which had become a routine during the week. However, he felt like a down home Sunday breakfast of eggs, grits, Virginia ham, red gravy and hot biscuits, but would have to go to Harlem to satisfy that craving and there was no way he was going down there. As he sat down with his New York Times and bagel with the radio playing soft instrumental music in the background, he felt at peace with himself. He opened the paper and there was the headline article about the campaign battles between Nixon and Humphrey. He turned the page without reading the article. There was another article about the war. He again turned the page and was confronted with an article about the ongoing controversy over community control of the schools in the city. He closed the paper and turned on the television in search of some baseball game while declaring he just wanted to relax before Monday morning.

CHAPTER 6

"Hello Reggie, how are you doing? I wanted to call you yesterday to see how you were doing, but it took all day to clean-up after the party. People didn't leave until four- thirty. Are you okay?" Harriett asked.

As soon as Reggie laid eyes on Harriett, his scalp began to itch. His hand began to travel toward his head to scratch but he pushed it back. There was no way, at that moment, he wanted to bring attention to his hair. He took a deep breath, hoping the movement in his face would relieve the itch.

"I'm fine. I just needed to sleep it off and I did a lot of that," he said, anxious to move on.

"Well, next time, we'll have to limit your intake. In the meantime, maybe we could put you to the test at lunch sometimes."

"Sure," Reggie said as he walked away thinking how do I get around this. I sure wouldn't mind having lunch. She could open my eyes to a lot of thing around here. But Lord knows I don't want to mess up my friendship with Jeff by having him think I'm trying to step into his territory. However, it's been a long dry season and maybe I could get it up even for this African queen. But she would probably turn into a Salem witch if she thought I was just using her. When I said I would meet each challenge with everything I have, I wasn't thinking of this kind. Anyway, I wonder if Harriett could ever be serious about someone who doesn't sport an Afro. It seems all her friends have them. Maybe she wants to try to change me.

"Good morning, Reggie. Give me a smile. Was your weekend as bad as the frown on your face?" Barbara asked.

"No, no, it was great. I guess my mind was some place else. How was yours?"

"Mine was okay. You and Gordon have a ten thirty meeting with the creative team on the Texas Oil campaign."

"Is Gordon in?"

"Not yet."

Reggie's mind shifted from troubled to excited. It was his opportunity to present his idea for the campaign, but, he wanted to discuss it with Gordon before the meeting and get his response and advice. He wrote down his idea and organized his thoughts so that he would come off as knowledgeable and well prepared. After reading his notes, he leaned back in his chair thinking this is not bad for the short time I have been here. If my idea is not accepted, at least they will have to respect that I am capable of making significant contributions. At nine thirty and Gordon had not shown up, he felt a bit nervous. He really wanted some feedback before going to the meeting. It was five minutes to ten when Gordon stuck his head in and said smiling, sounding almost out of breath, "Good morning, are you ready to go?"

"I'm ready," Reggie said.

"How are things going?" Gordon asked as he moved swiftly toward the conference room sipping his coffee and gripping the cup so that the coffee would not spill.

"Things are okay," Reggie said as he concluded there was no opportunity to discuss his idea before the meeting so he would have to take a chance.

"Good morning everybody. I hope you had the kind of weekend that made you raring to come in this morning and get started on this account," Gordon said laughing as he took his seat at the far end of the conference table, dropped a legal size note pad and pen on the table and leaned forward. Reggie was seated to Gordon's right. Rick was at the other end of the table and Jeff and Donald were on Gordon's left.

"The folks from Texas Oil are scheduled to be here Friday to hear our presentation on the new campaign so we need to organize ourselves," Gordon said in a more serious tone.

"I have an idea that might enhance our original idea and I think we can put it together before Friday," Rick said.

"Well, let's have it," Gordon answered.

"Why don't we get Hank Aaron, or Walt Frazier to do one of the monologues about the great community services the company is doing with emphasis on their impact in the Black community? They could use some image- building in the Black community and with the country still reeling from the assassination of Martin Luther King, it would be a sure winner," Rick said.

"Great idea," Gordon responded with enthusiasm in his voice.

"I know someone who knows Hank Aaron's agent," Rick said with a nervous slur in his voice.

"Well, let's go for it," Gordon replied raising his hand in a victory sign.

Reggie felt proud. He sat waiting for Rick to announce that he got the idea from him. Rick never looked in his direction. He sat smiling nervously as if he had saved the day. Reggie felt the muscles in his stomach tightening and beads of sweat forming on his forehead. That no good snake in the grass bastard, he thought.

After clarifying all that needed to be done and each person's responsibility for the presentation, Gordon ended the meeting. Reggie wasn't sure what he should do or should he do anything to get rid of the anger he was feeling. He wasn't comfortable discussing it with Gordon. He didn't want Gordon to see him as a weak complainer. Wouldn't it have been great to go to lunch with Harriett and get her advice on this, he thought. Maybe I should see if Jeff is free for lunch and discuss that bastard with him, but he had not had a chance to come up with the right lie to tell Jeff about his Saturday night behavior. What the hell, he thought, if the subject comes up I'll stick to the same story I gave him already.

Rick dashed out of the conference room with Gordon seemingly engaged in a discussion of the new idea. Reggie was the last to leave. He caught up with Jeff who was talking to Donald as they walked back to their offices. Donald stopped off to talk to a secretary.

"Hey man, are you free for lunch?" Reggie asked Jeff.

"No, man, I have to run down to Motor Vehicles to get my driver's license renewed. Let me take a rain check."

"Okay," Reggie said now wondering what to do with all the tension boiling in him. I need to get out of here for a while, he decided. He immediately thought of asking Harriett, but just as fast, remembered all the pitfalls of going there. He waited until twelve- thirty, the time Harriett usually left for lunch, before he left his office. He didn't want her to see him leaving alone. She might press him to have lunch with her and if he couldn't come up with a lie fast enough to turn down the offer and accepted, he would have to deal with Jeff. And he didn't want to add on any doubts Jeff may already be harboring about the two of them.

He left the building with no destination in mind and just started walking. There was an overcast sky with no breeze but a pleasantly warm temperature. He looked up into the sky as if to ask the sun to come out and lift his spirits. Disappointed, he bowed his head and put his hands in his pockets. He found himself on Park Avenue, a wide two- way street with rows of shrubbery down the island separating the two sides. The burst of openness caused him to lift his head and decide to walk up this street which was less congested than the one way streets.

As he stood on the corner of Park Avenue and Fifty-First streets waiting for the traffic light to change, he noticed the back of someone who seemed familiar, walking toward Fifty-Second. He batted his eyes and wiped them and looked again while becoming impatient with the slow changing light. His heart began to race and his hands which had been balled into a fist began to sweat. Dear Lord let it be, he mumbled while the person began to blend into the crowd. He looked at the traffic crossing the street in front of him to see if he could jaywalk, but it was too congested. He turned his head left and right and tightened his lips in frustration. When he looked ahead again the green light flashed. He wanted to run, but there were too many people in the block, so he walked as fast as he could whipping his way through the people as if he were going to put out a fire. The light at Fifty-Second turned red and brought the person to a halt.

Reggie slowed down and tried to compose himself before approaching and decide on exactly how to approach. The light changed and without a defined strategy, he just walked up behind her and said, "Hello, Miss McKay."

She turned around and paused for a moment seeming to refresh her memory then burst into a smile and said, "Hello, Mr. Morton, Where did you come from?"

"I've been chasing you for two blocks," Reggie said, smiling back at her. He remembered her blond hair hanging below her shoulders, her blue eyes and beautiful petite body, but didn't remember her disarming smile which magically washed away all the tension he had been feeling. All he could think of now was wrapping his arms around her and just holding her tightly and dancing. For a moment, it seemed the sun had burst through the overcast sky.

"How have you been adjusting to life in New York?" Carol asked.

"I can't complain. I have the excitement of Manhattan during the day and the quiet of Riverdale in the evening-the best of two worlds. I'm getting used to the commute which I wish was shorter, but it usually gives me time to anticipate my day in the morning and wind down time in the evening." He just wanted to burst out and ask, when can we get together, but restrained himself trying to project coolness instead of the boiling anxiety churning in him. He suddenly remembered that he was out to lunch even though eating was the last thing on his mind; it would be natural to invite her to lunch.

"Have you had lunch?" Reggie asked.

"No, but I plan to pick up something and take it back to the office. I just came back from a meeting and have a report that's due by the end of the day."

Reggie felt like a tire that had just run over a nail and gone flat. He could feel the blood flush from his face. My God, he thought, I hope she can't read my mind.

"Well, what about lunch tomorrow?"

"I'm sorry. The reason I have to finish the report today is because I have an early flight to Atlanta tomorrow. However, I will be back in the office on Monday. Why don't you call me and we can arrange to have lunch, okay? Did I give you my card? Here, take one. What a surprise running into you," Carol said with another disarming smile as she reached to shake Reggie's hand.

"I'll talk to you on Monday," Reggie said as he stood in a daze watching her disappear into the crowd. He seemed to be glued to the spot where he was standing while people, with great irritation, maneuvered to avoid running into him. He finally became conscious that he looked like he was renting the space where he was standing. He started to walk away as if he had just bought the last gift on his Christmas list the day before Christmas Eve. He unconsciously headed back to his office. When he stepped into the reception area, Harriett said, "You look like you had a fabulous lunch or did you find a million dollars?"

Reggie suddenly realized he did not have anything to eat, but felt like he had had a full meal. "Neither," he responded and gave Harriett the peace sign and continued to walk to his office.

"Hi Reggie, Gordon would like to see you," Barbara said.

"When?"

"He said as soon as you returned from lunch. He's in his office now. You can go right in."

"Hey, my man," Gordon said. Reggie was beginning to sober up, wondering what Gordon was up to with that forced smile on his face.

"The agency has been given the go sign to make our bid for the Navy account and the president has assigned me to the team making the pitch. We have to be in Washington for a presentation this Friday so I won't be able to be at the meeting with Texas Oil. You will have to take over the meeting. Sorry I have to throw this on you without warning, but that's the way things go around here. Let's get together for lunch Wednesday and I can go over things with you. Are you okay with this? I know you can handle it. You saw how I handled the last meeting with them."

"I'm fine with it," Reggie said although he felt his mouth go dry as the image of those Ku Klux Klan looking guys from Texas Oil flashed in his mind. He remembered they were professional and courteous, but not friendly toward him. He visualize them walking into the meeting with a rope in their hands pointing at him. However, it was a great opportunity to strut his stuff and maybe put Rick in his place, but if he messed up it could be a great opportunity for the agency to say we tried but it didn't work. He wondered if that was actually the plan especially since he wasn't sure about those guys from Texas Oil. The account had been with the agency for a while, so surely they don't want to jeopardize it by putting a new Black man in charge of dealing with them even though it might be just for a day. Well, he declared, I've got three days to get ready. I wish Gordon and I were having lunch tomorrow so I could hear what he wants to brief me on so I could have a couple of days to digest it. Well as I said, I would give it everything I got so here we go.

During the ride home that evening Reggie could not wind down. His mind was caught between the thought of seeing Carol again and the possibility of causing a disaster at the Friday meeting. If he could make it through Friday in good shape, he thought, life could be just beautiful. Oh God, let it be, he prayed. He then had the fleeting thought that maybe Carol was lying about her report and trip just to get rid of him and that she would not return his call on Monday. He again remembered his two failed relationships. He closed his eyes tightly trying to squeeze those thoughts from his mind. He told himself that Carol's disarming smile portrayed a warmth, honesty and sincerity that set her apart from the others.

Where will I take her to lunch? I don't know many places. Maybe she will have a suggestion, but I don't want to come off as unsure of anything. I know what- I will tell her we are going to the Cattlemen Club. I know about it and I will build it up as a place that impressed me.

What will I talk about? I don't want to scare her away by exposing my burning hunger to be with her. Maybe, if Friday goes well there will be something interesting to discuss, but I don't want to fit the stereotype that men like to talk too much about themselves and are not good listeners, he worried. Just thinking about the possibilities made Reggie feel like dancing.

The bus came to a sudden stop to avoid a collision and caused Reggie's thoughts to jump back to Texas Oil. The muscles in his neck and back tightened. He could only think of how things could fall apart if he screwed up. He told himself that he needed to put thoughts of Carol out of his mind and concentrate on the presentation. First of all, he decided, he needed to make sure he did not reveal his apprehensions about the Texas Oil men and that he project the perfect image of a professional, knowledgeable and cordial manager.

Reggie sat down at his table that evening with a legal pad and pen and began developing an outline of his strategy for the meeting. He jotted down some areas that needed to be planned: meeting with the team to lay out the presentation, deciding on the appropriate behavior for dealing with the representatives of Texas Oil, becoming thoroughly versed in the recommendations that were presented, and follow-up plans. He began to write notes under each area-meet with team on Thursday, decide on the flow of the presentation, come up with topics for small talk with the Texas Oil reps and prepare his summary remarks. He then arched his back, stretched his arms and yawned. The clock on the radio next to the table that had been playing soft music showed twelve-thirty. He felt exhausted and headed straight for bed where he tossed and turned most of the night.

Reggie arrived in his office the next morning as anxious as a prize fighter before the bell rings for his first round. He asked Barbara to give him Gordon's file on Texas Oil. He perused it cover to cover, soaking up every bit of data that would help him feel prepared to address any issue that might come up. He continued to go over the outline he had prepared. When

Wednesday came he was beginning to feel comfortable about the meeting and was looking forward to lunch with Gordon.

"Good morning Reggie. How you doing? Feeling any butterflies?" Gordon asked with a smile that covered his face.

"Yes, the butterflies are in action, but I sent down a bagel and coffee to clip their wings," Reggie said smiling back at Gordon.

"You'll be all right. How about lunch at twelve-thirty?"

"Sounds good to me."

"Okay, I will pick you up."

Gordon arrived at Reggie's door promptly at twelve-thirty. "Are you ready? I have to be back for a meeting at two. I want to introduce you to Dionycis, a hot spot you might want to keep in mind. You can get a great cheeseburger and martini at lunch time and enjoy Go Go dancers at other times. It's a favorite place of a lot of people from the office."

The bar, a "pieced together" space with a few cages for Go Go dancers and a small stage for dancing, was crowded and noisy. Gordon was smiling and pointing to the cages and saying, "You should see those when the dancers are there." A waitress chewing on a wad of gum came over to them and asked, "What can I do for you gentlemen?"

"This is my friend's first time here so why don't we start with a couple of your famous martinis." Gordon said.

"Two martinis coming up," she said and returned to the table with the drinks as if they were already made up.

"Fantastic," Gordon said as he reached for his and immediately took a sip.

"Would you gentlemen like to order now?" the waitress asked looking directly at Gordon with her order pad held loosely in her hand.

"Would you like to try one of those cheeseburgers I told you about?" Gordon asked Reggie.

"Why not," Reggie answered.

"We'll take two cheeseburgers with French fries."

"Two cheeseburgers and fries coming-up," the waitress repeated as she dashed away.

After taking a few sips of his martini, Gordon raised his glass and said, "Here's to you and your success with Texas Oil. Are you all prepared for the meeting? There's not a lot to do. They know the strategy, so all you all are doing is presenting them the status of our efforts to get the celebrities they have been informed about, going over the copy for their monologues and the projected shooting schedules for the commercials. The only thing new is Rick's suggestion about reaching out to the Black community which is a great idea. I am sure Rick will do a great job making that presentation and I can't imagine they will have any objection to the idea. Well, yes I can, but I don't think they will. Howard is the one to focus on. They will buy what he tells them. He's not as washed in Southern blood as the rest of them. I know you can handle it. Are there any questions you want to ask me?"

"I wanted to go over my plans for running the meeting." Reggie said as the waitress arrived with the food.

"Okay, take a bite and tell me what you think." Gordon said.

With Gordon's request for a verdict on the burgers and the idea of talking with his mouth full, and the level of noise surrounding them, Reggie thought he should give the food priority at the moment and pursue Gordon's opinion about his plans when they were walking back to the office.

"I'll recommend it to anybody looking for a great burger," Reggie said.

"I thought it would be a hit with you." Gordon then turned his attention to his plate and picked up a few fries with his hand and began charging into his burger. He didn't seem to remember or hear Reggie's comment about discussing his plan. The waitress came over and asked how was everything?

"Everything is fine. How about another round of drinks?" Gordon asked.

"Not for me," Reggie said.

"Okay, just one." When the drink arrived, Gordon looked at his watch which disclosed it was one –thirty five. "I got that meeting at two. We better get out of here. The president will fire me if I'm late." He gulped down the rest of his lunch and picked-up the drink and didn't put it down until the glass was empty. Reggie quickly devoured his food and finished the rest of his drink. Gordon beckoned the waitress and asked for the check. They walked out of the restaurant at a pace that didn't give Reggie confidence that Gordon would be able to give his plan much attention and if he pushed it, he might come off as too insecure for the job, especially after Gordon tried to reassure him that things would be okay.

When they arrived back at the office, Gordon said, "You are going to be okay, man, don't worry. You got what it takes," as he dashed to his office to grab the bottle of Listerine and headed for the men's room before going to the meeting. His compliment, however, had inflated Reggie's confidence.

Promptly at nine –thirty Thursday morning Reggie, still wearing his suit jacket, entered the conference room for the meeting with Donald, Jeff and Rick. None of the three was there. He took a deep breath and moved to the head of the table facing the door and placed the folder with all his notes and papers on the table, then sat down and opened it and began thumbing through the pages with his head down.

"Good morning, Reggie," Donald said as he entered with a donut and a cup of coffee.

"Good morning fellow. How are things going outside of this place? Do you still have hope for your Mets making it to the World Series?"

"You bet your bottom dollar I do," Donald said. At that moment, Jeff walked in.

"Hello boss," Jeff said with a smile covering his face.

"Just for the next two days," Reggie said, also with a smile. "We'll get started as soon as Rick arrives."

At nine-forty Rick rushed in and said "good morning," looking at everyone except Reggie and offering no apology for being late.

Reggie was irritated but went ahead and started the meeting by going over the logistics for Friday's meeting then reminding everyone the importance of being on- time. He then asked each person to go over their presentation. When it became time for Rick, he looked away from Reggie and spoke as if he were bored. Reggie had decided to take the high road with the thief because he was in charge and it might seem petty to dwell on what he felt about what Rick had done or his disrespect.

"We are ready guys. I'll see you tomorrow morning at ten," Reggie said. Rick bounced out of his seat and was the first to leave the room. Jeff looked at Rick and shook his head while David gave Reggie the peace sign seeming to ignore Rick. Reggie took a bit of solace in what he perceived as Rick's apparent discomfort with him especially since he had taken no action of revenge.

That evening Reggie couldn't get the meeting out of his mind. He kept trying to think if he had neglected to do something, but nothing came to mind. He stood in front of the mirror and practiced everything from small talk with the representatives to closing the meeting. He chased sleep the whole night and when the radio came on at six- thirty he was already wide awake. He jumped in the shower and quickly washed, then stood under the shower head letting the pulsating flow of water massage his back hoping it would relax the tight muscles from his neck to his waist. He stepped out of the shower feeling enough relief to let him focus on the clothes he had decided would make the best impression. He checked to see if he needed to make any adjustment and decided that the navy blue suit, the business white shirt, the red tie and black shoes would do the job. After dressing, he took one last look in the mirror and brushed his hand over his hair and, with a look of defiance, declared it was appropriate.

Reggie bypassed the deli where he usually picked up his coffee and bagel. He decided he was too jittery to add caffeine to his body and too many butterflies were flying around in his stomach to add food. A scotch and ginger ale would probably do the trick, he thought, as he imagined what it would be like for this Black man to walk into the meeting with slurred speech and out of balance. He imagined the reps from Texas Oil grabbing their briefcases and rushing out as he reached to shake their hands. He tripped one who fell on his face and broke one of his teeth. Reggie smiled as the fantasy caused the release of some of the tension he was feeling. He arrived at the office at eight-thirty with nothing to do. He closed his door and paced the floor for a while then took out his folder and thumbed through it. He walked around to the conference room to see that everything was in order. The Latin delivery boy from the deli had arrived with the refreshments. Reggie greeted him and watched to see what he had brought. He then walked back to his office where Barbara greeted him and asked if everything was okay for the meeting. He assured her things were fine and went into his office and took several deep breaths and sat down and looked out the window.

At nine-thirty, Barbara buzzed Reggie to let him know that Howard and the reps from Texas Oil had arrived. Reggie was flustered. He had not counted on them arriving early. His heartbeat began to escalate which he thought was not good for his first encounter with them. He wasn't sure whether he should greet them or let them wait in the reception area for a while until he pulled himself together.

"Do you want me to take them to the conference room and offer them some refreshments?" Barbara asked.

"Yes, could you do that for me?" Reggie asked. What he really wanted to say was, "you angel, thank God for you." He decided that fifteen minutes were enough time for small talk with them so he would lay low in his office for another fifteen before meeting them. He stood up and walked to the window and looked toward the sky and began to pray, "Dear God, please help me get through this meeting without looking like a dumb, shuffling Negro." He then began to take deep breaths and tried to recall everything he had planned to say. However, it all seemed to escape him so he mumbled to himself, "you got to have faith" and at nine-forty five he stepped into the conference room and walked over to the three men and extended his hand and said, "How are we doing today? I guess you have been informed that Gordon has been called away on an emergency project."

Yes, I spoke to Gordon Monday and he informed me," Howard said as he shook Reggie's hand and while the other two also shook his hand and said, "Good Morning, Mr. Morton" with a slight tremble in their voices.

"I hope our bagels, cream cheese and pastries are a good substitute for a hearty Texas breakfast," Reggie said with a smile.

The words were streaming from his lips like the flow of honey from an overturned bottle. It felt like the blood in his veins had been spiked by a shot of adrenalin causing it to massage his brain.

"It's just fine," Howard said. "If we had a hearty Texas breakfast, men of our age would probably not be able to listen to your presentation today."

"Well, I guess we ordered the right things. We will get started as soon as the rest of our team arrives which should be in about five minutes."

"I understand you all are staying at the Waldorf. Is it living up to its reputation for service and accommodations?" Reggie asked, trying to pull the other two men into the conversation.

"It's a pretty fine hotel that's conveniently located near the office. That's the most important thing," one responded without changing the matter- of fact expression on his face.

"I think you have met our team members," Reggie said as Jeff and David walked in the room.

"Yes, we have," Howard said. "How you all doing? Have you been working hard for us?" Howard asked.

"You bet your bottom dollar we have," David said as Rick walked in the room with a big grin on his face and proceeded to go to each man and shake his hand before taking his seat.

"I guess we can get started. We are all here," Reggie said then proceeded to summarize the history of what had occurred in the campaign up to the day's presentation and then provided an overview of what was on the agenda for the day's meeting and who would be doing what. He then turned it over to each member of the team. As each member spoke Reggie sat back in his chair thinking how he had not missed a beat. Everything he planned so far had gone as expected. Every minute of preparation was worth it, he declared.

Rick was the last one to present. His face lit up like a one hundred watt light bulb. He spoke with great enthusiasm about increasing their share of the Black consumers market and how the right Black celebrity spokesman would be ideal for a commercial. He said the agency had been working with the agents of Hank Aaron and Bill Russell and Walt Frazier as a back-up.

"You guys really have been working for us. Let's go with the campaign," Howard said while clapping his hands and bowing his head toward each presenter and to Reggie and without making any specific comment about Rick's idea. Howard's partners forced a smile and nodded to the group.

"Thank you all for coming. Gordon or I will follow-up with you next week about shooting, etc.," Reggie said as he walked them to the elevator.

"Thank you, Mr. Morton," Howard said.

"Please call me Reggie," Reggie said.

"Okay Reggie," Howard responded as they entered the elevator.

When Reggie turned and faced the receptionist station, Harriett was smiling and giving him the victory sign. He returned the smile and victory sign then walked back to the conference room where Jeff and David were waiting.

"You guys did a fantastic job. Thank you," Reggie said.

David and Jeff placed one of their hands on Reggie's shoulder and said, "So did you."
Jeff took Reggie's hand and placed it between both of his and said, "Right on, my brother." Rick had disappeared.

Reggie picked up a bagel smeared it with cream cheese, grabbed a cup of coffee and headed back to his office.

"From the look on your face, I assume it went well," Barbara said smiling.

"It did and thanks a million for helping me out."

"No problem."

Reggie went into his office, closed the door, turned his chair toward the window, leaned back and placed his feet on the desk and began nibbling on the bagel and sipping his coffee. He felt like getting up and dancing around the room, but he was afraid someone in one of the buildings across the street might call the president and report that there was a crazy Black man going mad in one of his offices. So instead, he raised his cup of coffee and said, "Here's to all of you. This Black man never missed a beat. Put that in your pipe and smoke it." At that moment, there was a knock on his door. "Come in," he said as he jerked his feet off the desk.

"Hey, man, Harriett and I want to invite you to lunch to celebrate your victory. Do you have plans?" Jeff asked.

"Thanks man that would be fine. I have no plans," Reggie answered without hesitation.

"Okay, we will see you around twelve-thirty." Jeff said as he turned away.

Reggie was still basking in his success when it occurred to him what he had just agreed to. He wondered if they might be still looking for an explanation of his behavior at Harriett's party or would they use this opportunity to try to talk him into letting his hair grow into a bushy Afro. The thought of dealing with either scenario made him anxious and even if they didn't bring up either subject, just sitting there looking at their Afros would make him overly conscious of the fact that he did not have one, he thought. He became irritated that he was even thinking of these issues on the day of his first success in demonstrating his ability to manage an account. He thought about telling them it was not any of their business how he wore his hair, if the subject came up. But that might result in the loss of the friendship of people he might need down the road. He took his fist and banged it on the desk several times. At this point, he thought, there was no way of getting out of this lunch that wouldn't raise more suspicion about him than what was probably already in their minds.

"Are you ready for lunch Mr. Account Executive?" Jeff asked leaning against the door with a smile on his face.

"I'm ready my friend," Reggie said hoping that greeting him as a friend would soften any criticism of his behavior or hair.

"You deserve a special lunch after showing those Southern "crackers" that there is more to a Black man than brawn. So we are taking you up to Harlem to one of our premier soul food restaurants, Sylvia's. You're going to love it. Where did you say you are from?" Jeff asked.

"Tennessee."

"Well, you'll probably think you are home again when you taste Sylvia's food."

Christ, Reggie was thinking, why must we go up to Harlem? Well, I know I am in for it now. This celebration just might turn out to be a hanging. "Do you think we have enough time to go up to Harlem and get back to the office without overdoing it?" Reggie asked.

"Hey man where have you been? There is no abusing lunch time around here, especially after the kind of meeting you just finished. Don't worry about it. Harriett is the only one who would need to be concerned and she has covered her behind."

"Okay, let's go up to Harlem and indulge ourselves," Reggie said, thinking at least he would get a meal worthy of a celebration or a last meal before a hanging.

"Well Reggie your handling of the meeting this morning is the buzz around the floor, as if they were all waiting patiently for you to fall flat on your face. You showed them, right on! I understand Rick dashed out right after the meeting. It was probably because he had to go to the bathroom after watching how well you managed the meeting. I'm really proud of you," Harriett said as they stood on the street waiting to hail a gypsy taxi willing to go to Harlem.

"Thanks, it was only a meeting. It's not as if I landed a new contract for the agency," Reggie said feeling confident and a bit more relaxed after Harriett's compliment.

"A hundred and twenty-seventh street and Lenox Avenue," Jeff said to the husky Black driver who was wearing a cap to cover his medium- length hair.

"You going to Sylvia's?" The driver asked.

"Yes, my man," Jeff answered.

"The reason I asked is cause I don't get many folks down here asking to go to Harlem. So, I wanted to make sure you knew where you were going. I didn't mean to get into your business."

"No problem. The reason we flagged you down was because we figured you would take us there without any trouble. If you know what I mean," Jeff said.

"I read you brother," the driver said.

Jeff turned to Reggie and said. "Yes man, today was a big step for the agency. They have never had a Black person in the position of account executive. That position has a lot of contact with the client and neither the agency nor the client is too cool with that kind of situation. They are a bit more comfortable with someone like me behind the scene in creative and I am the only one. Harriett is the only receptionist. There are a few in traffic and the mail room, but would you believe there are no Black secretaries. So you can see what happened today was like a bombshell. Gordon must have sold them on the idea. He's a cool guy and well- respected and I guarantee you he cleared it with Howard before they agreed to it and I would be willing to bet that Rick was asked to spy on you. And I am sure Howard called the office as soon as he got back in his office to report. But man, there is nothing they can complain about. Of course they don't need a reason to find fault," Jeff said. He then patted Reggie on the shoulder and said "Right on brother, we've got something to celebrate!"

"Thanks man," Reggie said as he began to feel he was among friends that he could go to to discuss things going on in the agency. He then set his mind on what he would have for lunch at this famous soul food restaurant. I haven't had any smothered liver with onion gravy in a long time, he remembered.

The taxi pulled up in front of the restaurant with a neon sign flashing Sylvia's. A group of men were milling around the entrance and a line of street vendors were stationed along the congested block, selling books, hats, socks, and sticks of incense. Jeff paid the driver and they hauled out of the cab and made their way through the men and entered the restaurant where there was a long counter with stools and a stream of waitresses dipping into pots and loading plates and calling to kitchen staff about an order that should have been ready. There was friendly chatter between the waitresses and the customers seated at the counter where there was a display of enticing cakes-coconut, chocolate and red velvet.

"How many?" a young man dressed in an open collar white shirt and black trouser asked Jeff.

"Three."

"Follow me," the young man said. He led them into a room behind the counter with a scattering of tables for four. There were pictures on the wall of famous people who had patronized the restaurant. He seated them at a table covered with a white table cloth which was then covered with a sheet of thick white paper. He then handed them a menu that listed the various specials served on specific days. "Your waiter will be with you shortly," the young man said.

Reggie looked over the menu and could not find liver and onion gravy anywhere on any day's specials. His eyes lit up when he saw chitterlings, but they were on the menu for Saturday. Disappointed, he turned his attention to Friday and spotted barbecued ribs and decided they would be a good substitute for liver or chitterlings and if he ordered some collard greens, potato salad, corn bread, iced tea, and for dessert, a slice of that coconut cake, that would make for a true celebration. He looked around the restaurant at all the Black people who seemed to be enjoying each other's company and the food. Harriett and Jeff were engrossed in the menu. Reggie glanced at them and thought how nice it was they wanted to celebrate his victory in spite of his strange behavior at Harriett's party. He felt a bit guilty about his doubts about having lunch with them in Harlem.

"I'm Ben. Are you ready to order?" the waiter asked.

"I'm Jeff. I'll take the ribs, with macaroni and cheese and greens and the sweet ice tea."

"I'll have the same except instead of the macaroni and cheese, I'll have potato salad," Reggie followed.

"Well, I think I am ready. How about the smothered chicken with rice, greens, corn and lemonade?" Harriett said.

While nibbling on the warm corn bread the waiter brought while they waited for their meal, Harriett asked Reggie, "What was life like in Chicago? Have you kept in touch with your friends back there since you came here?"

Reggie's feeling of comradeship with Harriett and Jeff began to dissipate as soon as the question rolled off Harriett's lips. He wasn't sure how to answer as Harriett looked at him smiling while her African designed earrings dangled from her ears. He didn't want to reveal that he circulated mainly in a circle of white people for the entire time he was there and that his best friend was a white guy he met in college. He wondered if Harriett's smile indicated she was digging for some intimate details of his life that might enhance her chances with him.

"My time in Chicago was mainly spent on building a reputation in the business world that would lead to a lucrative career in management. I developed a few friends who described me as a workaholic. I haven't had time to contact them since arriving here," Reggie said.

"Nobody special?" Harriett asked as she folded her hands together in front of her smiling face.

"Nobody special," Reggie said out of a dry mouth.

"What's wrong with those Chicago women? How could they let a handsome guy like you slip through their fingers?"

"I guess they had many other choices," Reggie answered as Jeff gave Harriett a stern look.

"Ribs with macaroni and cheese?" the waiter asked looking at Jeff.

"Then you get the ribs with potato salad," the waiter said as he handed Reggie his plate.

"And you get the smothered chicken," he said to Harriett.

The food muffled conversation except the occasional comments of approval. It brought back memories of those great meals his mother used to prepare, Reggie reminisced. But Harriett's inquiry had taken some of the joy out of eating it. During the ride back to the office, Jeff asked Reggie, "What's up with you this weekend?"

At that moment, Reggie had one of those experiences where the right answer immediately rolls off your lips with great authenticity as if it had been anticipated. "I've got to stick around the apartment for some furniture deliveries. That will take up Saturday and I will probably spend Sunday trying to put everything together." It was a lie, but he was certain he did not want to get too involved socially with Jeff and Harriett. Besides his present discomfort, he couldn't imagine they would be accepting of him dating a white woman.

"Okay man, I hope you get it all done and those delivery folks don't keep you hanging around all day. That can be a drag," Jeff said. Harriett looked at Reggie with a seductive smile.

During Reggie's bus ride home that evening, he replayed in his mind the meeting and every move he made and the reactions of everyone. He felt he was off to a great start and he wanted to share those feelings with someone who would understand, but there was no one. He felt lonely, but then his thoughts turned to Carol. With the meeting behind him, he could direct all his thoughts to Monday's lunch when he would have much to talk about.

CHAPTER 7

Feeling rested, fresh and energized, Reggie dashed past the receptionist desk giving Harriett, who was engaged in conversation with a visitor, the peace sign. After he greeted Barbara, she informed him that Gordon would not be in until the afternoon and that he had a meeting with the team bidding for the Navy contract at two. Reggie went into his office wondering what would be the best time to call Carol. Although he was anxious, he didn't want to turn her off by advertising it. She might think it's only a sexual thing and shy away. He decided ten o'clock should not be perceived as desperate and anyway that is about as long as he could wait. That should be a respectable time to ask for a twelve- thirty date, he decided.

He thumbed through papers, looked out the window and went to the men's room trying to kill the hour until ten. At ten on the dot, he picked up the phone and nervously dialed the number and took a deep breath in an effort to slow down his heart rate and calm himself so that his nervousness would not be reflected in his voice. The phone rang twice with no answer. He felt anxiety building. After the third ring, he felt sad. After the fourth ring, a hurried voice said, "Hello, Carol McKay." Reggie felt like a fifty pound weight had been lifted off his shoulder.

"Hello, Ms. McKay Reggie Morton here," he said slowly. He wanted to ask where were you? Are you busy? But he caught himself. "How are you today? Was your trip successful?"

"I'm fine. I just arrived in the office-problem with the subway. How are you?"

Not bad, he wanted to say. I'm riding on cloud nine now that I hear your voice, but instead asked, "Are we still on for lunch today?"

"Yes, could we make it at one?" Carol answered.

"That would be fine. I'll meet you on the corner of Park and Fifth. See you then." Reggie answered then hung up the phone and said, "yes!" as he hit the desk with his fist. Leaning back in his chair, he suddenly remembered the last time he felt this way was in high school when Mona, the most beautiful girl in his class, agreed to be his girlfriend. However, many years later, when she decided to dump him for that white guy, he declared that being in love was more than he could handle. He never thought this day would come.

His fast- moving thoughts shifted and he wondered whether Carol really liked him or was she just exploring what it was like to be involved with a Black man just like Betty, the white girl in college who dumped him after he became too serious. I can't believe Carol is that way, he thought. She is more mature than the others. She is too nice. I pray she is not playing with my head, he pondered. He decided all those thoughts and doubts were stealing his joy of meeting Carol, so he decided that he would leave the office early and walk around before lunch time. Walking tended to ease his mind and help him think more positive, he remembered.

"Hello Mr. Morton," the soft gentle voice behind him said. It sent his heart into a rapid pace as he turned around and became mesmerized by her smile.

"Well, hello Miss McKay. You are looking fine today." He wanted to say, good enough to eat, but restrained himself. "How about calling me Reggie?"

"I will if you will call me Carol."

"Okay Carol, now that we have that all taken care of let's go and have a meal together. I was thinking about the Cattlemen Club," Reggie said.

"I have a better idea. There is a delightful Chinese restaurant just a few blocks away. Why don't we go there? The food is great for lunch."

"Sounds good to me," Reggie said. But, he wondered if he had to eat with chop sticks as he had seen some folks doing in Chinese restaurants. If he had to, he imagined the embarrassment he was likely to experience trying and how much he didn't want to make a bad impression on his first date. As they walked, Carol asked Reggie if he had had an opportunity to explore the area. She described it as the heart of the city where it is convenient to walk to Broadway theaters, the Museum of Modern Art, great stores and fine restaurants.

"I haven't had much time to tour during my first weeks on the job. Things move fast at the agency and I have been trying to keep up. Maybe I can intrude on your time to guide me through the area," Reggie said.

"Of course," Carol said as if she were responding as a courtesy to something she really didn't hear, while looking directly ahead. "Here we are," she said, pointing to the door of the restaurant.

They were greeted by a Chinese man wearing a white chef's jacket and dark trousers. After bowing to them and saying, "Welcome," he ushered them to a table next to a window lined with crawling plants and facing the street which allowed in the bright sunlight. He then asked, "Okay?"

"Fine," Carol responded with a slight smile. Reggie thought that it was probably considered a choice spot since those tables that were not next to the window were lined up in the center of the room. However, it did not create a romantic atmosphere as he had hoped for. But some of his discomfort evaporated when he glanced a fork next to his napkin. The waiter handed them a menu then disappeared and returned with a pot of tea and asked if they were ready to order.

"Give us a few more minutes," Carol said. "What about you? Are you ready?" she asked Reggie.

"I'm going to have number seventeen, the shrimp and vegetables."

"Then we are ready. I'm having number ten- the chicken with peanuts." She then summoned the waiter and placed the orders. Reggie felt a bit ill at ease. Carol appeared to be in charge and he was just sitting back like someone needing to be led. He wasn't sure how he must appear to her.

"What has it been like trying to keep up at Benton, Barnes and Fowler? That is where you told me you were going to work, isn't it?"

"Yes it is. Well, I think I'm off to a good start. I just managed my first client presentation of a new campaign. Everyone says it went well, including the client," Reggie said with a nervous smile.

"What was the campaign?"

"Texas Oil is trying to improve their community service image and we have come up with a range of testimonies from ordinary people and famous people focusing on charitable contributions the company has made, community service projects they have promoted, and staff they have loaned to organizations needing their expertise," Reggie said as he sat back in his chair looking directly at Carol as if she were his student.

"That sounds very interesting. I hope it works for them. The oil companies need a lot of image- building, especially when it comes to jobs for women. How many people were involved in the presentation?"

"There were four of us representing creative and management."

"It does sound like you are off to a good start. That's really wonderful. You have obviously impressed your bosses in a short period of time and that bodes well for your future there," she said as she leaned forward with a look of concern and approval on her face.

Carol's words gave Reggie the feeling that he had gained a level of respect and he was hoping that would bode well for his future relationship with her. Feeling a bit more secure, he asked

Carol what kind of work she did that requires her to travel around the country so much.

"I work for Bitterman Management Consultants. We analyze employer management practices and design systems to meet the particular needs of a company and we spend time with them during the initial implementation of our recommendations."

"What kind of practices are you asked to analyze?"

"It could be how they evaluate employees, wage distributions, developing job descriptions, record keeping."

"Well, you really need a lot of expertise to do that job."

"Our staff has a range of expertise."

"Chicken dish for you and shrimp for you," the waiter said as he laid down the plates and a bowl of rice to be shared.

"It smells rather inviting," Reggie said.

"I think it will taste as good as it smells," Carol said.

Reggie picked up his fork, pierced a shrimp and tasted it and said, "It is indeed as good as it smells." At one point he and Carol reached for the rice bowl at the same time and his hand rubbed against hers. They both smiled and said, "after you." The touch sent an erotic wave through Reggie that elevated his feeling of relaxation and his desire for further contact. As the restaurant filled up, the level of noise rose and made quiet conversation a challenge so they ate their meal in silence, occasionally glancing at each other with a smile. After the meal, and when the waiter brought the check, Reggie snatched it up off the table as Carol reached for it. "It's my treat," he said.

"If you insist," Carol said with a smile.

As they headed back to their offices, Reggie was wondering how to follow up on this. He didn't want to wait another week to get together again; but he also didn't want his anxiety to scare her away. When they reached the point of going their separate ways, Reggie asked, "When can we get together again?"

Carol hesitated and said, "Well, things are pretty hectic this week." Before she could say another word, Reggie asked, "What about dinner Friday night?"

"Let me get back to you on that," Carol answered.

"I'll be waiting for your call," Reggie said as he reached to shake Carol's hand.

"Thanks for the lunch, I really enjoyed it," Carol said with that disarming smile as Reggie slowly released her hand. Carol walked away and Reggie just stood there watching her until she disappeared into the crowd. As he walked back to the office, he wondered if she was waiting to hear back from someone regarding another date before she called him. He wondered if he would have to wait until Friday to get her decision or if he should call by Wednesday and check. "The hell with it," he said out of frustration. "If she likes me she likes me; if she doesn't, she doesn't." But he couldn't wipe away the image of her smile, the compliment she gave him about his work, and that fleeting touch of her hand. He bit his bottom lip, converted his left hand into a fist and slammed it into his right hand and said, "This is crazy!"

The rest of the day Reggie was in somewhat of a daze. He met with Gordon who praised him for his performance at the meeting with Texas Oil and told him that he would have to follow up with them because he was going to be busy working with the team pitching for the Navy contract. Reggie heard what Gordon was saying but he wasn't really internalizing it. He told Gordon, in a very somber voice, that it was fine with him and that he would keep Gordon updated on what was going on. Gordon shook his hand and said, "Right on," in an effort to show his coolness with current Black culture.

When Reggie was leaving the office, it occurred to him that he had not seen Harriett and had not run into Jeff all day. Harriett must be out today, he decided. In any event, he was glad that the day had passed and he did not have to deal with any guilt about the lie he told them about how he planned to spend his weekend. On the bus ride home, he took a window seat, leaned back and felt his muscles relaxing. He closed his eyes and his doubts about Carol began to float away. He could only see the two of them together in a cozy corner of a quiet restaurant with flickering candles and Jerry Butler singing "For Your Precious Love."

He spent the evening relaxing, reading the newspaper and listening to the soft music of WPAT-FM. He didn't want to turn on the television and get any news about how Richard Nixon was going to win the election or how many people were killed in Viet Nam, or the latest move of the Black Panther Party. Any of that would spoil his fantasy about Carol. He wanted to share his feelings with someone, but there was no one safe in his life at the time. He wondered what happened to his friends from high school. His mother told him that the latest news about Arnold, his militant friend who went to Howard University, was that he dropped out of school, but remained in Washington where he joined the Black Panther Party and that he had been arrested for weapon possession. His other friend, Alfred, she said, had settled down, got married and was an executive at the Black insurance company. She said she had run into Beverly's mother at the shopping center and she told her that Beverly had moved to San Francisco and was teaching in a high school there. He wondered what happened to Beverly's white friend that she brought home with her once. He wished he had Beverly's telephone number. He felt he could share with her news about Carol and she would understand. He suddenly remembered that bottle of Almanden white wine he had stored in one of the cabinets in the kitchen and decided to pop the cork and raise a toast to the future that would bring about a beautiful relationship with Carol and a promising career in advertising.

Shortly after he put down the glass, the excitement of the day began to weigh heavily on him and his eyes began to cash in on the support they had given him all day. He drifted off to sleep with thoughts of making love to Carol. In the middle of the night, he awoke with his pajama top clinging to the perspiration sailing down his back. He turned his head and noticed his pillow was also wet. He sat up in the bed and, for a moment, was confused then remembered he was dreaming that dream again. He wondered why it happened on this day of all days and why it kept coming back. After changing into something dry, he lay back down trying to forget the dream and focusing on what was on the agenda the next day at the office. However, the only thought he could muster was how to interact with Jeff and Harriett without revealing his relationship with Carol. He tossed and turned the rest of the night, searching for sleep that he hoped would give him rest that would bring back his feeling of optimism that had been damaged by the dream.

CHAPTER 8

Eight o'clock found Reggie in the office ahead of most everyone. He wanted to get a head start on developing his strategy for overseeing the remaining work to be done on the Texas Oil account. He had not taken time to focus on it since Gordon informed him he would have to take charge. As he walked on carpeting through the quiet halls and empty offices, he wondered if someone were to see him they might conclude this Black man was a thief, searching for loot wherever he could find it, and summon security.

He anxiously tried to project the image of "I belong here" and stepped briskly into his office and shut the door behind him. He sat at his desk and took a deep breath then slapped his head several times and said, "Don't be stupid. Focus! focus!" He leaned back in his chair, looked out the window for a few minutes then took out a legal- size pad and pen and began to jot down an outline and timeline for securing a commitment from the celebrities identified for each commercial, confirming place and time for shooting, making sure the copy work had been done and agreed to and working with media to buy time for airing. He identified each contact person for each phase of the project. It was at this point he hesitated. He needed a particular strategy for dealing with Rick, that underhanded thief. He wondered if this was one of those times the preacher at his high school baccalaureate graduation service was referring to when he said, "If you can take it, you can make it."

Reggie felt Rick must be feeling like a wild animal cornered with no place to go except to charge forward and face the consequences. His delayed arrival at the presentation and his quick exit when the meeting was over were indications of his discomfort, especially since he had to make his presentation before the person from whom he stole the idea. And now that person was in charge of the whole project. Reggie decided it was better for him to continue to take the high road in dealing with Rick because he was probably suffering already considering he had to recognize Reggie's position in order to get his job on this account done. Reggie was also thinking that he would have to dance around Jeff to keep his relationship with Carol top secret. This, he thought, might be more challenging than taking the high road with Rick.

Around ten o'clock Reggie emerged from his office looking for Gordon to get his opinion on his strategy. As he approached Barbara's desk, Gordon's door opened and he emerged with his arm around Rick's shoulder as the two appeared to be engaged in friendly conversation with Gordon patting Rick's shoulder. When Gordon saw Reggie, he immediately let go of Rick's shoulder as Rick hurriedly walked away.

"Good morning, buddy," Gordon said as his face went from friendly to serious. "How are things going?"

"Not bad," Reggie said from a mouth that had gone dry. "I was wondering if you had time to go over my ideas about strategy for going forward with the Texas Oil project."

Gordon wrapped his arm around Reggie's shoulder and said, "I won't be able to do it today. Have Barbara set up a time later in the week. I'm off to Washington today for a meeting. Okay buddy?"

"Fine," Reggie said, trying to control the muscles in his face to hide his unsettling discomfort. He walked back into his office wondering if there was anything else they were talking about other than him. He tried to convince himself that they knew each other before he started working at the agency and there were other accounts they could be collaborating on, but it was not convincing. After standing and looking out the window for a while, he concluded he could not let something like that consume him. After all, Gordon had given him no reason to distrust him and he was probably trying to counsel Rick to cooperate with him.

He took a deep breath, sat down and began to read through his notes again when he overheard Barbara ask Gordon if he returned Howard's call from Texas Oil and Gordon answered, "Yes," as he dashed past Barbara's desk on his way to the airport. Reggie sat staring at the wall. He finally rationalized that the call probably reflected the fact that he was assigned to the position temporarily and it was natural for people to seek out Gordon for advice until they were comfortable with him or until Gordon resumed the responsibility.

He concluded it was up to him to establish himself. After all, he had presided over a successful presentation of the strategy for the campaign. He decided to go forward with his implementation strategy and brief Gordon later instead of seeking his advance approval. He then asked Barbara to set up a meeting with Gordon and meetings with each of the relevant people involved in executing the campaign. He decided he would quiz Barbara about the various people he had to meet with. Barbara was anxious to help and showered him with as much gossip as she could about everyone on his list.

Over the next two days Reggie worked closely with Barbara in preparing for and scheduling meetings. After each meeting she was always ready to hear his assessment of what occurred and what he might need her to do as follow –up. Barbara became a great source of comfort. He felt she truly had his interest at heart and her longevity at the agency made her a great source of information on how it operated. In addition, she would likely have a different perspective on things than Jeff and Harriett and that could be helpful.

Everyone Reggie met with was cordial and greeted him with a smile and a friendly handshake and was very cooperative. He shared that account with Barbara, but he was reluctant to share his feeling that most of the people seemed to be condescending in their responses. He thought he might be overreacting or overly sensitive considering what he had decided might be his misperception of what happened with Rick and Gordon and Howard. Anyway, he wasn't sure how Barbara would react to such an observation.

He met with Gordon when he returned from Washington and briefed him. Gordon approved of the progress that was being made and offered no suggestions for change. However, he told Reggie, with a very serious look on his face, that he should be sure to keep everyone involved informed about the progress of the project, especially Howard. Reggie assured him that he would but wondered if that was just an off the cuff recommendation or was there something behind it, considering he had emphasized the point in his briefing. Gordon made no mention of his meeting with Rick or his call to Howard. Reggie thought maybe one day he would take Gordon to lunch and give him a couple of drinks and ask him what happened and wait and see what comes out of his mouth.

CHAPTER 9

It was now the middle of the week and there was no call from Carol. Reggie was feeling anxious. He wanted to call her but was afraid he might face a polite excuse about not being able to meet him for dinner and he wasn't ready for that kind of rejection. On the other hand, he thought, a call could demonstrate confidence and women love a look of confidence. But it could reveal his anxiety which might turn her off. He went over and over the different alternatives and finally said, "Who needs this!" and then decided if she hadn't called by Thursday morning, he would call her and deal with whatever the consequences. After all, it was not a matter of life and death or would it just feel like it was.

When he left work on Wednesday he felt restless. He decided to take the subway home instead of the express bus. He thought it would be a good distraction watching a group of people who would probably be different from those on the bus. He walked over to Broadway and Fiftieth streets and caught the Number 1 train. He was indeed distracted. The car he was in was packed body- to- body. If you did not have a seat or were not near a handrail, you didn't have to worry about falling; the bodies around you would keep you in balance when the racing train came to sudden stops. As he stood in the middle of the crowd with bodies pressing against his and his hands locked against his thighs, he could see mostly the back of heads. The faces he could see seemed either preoccupied or angry. What he was able to discern, however, was at the Seventy- Second Street stop, a herd of white people hauled out of the train. Another herd left at Ninety- Sixth and another at 116th Street. At 125th Street, the majority of Blacks left and the "straphangers" then became mostly Latinos and just a handful of whites and Blacks. By this time Reggie had a seat. As he sat looking up at the billboard on the wall above the seats advertising Dr. Zizmore's guaranteed ability to transform your complexion, he had a feeling of serenity about his apartment in the quiet suburban- style neighborhood of Riverdale surrounded by well- to- do white people.

When Reggie left the train at 242st Street, the last stop, instead of taking the bus, he decided to walk the rest of the way to 256th Street near his apartment. It was a cool fall day. Some of the leaves on the trees in Van Courtland Park were beginning to turn a rusty brown. Some of the houses along Broadway had a wreath made of dried corn cobs and leaves attached to their doors and pumpkins and carved "Jack O Lanterns" arranged on their porches or doorsteps. Reggie was reminded of the upcoming holidays and wondered if he should plan to go home for either Thanksgiving or Christmas. He imagined Carol cooking a traditional Thanksgiving dinner and inviting him over. He would bring champagne and they would eat, drink and make love on a warm blanket in front of a fireplace with a crackling fire. He wondered what would be the best gift to give her for Christmas. A diamond, maybe.

When Reggie enter his apartment, he went directly to his album collection and pulled out Arthur Prysock's "Silk and Satin" and placed it on the turntable and flipped the switch and out came, *"I blessed the day I found you. I want to stay around you now and forever, let it be me….."* He closed his eyes, leaned his head back pointing toward the ceiling and danced around the room holding out his arms as if he were embracing a partner.

The music stopped and he opened his eyes and began to walk toward the kitchen when Arthur Prysock's velvet voice began to flow through the apartment, filling the room with the words, *"Sun, sun go away let it be a rainy day, she can't see my tear drops in the rain. Here she comes with her new love. She must not know I still love her so. I just got to cry to ease the pain. She won't see me crying in the rain..."*

Reggie stood in his tracks holding onto to the refrigerator door feeling like a sharp pain had gone through him. This is crazy, he thought, then pulled out some leftover chicken with snow peas he had picked up a couple of days ago at the Chinese restaurant, threw them in the oven and sat in silence waiting for them to warm up as the needle on the album ejected. He poured himself a glass of wine. He figured it would help the leftover food digest and would relax him. After dinner he shed his work clothes and changed into lounge attire and lay across the bed for a moment of relaxation. When he awoke, he felt rested and invigorated. He noticed all the lights were on, so he decided he would pull back the covers on the bed and go back to sleep when he looked at the clock and noticed that it was eight- thirty. He was a bit confused about the time so he pulled back the drapes and saw full sun light. He dashed into the shower with his heart racing. He had never been late for work before and wondered if they would think he was a disciple of BP (Black People) Time if he walked in more than an hour and a half late, although he realized that was not unusual for Gordon. But of course Gordon is white. As the bus trekked through the congested traffic, Reggie swore under his breath every time it stalled. When he finally arrived at his stop, he dashed through the crowds on the streets looking back at each person he bumped into with a tense "excuse me." When the elevator arrived at his floor promptly at ten o'clock, he took a deep breath trying to erase the tension that he felt was plastered on his face. He thought Harriett's greeting might be an indicator of how his late arrival might be viewed by some; but, she just smiled and said, "hello" in a very friendly manner. He felt a bit relieved but wasn't sure that was an accurate assessment. Barbara was not at her desk and Gordon's office was dark. Thanks God, Reggie thought. When he stepped into his office, there on his desk was a note from Barbara that said a Carol McKay had called at 6:15 the night before. At that moment all his thoughts and fears about being late disappeared. He felt like a shot of adrenalin was racing through his body. He picked up the phone to dial her immediately then put it down. He wanted to prepare himself for whatever her response would be without exposing his anxiety. He held the phone in his hand trying to think of a strategy, but was too anxious to think so he just dialed the number.

"Hello, Carol McKay here," came rushing through the wires landing in his thirsty ear. He felt a burst of euphoria thrust through his body. He visualized the beautiful blue eyes, blond hair and disarming smile and squeezed the phone as if he were holding her in his arms.

"Good morning, Carol McKay. This is Reggie Morton on the other end of the line," he said in a playful voice. "How are you on this beautiful fall day?"

"I'm busy but doing well. How are things going with you?"

"I'm doing okay, but I will be doing much better if you tell me you are available for dinner Friday night."

"Well, you can consider me your medicine for the day. I am available."

"Well, I just saw the sun shine through my window out of a cloudy sky. Your medicine worked."

"Well, I am glad I have done some good today."

"Will you be ready to go directly after work or later?" Reggie asked.

"I'm fine right after work. I will be able to leave here around six. Is that good for you?"

"Sounds excellent, I'll meet you at Park and Fifty- First."

"Good, I look forward to seeing you then."

Reggie hung up the phone and leaned back in his chair rested his feet on his desk and cupped his hands behind his head and with a big smile on his face said, "Yes!" and began to hum Jerry Butler's "For Your Precious Love." At the same time, thoughts began to enter his mind about where to go for dinner, how to freshen-up before leaving work and how far to go in expressing his feelings on the second date without appearing too needy. No answers were revealing themselves. However he was still resting on Cloud Nine thinking it will all soon come to him when there was a knock on the door. He immediately tumbled from Cloud Nine and rose to open the door instead of inviting the person in.

"Good morning, Reggie," Barbara said. "Did you get my message?"

"Yes, I got it, thanks," Reggie said as the urge to share with her his excitement bubbled in him while at the same time the possible consequences of doing such a thing gripped him. He was sure Barbara would not be able to sit on any information about someone he was dating. That would be one sure way for

Jeff and Harriett to find out and they would probably be insulted that they did not know let alone that this woman was white.

"By the way Gordon won't be in today. Do you need anything? I'm going out for a few minutes on an errand."

"Thanks, Barbara. I'm okay for now. I'll see you later."

Reggie went about his work with added confidence the rest of the day and Friday. He connected with all persons involved with shooting the commercial and they all continued to cooperate with smiles that he wanted to believe were legitimate signs of approval.

When Friday afternoon rolled around he lost interest in everything except what would happen at six. He hung up the phone from the last call he had to make before leaving the office and looked down at his watch. It was five-thirty. He dashed into the men's room with the shaving kit he brought in that day and took out the Listerine and took in a gulp and swirled it around his mouth before unloading it down the sink. He then slapped on just a dash of English Leather cologne then looked around to make sure he was in the bathroom alone before reaching into the shaving kit and pulling out the brush to tame any strings of hair that may have gone astray during the day. He took one last look into the mirror, adjusted his tie and turned from side to side to test his looks from different angles. He nodded his head in approval and grabbed the shaving kit and tried to walk at a normal pace back to his office.

Barbara was gathering her things to leave when he approached her desk. She looked up at him and said smiling, "Big date tonight?" He was taken by surprise and immediately said, "no,no" wondering what had given him away. "My God she's nosey," he said to himself. He waited until she was gone before he emerged from his office to leave. He arrived at the designated meeting spot at five minutes to six and looked and saw Carol approaching. He had decided to take her to the place he knew best-the Cattlemen Club. He remembered it had a cozy romantic ambience that would set the mood for the evening.

"Hello Reggie Morton. You are looking rather snappy this evening. How do you manage to keep it all together after a full day in the very competitive business of advertising?"

" Well, I guess its just a matter of keeping things in perspective. A college professor of mine who was trying to encourage a group of us who were struggling with student teaching once said, 'Night between two days was made for teachers.' I've taken that to apply to any profession. Things could look altogether different tomorrow."

"Well, I think I need to adopt that perspective, especially since it works for you," Carol said, looking seductively into Reggie's eyes. The urge to grab and hug her had to be contained when Reggie took note of that look.

"Why don't we take the subway down to the Greenwich Village? There is a restaurant called The Jamaican. It's one of my favorite. I think you will like it."

"Let's go," Reggie said, disappointed that he did not again seem to be in charge. I hope it is as cozy as the Cattlemen Club, he contemplated.

The subway ride down to Greenwich Village was not as amorous as Reggie had envisioned for the beginning of the date. The car they were pushed into was so crowded that they were separated by six or seven people. Each time Reggie turned to get a glimpse of Carol, she seemed unfettered by the two Black men and one Latin who were pressed against her. Reggie was beside himself and wanted to move closer and push at least one of them away, but each time the train stopped at a station others embarked and prevented him from moving in closer. When the train finally stopped at West Fourth Street and Carol signaled that this was their stop, he pushed himself through the crowd and, with a look of frustration in his eyes, grabbed Carol's hand. She looked up at him and smiled as they walked silently up the stairs onto the streets that were almost as crowded as the subway but with much more space to maneuver.

"Have you made it to the Village before?" Carol asked.

"No, this is my first time, but I have heard it is one of New York's hot spots for cool night life and from the looks of all these people on the streets, I'm convinced," Reggie said with a bit of excitement in his voice.

"I would say it is more Bohemian than the rest of the city," Carol said portraying a sense of satisfactory achievement in her voice as she squeezed Reggie's hand. Reggie's heart began to pound a little faster and the frustration he felt on the subway seemed miles away.

"Good evening, madam. Do you have reservations?" the elderly light brown skinned man with a Caribbean accent asked.

"Yes, I'm Carol Mckay with a reservation for two."

After taking his time reviewing the reservation schedule, the elderly man said, "Come this way Miss Mckay. Your table is ready." Carol followed with Reggie trailing her through the green and yellow ribbons adorning the restaurant. "Your waiter will be with you shortly," the gentleman said while handing them the menu.

As they sat reading the menu Reggie took in the scenery. The crowd was mixed, but the majority of the customers were white. The chatter was a tone higher than what Reggie would consider conducive to a romantic quiet corner with a candlelight flickering on the table as he had envisioned it would have been at the Cattlemen Club. He noticed the tables where there were couples. They all seemed to be engaged in animated conversation with laughter. There were palm trees strategically placed in corners near windows which gave the place a relaxed feeling. Reggie felt that maybe this kind of restaurant was Carol's way of saying this is the only kind of evening that she was ready for. So, he decided to play along with the program. Otherwise, she might see him as more anxious than she was willing to handle or maybe she just wanted to know he was interested in something other than her drawers.

A tall, dark-skinned waiter standing over them asked, in his Caribbean accent, "Would you like drinks before dinner?" Reggie decided to assert an appearance of being in charge and nodded to Carol who ordered white wine. Reggie asked for a scotch and ginger ale. As the waiter walked away, Reggie leaned back in his chair feeling more relaxed than he had since leaving the office.

"Have you eaten Caribbean cuisine before?" Carol asked.

"No, I haven't", Reggie answered looking quizzically at the menu.

"I recommend the jerk chicken. It's spicy with a well-seasoned taste. I am not sure what seasoning you would find in those delicious rice and peas. However, I can taste some bay leaves. You should also try the fried bananas called plantains. I have never had the curried goat, but I have heard it is really good if you don't mind goat meat."

"I think I will try the chicken."

"The first time I came here my mother and I had come into town to do some shopping and had come to this restaurant at the recommendation of Phyllis, our housekeeper, who is from Jamaica. My mother, who has always been a person interested in new things, loved it so much we used to make it here whenever we were in the city. I remember one time she was bored and had Charles, our chauffeur, drive us from Ridgefield, Connecticut into Manhattan just to have lunch at this restaurant. She convinced my father that we should add Jamaica to our winter vacation "Getaways" after hearing Phyllis' descriptions of life there. We used to take packages for Phyllis' relatives whenever we traveled there. It was like they were relatives we were visiting. They usually had us over for a meal. Phyllis' aunt was a great cook. She had a great way of seasoning fish. The fish here is not quite the same as Phyllis's aunt's. But I did have some that came close at the West Indian festival on Eastern Parkway in Brooklyn on Labor Day. By the way, that's an experience you must have. The costumes they wear in the parade are some of the most creative and beautiful I have ever seen and the steel drums are fantastic. All of the Black Caribbean islands participate in the festival." Carol spoke in great animation smiling, with a sparkle in her eyes and her hands going up and down and sideways.

"Do you usually go to the festival with friends?" Reggie asked attempting to fish out if her circle of friends included any Black people.

"Oh yes, there are three of us. We rely on Jenny to lead us. She is from Trinidad and swears that that's where you will find the Carnival of all Carnivals every year just before Ash Wednesday. We all plan to go one year."

"Well, we'll have to go to the Brooklyn festival next year," Reggie said. He concluded Jenny was Black and wondered if she sported an Afro. He had very little knowledge of the West Indian culture and how they responded to the Black Power movement. He wondered if Jenny was into the movement and if she was, what would that say about Carol with that kind of friend.

The waiter arrived with the drinks and asked if he could take their orders. Reggie again looked toward Carol, signaling her to give her order. "I'll have the jerk chicken with rice and peas and a salad."

"I'll have the same but I would also like to add plantains to my order," Reggie said as he looked over at Carol with a smile and said, "I'll be adventurous." She smiled back and said, "You won't be sorry."

"I'd like to make a toast," Reggie said raising his glass to cling to Carol's, "To Carol and Reggie, may our days ahead be smooth ones."

"I'll drink to that," Carol said, projecting that smile that melts Reggie's heart. He felt like reaching across the table and landing a kiss on her soft, thin lips.

"Have you been able to get around and see some of the city since we had lunch?" Carol asked trying to tone down the conversation to something less intimate.

"Yes, I have done a few things, but it seems like all my free time is spent preparing for the next thing that needs to be done at the office," Reggie said, suddenly wondering if or how to reveal his relationship with Jeff and Harriett. If she likes the West Indian Festival and this restaurant, maybe she would expect me to introduce her to a Jeff or Harriett and take her to Harlem to a restaurant like Sylvia's.

"Did you know anyone in the city before you moved here?" Carol asked.

"No, I didn't. I just knew I was coming to a great city with eight million people."

"Well, have you been able to make friends with any of the eight million?" Carol asked jokingly while fishing for details about his social life and relationships.

"Not yet," Reggie answered, beginning to feel off balance by the questions.

"What about your friends back in Chicago? Did you leave behind someone special?"

"I'm in touch with all my friends in Chicago and they are all special," Reggie answered with a smile on his face.

"Touche," Carol said, flashing a smile right back.

"Chicken, rice and peas and salad, I believe that is for you and this one with the plantains for you, sir," the waiter said, carefully placing the dishes before their rightful owner.

"I hope it tastes as good as it smells," Reggie said as he pierced his knife and fork into the dark brown pieces of chicken separating a sliver that he began chewing slowly and then more rapidly as he tasted the spicy peppers that set off a small flame in his mouth. "This is delicious," he said as he reached for his glass of water and took a sip. The water did not quite cool him down so he took his fork and cut a piece of the plantain and devoured it. It was sweet, soft and soothing.

"I'm glad you like it," Carol said laughing at the look on Reggie's face. "I thought you would appreciate some good spicy food. Aren't you used to that kind of food?"

"I love spicy food. However I wasn't really expecting to find it here as spicy as this is, but I love it," Reggie said as he cut another piece and began chewing it.

"At first I had a problem eating it in spite of the great seasoning, but I got used to it," Carol said as she took another sip of her wine after each bite.

Reggie's adventurous indulgence in the food before him consumed his attention until he had taken the last bite while Carol, in amusement, continued to watch the expressions on his face as his fork brought each dish to, what seemed like, his reluctant lips.

"Well, did you really enjoy it?" Carol asked, almost laughing.

"It was a new journey for me, but it was good."

"Well, I'm glad you did," Carol said as she laid down her fork after cleaning out her bowl of salad and all the chicken and about two tablespoons of rice and peas.

"May I take these?" the waiter asked.

"Yes," Carol responded.

"Would you like dessert or coffee?" the waiter asked looking directly at Carol.

"No," Carol answered and looked at Reggie and asked him if he would like some.

"No, I'm done," Reggie said.

"You can bring the check," Carol said looking directly at the waiter.

Reggie was beginning to feel embarrassed that the waiter seemed to ignore him and Carol seemed to be comfortable with it in spite of his efforts to assert himself as being in charge. However, he was not sure how to deal with the feeling except to ignore it for fear of saying something that would spoil the prevailing good mood he and Carol were sharing.

"Thank you," the waiter said as he handed the bill to Carol. Reggie politely reached across the table and retrieved it immediately so the waiter would not miss his action. Carol suddenly seemed embarrassed, but said nothing. The waiter seemed equally embarrassed as he dashed away. Reggie studied the bill and pulled out his Master Card and placed it over the bill.

"Thanks Reggie for a lovely meal," Carol said flashing a well-contrived smile.

"It was indeed my pleasure and thanks for expanding my cultural horizon," Reggie said with a slight smile.

After paying the bill, they walked out of the restaurant this time with Carol following Reggie. It was a cool fall night, conducive to being outside without an extra layer of clothing. The streets were bustling with folks seemingly ready to declare their freedom from a week of suppressed anxieties. Reggie felt exhilarated. This was the first time he felt a part of the fast-moving night life of the New York he had always envisioned. As they walked down Sixth Avenue toward the Fourth Street subway station, Reggie reached for Carol's hand which she offered freely. He realized they were walking toward the subway and he wondered if that meant Carol was ready to bring their date to an end and, if she were, would she invite him up to her place for a drink or should he invite her to his place. Before he could scratch his head with his free hand in search of an answer, Carol asked, "Would you like to hear some jazz?"

"Yes," Reggie said without hesitation although he wasn't that interested in jazz.

"They usually have some good performers at a place called Blue Note Jazz Club. Let's walk over there."

"Great idea," Reggie said. Still, he wondered how the evening would end. The smoke- filled club was crowded with small tables squeezed into the space. The performers were an up and coming group that mixed their jazz with blues which met with great approval from the audience. Carol thumped the table as the music played. Watching her apparent enjoyment added to Reggie's enjoyment. When the band ended their first show, Carol looked at her watch. It was ten- thirty. She turned to Reggie and said, "This has been a lovely evening and a long day. I need to get some sleep before the carriage turns into a pumpkin." Those words spoke clearly to Reggie how the evening would end.

"Well, you wouldn't need to worry. I would take that glass slipper and travel all over the city until I found you," Reggie said looking directly into her eyes and smiling.

"I'm impressed," Carol said as she rose from her chair and began to maneuver through the crowd toward the exit. This time Reggie followed, feeling more and more secure that Carol was experiencing some of the same feelings he had. As they walked over to the Christopher Street subway station on the Number I line, Carol asked Reggie if he enjoyed bike riding. Reggie said, "Of course."

"A group of us plan to go bike riding in Central Park on Sunday if you would like to come along. You can rent a bike if you don't have one."

"I look forward to it."

"I'll call you and give you the details as soon as everything is confirmed with my friends."

"I'll be waiting for your call."

Carol squeezed Reggie's hand and said goodnight at the Seventy-Second Street station. Reggie sat in a state of bliss as the train made its long journey to the Two Hundred and Forty Second Street stop. He closed his eyes and retraced the evening from start to finish. As soon as he entered his apartment, he went directly to his pile of albums and pulled out Della Reese's, "Waltz with Me Della," and sang along with her as her very strong but soothing voice backed by an orchestra filled the apartment with "Don't You Know I'm in Love with You."

Reggie awoke Saturday morning feeling renewed. He remembered he needed to pick up laundry and do some grocery shopping. He wondered when to do those chores. He didn't want to miss Carol's call. She probably won't call her friends early on a Saturday morning, so maybe I should get up and get out now, he thought. But maybe she also has chores and will want to get this decision behind her. As he lay there pondering what to do, he began to wonder about Carol's friends and what they might be like. If they are all white, what would they think of her dating a Black man? If they don't know any Black people, how would they treat him? Would Jenny be in the group? Surely, he thought, Carol would not have invited him if she anticipated an embarrassing situation, but often, he concluded, white people like Carol don't think about these kinds of things like Black people do.

He took a deep breath and decided whatever happens, he would do nothing that would embarrass Carol and he would endure whatever happens just to be with her. He rolled out of bed and headed for the grocery and cleaners. It seemed shopping early on Saturday was a popular trend. The lines at the grocery's check-out counter were long and the clerks were not in danger of a heart attack because of their pace of work. Reggie stood in line shifting his weight from foot to foot and swearing under his breath at the cashier and praying Carol would not call while he was out.

It suddenly occurred to him they only had each other's office number and he wondered how Carol would find him. He wasn't sure how many Reggie Mortons were listed in the phone book in The Bronx. Also, if he wanted to call her, he would have to look up her number in the very large Manhattan book and who knows how many Carol McKays were listed. He began to feel anxious and more impatient with the check-out clerk, realizing he still had to pick up his laundry. When he finally made it to the front of the line and paid his bill, he grabbed his bag and dashed out as the clerk said, "thank you", to his back. He nervously ran to the cleaners and encountered more speedy service and this time he uttered a hearty, "Thank you!" to the attendant as he wasted no time plowing through the door.

The weight of the grocery and laundry slowed his pace, but his steps were very deliberate and his focus was straight ahead until he stepped into his apartment. One hour later the phone still had not rung. To kill time and reduce his anxiety, he took out that ten pound Manhattan telephone directory and began to search for Carol McKay somewhere around Seventy-Second Street. He counted twenty and wondered where to start. There were four that lived somewhere between Eighty-Second and Sixty Sixth. He decided if she did not call by twelve, he would start calling the four. As soon as he had decided on the strategy, the phone rang. He prayed it was her and when he heard her voice, it felt like he had just been exonerated from a charge of rape.

"Reggie Morton?" the voice asked.

"You've got him," Reggie answered.

"Thank God. I just realized this morning that I didn't have your home number and I had to ask the operator for Reggie Morton in Riverdale. It seems you are the only one. I hope I haven't awakened you. I have a lot of chores on my list today so I started early with my calls to confirm Sunday."

"I am wide awake just waiting for your call to make my day."

"Well, I hope it works. My friends and I have agreed to meet at the fountain in Central Park at one-thirty Sunday. There is a bicycle shop at Broadway and Ninety-Sixth streets. You can rent a bike there so why don't we meet there around a quarter to one."

"I'm counting the minutes," Reggie said holding the phone tightly to his ear with his eyes closed and his lips puckered as if he were holding Carol in his arms.

"I'll see you then," Carol said then put down the phone with an approving smile on her face.

Reggie hung up the phone, took a deep breath and exhaled slowly, then threw his right fist into the air and yelled, "Yes!" Feeling a surge of confidence, he began to whistle Dionne Warwick's "A House is Not a Home" and, without reservation took on the hated task of cleaning the bathroom and making up his bed. As the surge began to ebb, he became aware of hunger pains and decided he felt like walking down to the International House of Pancakes for a hearty breakfast. On his way to the restaurant on this cool, cloudy day, he fantasized that it would be a bright sunny Sunday and wondered if there would be opportunities to hold Carol's hand, or hug her, or hold her in his arms and kiss her. The need in him for intimate contact had intensified after what he perceived as go- ahead signs from Carol last night and he wondered how long it would take before she was ready to go all the way. Just the thought of it excited him.

Reggie slept well that night and awoke with the sun shining through his window. He yawned, stretched his arms and said, "This is the day that the Lord has given and I am more than happy in it." He reached for the New York Times that he had picked up the night before and began thumbing through the first section, eliminating all articles dealing with Viet Nam and the campaigns for president-too sobering, he concluded. There was nothing there that captured his attention. His mind couldn't make a transition from thoughts of spending the day with Carol. He rolled out of bed and headed for the shower and after a careful inspection of his face to make sure last night's Magic shave had given him a clean shave, he jumped into the shower. As he enjoyed the pulsating water piercing his body, hidden thoughts of unpleasant memories flashed back. He remembered his first shower in the dormitory in college when a parade of white boys paced by the shower to see if it was really true that Blacks had tails. For a moment, he wondered if Carol held some absurd stereotype about Black people. He didn't mind if she held on to the one about Black men in the bed because he figured he could live up to that one. Feeling a moment of conquest, he smiled and dismissed the bad memory.

He stepped out of the shower and was careful to put on just the right amount of Old Spice after shave lotion and English Leather cologne. Wrapped in his terry cloth bathrobe, he decided some breakfast was in order, so he whipped together some eggs and bacon, poured a glass of orange juice and boiled water for some instant coffee. As he sat eating, he wondered what would be a good outfit for the day. Carol had not seen him yet in casual clothes. The sport coat and trousers he wore on the flight from Chicago was the closest she had even seen. He decided his brown bell bottoms and the brown and white turtle neck wool sweater would do the trick. When the time came for him to dress, in his usual fashion, he posed from side to side in front of the mirror, pressed his hair down with his hand, nodded his head in approval then dashed out to meet the public, this time a public that really mattered.

The train finally arrived at the Ninety-Sixth Street station after the long ride. Reggie bounced up the multiple set of stairs taking two at a time from the deep underground station. He stepped out into the bright, cloudless sky encountering a light breeze gliding up from the Hudson River. He felt invigorated as he crossed the street to the bicycle shop. He looked at his watch and saw that it was only twelve. Carol was not waiting, so he walked into the shop and began to examine their inventory.

After a thorough survey he identified a ten- speed blue and red that felt comfortable. He went ahead and rented it and parked it outside as he waited for Carol. At exactly twelve-forty-five, Carol rolled around the corner on her bike waving at Reggie and flashing a somewhat nervous smile as she looked to estimate the flow of traffic in her path.

"I see you are all ready to go. Nice bike", Carol said.

"I might be a little rusty, but you know what they say, you don't forget how to ride a bike," Reggie said as he saddled his bike, steadied himself and adjusted the gear for climbing the hill up Ninety-Sixth Street.

"Well, follow me," Carol said pulling off up the hill seemingly without any unusual effort. Reggie followed, a bit nervous as he adjusted to bike riding- maneuvering around cars that had the right-of-way and were not particularly sensitive to bike riders. Carol was not hard to follow. She peddled slowly. When they finally turned into the park at Seventy-Second Street, Reggie breathed a sigh of relief as they joined a flow of bike riders rapidly traveling on pavement without automobile traffic. As they approached a crowd mingling around the ever-popular overpass overlooking the Bethesda Fountain, Carol waved to three girls parked together. One was Black and Reggie concluded that must be Jenny. She was wearing blue jeans and a bulky sweater. The other two were white and dressed in knee length shorts and fitted sweaters. Both were waving and grinning.

"I see we are all here on time," Carol said as she brought her bike to a halt.

"Indeed we are," one of the white girls said with a huge grin on her face as she looked at Reggie.

"Reggie, this is Madeline, Rose and Jenny," Carol said.

"Hi Reggie," they all greeted him. Madeline and Rose, with welcoming but somewhat nervous grins on their faces, reached out to shake Reggie's hand while balancing their bikes. Jenny was too far away for a hand shake. She waved, flashing a very sober look.

"Nice meeting you all. Thanks for letting me join you today," Reggie said as he shook Madeline and Rose's hands and waved back at Jenny.

"Our pleasure," Madeline said. "Is this your first trip to the park?" she asked.

"As a matter of fact it is," Reggie said.

As he was about to say it looked like the great place to gather on a beautiful Sunday, Carol interrupted.

"Reggie hasn't seen much of our city yet. He works for Benton, Barnes and Fowler advertising agency and they have been keeping his nose to the grind and after work he is out of Manhattan and up to Riverdale."

"Well, today you will get a good dose of what Manhattan has to offer," Madeline said.

"All right gang, let's start the tour," Jenny called out as she began to peddle away. Madeline and Rose followed directly behind Jenny while Carol and Reggie brought up the rear. The crowd of bikers was almost as much an obstacle to riding as cars, so Reggie was consumed with watching where he was going. The tour took them around the park from east to west with bikers in a festive mood. Reggie kept thinking this ride could be a lot more fun if I were more comfortable on this bike. He was relieved when they rolled back into the area of the fountain that seemed to have become more crowded.

"Let's introduce you to another New York institution-the 'Dirty Dog' " Rose said as she parked her bike near a hot dog vendor. "What would you like on yours? Onions, sauerkraut, mustard or ketchup?"

Reggie felt embarrassed that she wanted to buy him a hot dog, but didn't want to make an issue of it. "I'll take mustard," he answered.

"And what to drink?"

"I'll take a Coke."

"Okay, guys, I'm buying. Line up and give the man your orders," Rose commanded.

The group ate their hot dogs in silence as they listened to the man standing in front of the fountain occasionally looking up at The Angel of the Waters while blowing out romantic melodies from his saxophone. Reggie felt a moment of being at peace with the world as he stared at the jovial revelers dancing around the fountain and the romantic couples rowing on the lake.

"Okay guys, I have to go. I promised mother I would be home for her early Sunday dinner. She wouldn't forgive me if I didn't show up for her stewed chicken and macaroni pie. I'll see you all," Jenny said as she began peddling off without any specific farewell to Reggie.

"I have to go, too. Barry and I are going out to dinner and I need to do some grocery shopping for next week. My refrigerator is empty. Reggie, it was nice meeting you and I assure you that we have much more of Manhattan to show. So, I look forward to our next meeting. Carol, I'll talk to you during the week. What about you Rose? Are you hanging around or riding with me?" Madeline asked.

"I'm going along with you. I look forward to seeing you next time Reggie. I enjoyed your company," Rose said as she jumped on her bike.

"Okay, guys, we will talk," Carol said.

"I really enjoyed getting together with you all and I look forward to the next time," Reggie responded as he waved them good-bye. He felt he probably passed Madeline and Rose's inspection, but he wasn't so sure about Jenny. She was not as friendly as the others. In any event, he was glad to finally have Carol to himself.

"Would you like to go over and sit on one of the benches and listen to those steel drummers playing in front of the band shelter?" Carol asked.

"Sure, would you like something to drink?" he asked.

"No, I'm fine. Go ahead if you want something."

"I'm going to have another Coke." Reggie returned to the bench and parked his bike next to Carol's and then sat close to her and reached for her hand which she gave.

"I like your friends," Reggie said without revealing any doubts about Jenny.

"They like you, too," Carol said.

"How do you know that?" Reggie asked with a mischievous smile.

"I know my friends," Carol said looking directly into Reggie's eyes.

"Well, I guess I passed the test," Reggie said as he raised his can of Coke in the motion of a toast.

"I guess you did," Carol replied with a big smile on her face while squeezing his hand. The drummers began to beat out the tune "When you walk through a storm, hold your head up high and don't be afraid of the dark......" Carol's eyes turned away from Reggie and a sober look covered her face as she tightened the grip on his hand. They sat in silence for the duration of the song. When the drummers changed tunes Reggie asked, "Who broke your heart?"

Carol loosen her grip and turned her head back in his direction and asked, "What made you ask that question?

"Just a hint," Reggie answered. "I figure a woman like you may have broken many hearts and just maybe you might regret one of those times or just maybe someone broke your heart."

"Are you a trained therapist?" Carol asked with a smile returning to her face.

"No, just a man trying to figure out things."

"Well, if you must know. I broke off my engagement last year. However, I am not having second thoughts. It was clear to me that Nicholas and I were not destined to spend our lives together. I tried but my heart was not in it. We met during our senior year in college. Strangely enough, we were both from Ridgefield but went to different high schools. Both our parents were excited about the engagement. They saw us as the perfect couple as did Nicholas. I am an only child and my parents were looking forward to this beautiful wedding. But after a very exciting beginning, I came to realize that I didn't have the feelings for Nicholas that I would like to have for someone I want to be with for the rest of my life. He was really a nice guy, but the chemistry wasn't there. Well, what about you, Mr. Handsome, up –and- coming advertising executive? How many hearts have you dropped along the way? "

"None. Absolutely none. But, I probably know how Nicholas felt when you broke off the engagement. I have never reached the point of engagement, but I have lost two women that I cared a lot about, one from high school and one in college. I don't know, maybe both were infatuations and not love, anyway both times it hurt,." Reggie said avoiding too many details for fear he would have to reveal that the one in college was white and he was not ready to unload that information. However, considering Nicholas was from Ridgefield and Carol's family approved of him, Reggie felt sure he was white. After hearing his story, Carol again squeezed Reggie's hand.

"Have you ingested enough New York culture for one afternoon?" Carol asked as she tried to let go of his hand.

"Only if you have completed being tour guide for today," Reggie said looking seductively into Carol's eyes and grasping her hand tightly.

"Well I think we have completed the highlights for today and now I will guide you back to turn in your bike," Carol said smiling and looking away and then back into Reggie's eyes. She gently slid her hand away from his and stood up. Reggie followed as he began to be haunted by an erotic feeling. They rode with Carol leading through the threatening traffic; but this time Reggie was feeling more relaxed watching Carol's hair wave in the air.

Carol waited outside while Reggie returned his bike. Reluctant to end the date, but not wanting to push his luck, Reggie walked out of the bicycle shop and up to Carol, ready to tell her he had had a great time and to make his case for another date when she asked if he would like to go to her apartment for a drink. Reggie was caught off guard. His mouth went dry. He almost stuttered trying to roll out his emphatic, "Indeed I would."

"I should have thought to ask you what you prefer to drink before I offered the invitation."

"I'm rather flexible," Reggie said grinning, unable to disguise his elation at receiving the invitation. He now began to wonder what would happen and what he should do that would leave the best impression.

"We can take the subway downtown," Carol said.

"What about the bike?" Reggie asked.

"It's permissible to take it on the train."

"Really? Then let me help you." He then lifted it from Carol and marched down the stairs like a Roman soldier hoisting his heavy gear. When the train rolled into the station and the car door opened, Reggie stood guard over the bike while annoyed passengers exiting pushed around him. Once in the car with the bike positioned to stand firmly, Reggie took a deep breath and exhaled while Carol placed her hand on his shoulder. Reggie felt he had successfully taken charge, but the moment was fleeting.

He immediately began to wonder what he should do when he got to Carol's. Should he try to demonstrate coolness of give in to his yearning to be with her? The time for coming up with a strategy evaporated. The conductor announced the next stop would be Seventy Second and Reggie's priority then would be getting the bike out without injuring someone. When the train stopped and the doors opened, he flexed his muscles and lifted the bike and held it in that position until he got to the top of the stairs and onto the street.

Embarrassing beads of sweat began popping up on his forehead. He wanted to wipe them away, but felt it would bring undue attention to them and that might destroy Carol's perception of him as her strong knight. Maybe the wind would dry them, he thought. Carol had gone ahead. When they reached the street, she looked back for him and said, "this way."

Carol's apartment was on the fourteenth floor with a view of the building's tree- lined courtyard surrounded by a driveway that extended from the street to the entrance of the doorman secured building. The apartment had a spacious area as you entered that was divided between living and dining sections. There were pieces of African sculpture on the two tables next to the sofa. Down the hall from the entrance was a bedroom and at the end of the hall a bathroom.

Carol invited Reggie to take a seat on a cushioned flower designed sofa facing a glass top coffee table. There on the table was "The Feminine Mystique," a novel by Betty Freidan that had been promoted as the catalyst for the liberation movement for women. Although Reggie had not read it, he was familiar with the controversy it had stirred. It was enough to give him pause about the possibilities for the evening. He wasn't sure what impact it had had on Carol. In any event, his desire to fulfill his animal caveman instinct, he decided, should be curtailed somewhat. He needed something clearer than an invitation to stop by for a drink to pursue an erotic evening. At the same time, he wondered what she would think if he did not make a move toward some serious intimacy.

"I'm afraid all I have in my bar is vodka and white wine. Can I interest you in either?" Carol asked. Reggie felt he needed something strong to help him seem cool while feeling anxious.

"If you have any orange juice, give me a vodka and orange juice."

"One vodka and orange juice coming up," Carol said as she disappeared into the small kitchen, just off the dining area. She reappeared with his drink and a glass of white wine and sat down next to him, pulled her feet up on the couch and faced him. Reggie felt nervous, but excited. He took a gulp of his drink then leaned forward to place his glass on the coffee table. When he leaned back, Carol had inched closer to him and was flashing a mischievous grin. At this point, instinct overwhelmed Reggie and he pulled her into his arms and landed a hungry kiss on her inviting lips. Carol wrapped her arms around his shoulders and gave in to his hunger then led him into her dimly lit bedroom. Carol was as unrestrained in pursuing her desire as Reggie which sent him into a state of ecstasy and his response sent her into a mad embrace that glued the two together. Their entangled bodies rolled around the bed until what seemed like a flash of lightning struck, causing a climatic burst of ecstasy.

Carol laid her head gently on Reggie's chest as it rose and descended in rhythm with his heart beat. Reggie stroked her hair while staring at the ceiling wondering what else life could offer that could beat what he had just experienced.

When Reggie awoke, he reached for Carol and realized she was not there. At that point, he heard the running of water in the bathroom. He looked at the clock on the table next to the bed and saw that it was five-thirty. His first thought was an invitation for a drink and a gift of glory did not necessarily mean an invitation to spend the whole day and night. He reached for his clothes and dressed as a gesture to say he was not taking for granted he was welcome to stay. Carol walked into the room in a full length bathrobe, walked over to the fully dressed Reggie and kissed him on the cheek without speaking.

"Would you be interested in going out to get something to eat?" Reggie asked.

"I think I had better get some work done. I have a major presentation to do tomorrow and I don't feel ready yet," Carol said in a very sober voice.

"I can understand that. Well, I'm going to head up to Riverdale. Thank you baby for a day that I shall never forget," Reggie said in a seductive tone as he kissed her on the cheeks.

"It was wonderful for me too," Carol said as she hugged Reggie.

"I'll call you tomorrow."

"Okay," she said as she released him from her arms.

Reggie walked away convinced he had a good idea what people felt when they said they were floating on a cloud. The long subway ride to Riverdale seemed like one short leap as he sat in a daze of self confirmation uttering under his breath, "God is good."

CHAPTER 10

Reggie stepped off the elevator quietly humming Dionne Warwick's "Our Day Will Come…and we will have everything." He was stepping with the confidence of a man who had just witnessed the delivery of his first son, totally unaware that his inner joy was on display for others to interpret. As soon as he entered the reception area Harriett said with a mischievous smile, "And a good morning to you. You look like you had a great weekend." Reggie was shaken by the greeting and immediately responded with a change in his countenance, "It wasn't bad. How was yours?" He asked trying to appear unflustered.

"Mine was okay, but I would be willing to bet it was nothing like yours."

"I would doubt that," Reggie said as he kept walking to his office. This time as if he had just been disciplined by some authority figure. He had not had time to take his coffee out of the bag when there was a knock on the door. When he opened it, there stood Jeff with a hearty, "Hey man what have you been up to lately? Are you hiding out in Riverdale on the weekends? I can't imagine what could keep you up there. What did you do this weekend?" Jeff asked rather nonchalantly.

Reggie felt cornered, realizing a moment of truth could be facing him. He certainly wasn't ready to come clean with Jeff about Carol. But he needed to come up with some explanation that was believable or risk raising unnecessary suspicion.

"Some friends of mind from Chicago came into town for a day and we hung out." Reggie said in as calm a voice as he could as he took a sip of his coffee. "What did you do?"

"Harriett and I checked out some jazz at Birdland. You should come with us sometime. You can get some good shows on the weekend."

"Let me know the next time you are going," Reggie said as he took another sip of his coffee and thumbed through some papers on his desk as if he were looking for something that needed immediate attention.

"Hey what are you doing for lunch today?" Jeff asked as he got up to walk out of the office. Reggie felt a lump rise in his throat. He wondered If Harriett had discussed with Jeff her brief conversation with him. Maybe Jeff was on a fishing tour at the request of Harriett and a lunch would give him more relaxed timed to probe. He felt unnerved at the thought of revealing his relationship with Carol.

But just as unsettling was the thought of starting to add lies on top of lies and later trip up on one which would probably make Jeff and Harriett less trusting. That, he figured, could make him feel more isolated. He also didn't want Jeff to get the impression that he was trying to avoid him. That could be as damaging as telling the truth about who he was dating. He felt angry with himself for having to deal with the situation. Why in hell can't I just live my life without worrying about what someone else might think. I couldn't give a shit about how they live their lives. What the hell were those judges thinking when they ruled in the Brown V Board of Education case and Martin Luther King's messages except to bring people together. So what's wrong with Carol and me coming together if we feel it? He wanted to say to Jeff, Man, I don't mind doing anything with you if you can accept the woman of my choosing, but all he could permit to part his lips was, "I don't have any plans. What's up?"

"Nothing in particular. Harriett and I just thought we would get something in the neighborhood and you might want to join us," Jeff said.

At the sound of Harriett's name, Reggie felt the knot that had risen in his throat had traveled to his stomach. He was certain the two of them were up to something that could embarrass him. He wanted to say to Jeff, Why don't you two coons go some place and rub your furs together and leave me alone? But thinking he had no escape, he sucked in that emotion and said, "What time do you want to meet?"

"How about Twelve-thirty?" Jeff said as he began to walk out of Reggie's office.

"I'll meet you all at the elevator," Reggie said as he folded his hands into a ball and proceeded to strike his thighs in frustration. He thought about the first time he was home for Christmas from college and his brother enthusiastically questioning him about whether he had indulged in the "forbidden fruit?" He would probably admire him for capturing the affections of Carol.

Reggie spent the rest of the morning trying to anticipate the various scenarios that could occur during lunch that would confront him with having to confess or lie. None of the responses he imagined made him comfortable. He then worried about demonstrating some unconscious behavior that would raise a red flag to Jeff and Harriett that he was trying to hide something. "Oh, fuck it! fuck it!" He mumbled.

A knock on the door startled him. He wondered whether whoever was on the other side of the door could have heard his utterance. That kind of language was not the kind of image he wanted to project, especially in this environment. Instead of saying, "come in," which would immediately reveal his voice and maybe confirm to the person that he indeed utter those forsaken words, he nervously opened the door.

"Good morning, my man, what's up?" Gordon said as he detected some stress in Reggie's face. "Everything alright?"

Reggie forced a hearty, "Come on in, man. Things are fine. It's good to see you. How are things going down in Washington?"

"It takes some adjusting to deal with those guys responsible for running our government. But I think we are ahead of our competition in landing this contract. They have all kind of hoops you have to jump through before awarding a contract. You know what they always say, 'we are spending taxpayer's money and we have to be accountable to all taxpayers so here is another hoop you have to jump through. How are you making out with all the characters involved in the Texas Oil account?" Gordon asked with a kind of sober look on his face.

"So far so good. We are targeting Thanksgiving for the ads to hit the media," Reggie said with a tone of great confidence.

"Great man, keep at it," Gordon said as he stood up to leave the office. "Oh, by the way do you know anything about developing an affirmative action plan."

"Not really," Reggie said. "What's up?"

"That's one of the requirements for being awarded a government contact the size of the one we are bidding for."

"No man, I'm sorry I can't help you," Reggie said.

"Okay, I'll see you around," Gordon said with the same sober look he showed when asking about Texas Oil.

Reggie leaned back in his chair. He wondered if the stress on his face when Gordon entered his office caused those sober looks he detected in the usually jovial Gordon or was he being overly sensitive to Gordon's look because of the frustration he was feeling about lunch.

"Well, I am glad you were able to take time out of your busy schedule and have lunch." Harriett said in a sarcastic tone as she stood alone in the hall in front of the elevator bank in a trench coat with the belt tied tightly around her narrow waist accentuating her "Coca Cola" bottle figure.

"I'm glad you were able to do the same," Reggie said as he mustered up a flirtatious smile. "You are looking fine as usual. Does that mean the hustle and bustle of this place doesn't get the best of you?" He asked in an attempt to flatter her and divert any conversation about himself.

Before she could answer, Jeff arrived on the scene and said in the tone of a general leading his troops into battle and with a slight smile on his face. "I see I am the late one. Well, now that I am here we can proceed."

As the door of the elevator opened, Jeff stepped in followed by Harriett who turned her head and gave Reggie a wink. Reggie managed a nervous smile thinking maybe he just might escape Harriett's grilling about his social life since she appeared to want to be a part of it.

As they walked out of the building into the cool autumn day with the sun shinning bright, Reggie hoped the beautiful weather would brighten everybody's mood and make them very cordial. Harriett looked up at the sky and said, "What a beautiful day, I wish I could stay out all day and bask in it, but a poor girl has to work and I really need to be back no later than two. So let's go somewhere we won't have to spend the time waiting to be served. How about Binihana? Its only a few block away."

"Fine with me," Jeff said.

Reggie had never heard of Binihana, but he was so pleased with Harriett's comment about the weather, which he felt was a good indicator that things just might go well. He said. "I'm game." They walked three abreast the few blocks with Harriett in the middle. She reached for and held each of her partners' hands. Jeff swung his while Reggie kept his at his side. Harriett squeezed his hand. Reggie felt a bit erotic but refused to return the squeeze or to have any eye contact with her.

As they approached the entrance to the restaurant, Harriett let go of their hands. Reggie let it go and looked straight ahead as if nothing had happened. When Reggie saw the family- style seating around the tables with strangers mainly focused on the individual chefs at each table engaged in their theatrics of preparing and serving the food, he felt a great sense of relief-convinced that the setting was not conducive to the kind of conversation he was dreading. However, at the end of the table opposite where they were seated, there was a handsome Black man with short cropped hair and dressed in a tailored blue suit sitting next to a white woman with long brown, thin hair trailing down her back and with undistinguished facial features and wearing an unpretentious dress. Every now and then she would lean in close to the Black guy and whisper in his ear. He would turn toward her with a smile and adoring eyes. Out of the side of his eyes Reggie could see the frown on Harriett's face whenever she looked in the direction of the couple. Her look took away Reggie's appetite. He was thinking he might have missed the discussion about who he was dating but he had not missed the verdict. When they walked out of the restaurant, Harriett couldn't wait to comment on the couple.

"When will the brothers ever learn that these white women are only looking for a toy to play with? It seems they think the ultimate sign of success or validation is to have a white woman on their arms. I wonder what our slave ancestors would say if they could see this. It's a shame."

"They would probably say, what's that stuff like?" Jeff said in loud laughter.

"Oh shut up Jeff. What more could I expect of you."

"You know there is no white woman as good as you, mama," Jeff said as he hugged Harriett.

Reggie walked in icy silence praying he would not be asked to identify which side he would fall on. Just as Harriett turned toward him seeming to solicit his input, they stepped off the curb and a fast- moving taxi almost hit Reggie. Jeff said, "Where the hell does he think he is going? These cab drivers think they own the streets. Are you okay man?"

"I'm okay. Just a little shook up," Reggie said in an effort to portray himself as a sympathetic character and assure he would not be put on the spot for the rest of the trip back to the office. Whoever heard of an angel coming in the form of a taxi cab driver, he was thinking.

When the three were about to go their separate ways back at the office, Jeff said to Reggie, "If you don't have plans for this Saturday, you may want to hang out with us down at Birdland and listen to some great jazz."

"Okay man. Let me get back to you on that," Reggie said as he felt anger boiling in him again at the thought of having to deal with the invitation.

Back in his office, Reggie felt like he had just finished digging a dozen ditches. He realized this situation would continue if he did not find a way to confront Jeff and Harriett with the truth, but he didn't know what or how to do it. There were risks any way you tackle it. They were the only Black people he had gotten to know and if they abandoned him, he would be left with just Carol and her friends. Maybe that's not a bad idea, he thought. But he could lose a valuable resource of guidance in the agency and that might be what the folks back home call cutting off your nose in spite of your face. As he sat leaning back in his chair with his feet on his desk looking out the window as if some message revealing what he should do would suddenly flow through the sky and into his office, he remembered he promised to call Carol. His stress began to dissipate as he reached for the phone to dial her number.

"Well, hello Miss McKay and how's your day going? How did your presentation go?"

"It's good to hear from you. Things are fine here. How about you?"

"Well, after hearing your voice, everything on this end is also fine. I'm counting the moments until I see you again. What about lunch tomorrow?"

"Nothing would please me more, but I will be traveling the rest of the week. I'm going to Atlanta and Houston. I'll be back Thursday night. I was going to call you about next Saturday night. I have tickets to 'The Great White Hope' which is playing on Broadway and I thought you might be interested in going. Are you free then?"

"You name the time and place and I will be there."

"I'll call you Friday to finalize plans."

"I'll be waiting by the phone."

Reggie resumed his position. However, this time as he gazed out the window, his thoughts were focused on holding Carol in his arms and saying the hell with the world. He could tell Jeff without a conscience that something had come up for Saturday and surely he would not have the nerve to ask what.

There were just a few patchwork tasks to be done on the Texas Oil commercials and since Gordon was in Washington most of the week, Reggie cruised through the days anticipating the weekend. Carol called early Friday morning and made arrangement to meet on Saturday. Jeff stopped by the office around noon to see if Reggie was interesting in going to

Birdland. Reggie took the rain check he had planned and Jeff said okay and wished him a happy weekend without probing. Reggie took a deep breath and exhaled as soon as Jeff closed the door behind him.

Reggie, all decked out in suit and tie, arrived promptly at six o'clock at Carol's door. Carol, in a bit more casual attire, was wearing a fitted dark brown dress with a string of pearls. She greeted Reggie with a light kiss on the cheek. Reggie grabbed her around the waist, pulled her into his longing arms and pressed his burning lips over hers as his hunger drove his tongue to engage hers. Carol surrendered to the power of his will, but quickly regained her composure and pulled away and said, "Now, now, we want to have time to grab something to eat before the play."

"I've lost my appetite," Reggie responded.

"You probably wouldn't say that four hours from now," Carol said.

After a brief meal at a restaurant in the theatre district catering to rushed theatre goers, they arrived at the theatre ten minutes before curtains and were seated in the center section in the mezzanine. As Reggie sat in the crowded row of seats, he had a flashback to his first theatre experience when he was in college and went with a white friend to see "A Raisin in the Sun." It had been an embarrassing experience watching the trials and tribulations of a poor Black family as he sat next to a white person that he did not know very well.

As he looked around the theatre this time, he took note that the audience was overwhelmingly white. Although he did not know what the play was about, he concluded it was not likely to embarrass him. So, he sat back and began to thumb through the playbill. He had not reached the part showing the actors in the play before the lights began to dim. When he began to see the Black actors on the stage, he cringed and wondered what was the meaning of the title, "The Great White Hope." His anxiety did not dissipate as the play unfolded. It was based on the life of Jack Johnson, the first Black heavyweight champion prize fighter who asserted his rights to live life as he saw fit which included having a white woman at his side. The plot unfolded, revealing the tragic results of his determination to hold on to her in a world of legalized racial prejudice. Reggie was uncomfortable watching it, wondering what Carol was thinking and why she wanted to see the play since he was certain she knew what it was about. To find some comfort sitting there, he rationalized that his situation could not be compared to Jack Johnson's because he lived in a different time when legal segregation had been outlawed and there was the well respected Sammy Davis Junior who had fame, wealth and a white wife. And there was the respected Senator Edward Brooke from Massachusetts. He is married to a white woman.

As this thought disappeared, the curtains fell and the lights were turned up announcing intermission. Reggie was not ready to talk about the play, so he quickly announced he wanted a drink and asked Carol if she would like one. Carol said "no" as Reggie stood up to head for the refreshments stand. The bar was crowded which did not bother Reggie since he was in no rush to return to his seat before the play resumed. He arrived back at his seat just as the lights were dimming again. When he sat down, Carol placed her hand over his which sent a spark through him that gave him a feeling of validation and enough comfort to sit through the rest of the play without a high level of anxiety or guilt.

As the curtains fell after the last act, the audience rose to its feet with roaring applause. Reggie followed Carol's rise and clapping; however, his response was more a reflection that the play had come to an end.

"I think the critics got it right. This play is bound for a Tony Award. Jane Alexander was magnificent. Her portrayal of the impact love can have on one's character was brilliant. James Earl Jones did a great job. I have never seen such a great portrayal of man's struggle against the forces of society." Carol said as she wrapped her arm around Reggie's. "Did you enjoy it?" she asked.

"Yes, I enjoyed it. I thought it showed a realistic picture of life in the country at that time. Thanks for inviting me," Reggie answered while tightening his grip on Carol's arm. As they walked to the subway, Reggie turned his head to face Carol and said, "You make me happy."

Carol stared at him with an adoring smile and said, "me too."

When the uptown express train pulled into the Seventy-Second Street station, Carol just took Reggie's hand and pulled him behind her. As the train pulled out of the station, the downtown local train pulled in. Jeff and Harriett sat on the local train facing the uptown platform. Jeff couldn't believe what he was seeing. He immediately dropped a coin on the floor to distract Harriett so she would not see what he had seen. There before his wandering eyes was Reggie being led out of the station by this attractive white woman. That sneaky bastard, Jeff thought. He's into "Snow White," Thank God Harriett didn't see them. She would be totally, completely, unadulterated finished with him.

CHAPTER 11

"Good morning Reggie. How are things going, my buddy?" Gordon said as he stuck his head in Reggie's office. "Got a minute?"

"Yes, come on in and have a seat. How are things going with you?" Reggie asked in a very jovial manner.

"Well, I have good news. We landed the Navy account. It's a big one and everybody is as happy as a pig in shit," Gordon said as he leaned back in his chair and crossed his legs.

"You should be really proud. Hats off to you."

"It was a team effort, but I do deserve a pat on the back," Gordon said as he leaned forward laughing. He then leaned back with a slight grin on his face and said, "There is a role for you on this team."

"What in the world can I do?" Reggie asked smiling, but with a puzzled look.

"Since things are quiet with the Texas Oil account, the boss asked me to ask if you wouldn't mind taking a shot at developing an affirmative action plan. The Department of Labor is giving us a deadline of thirty days to come up with one. I'm told it's a fairly easy thing to do. It's just writing down our personnel procedures and making sure they reflect equal treatment for all. A member of the Department of Labor is willing to meet with you to go over the requirements. You would be doing a great service for the agency which usually results in great rewards," Gordon said with a tight smile.

"I guess I could give it my best shot." Reggie said while thinking isn't that a job better suited for someone in personnel. I don't want to be known as the Affirmative Action Guy. That reputation could brand me as a trouble- maker with everyone except the few minority employees and that does not fit into my career plans. Still, there is no way I can object to the assignment. It would seem like I am not a team player and that would not go over well for my future here. Maybe if I do it well and have no responsibility for implementing it, I could be branded a valuable asset to the agency. It sure would be a great boast to my reputation back home. Mom would love to announce that in church. Maybe it's an opportunity not a put down.

"How will this work? What about the follow-up on the Texas Oil account?" Reggie asked.

"Well, during the thirty days you will be working on the plan, you will be on loan to personnel and I will take over your responsibilities on the Texas Oil account."

Reggie wasn't totally comfortable with what he was hearing. He wished this conversation had taken place over lunch after Gordon had had a few drinks under his belt. It might have come out differently than what he was hearing now, but he reminded himself that this could be an opportunity and he should take on the project with that thought. "When do I start?" Reggie asked trying to project enthusiasm.

"Immediately. I will take you to personnel as soon as you are settled. They will guide you. Thanks Reggie," Gordon answered with a very sobering look on his face while extending his hand for a shake then patting Reggie on the shoulder.

They approached a reception area where this white woman in her forties with her hair in a pony- tail was seated. "Hello Sandra, how are you on this lovely Monday morning?" Gordon asked with a bit of sarcasm in his voice.

"It's Monday. What can I say?" she answered lethargically while raising a steaming cup of coffee to her pursed lips.

"Could you tell Henry I am here?"

"Go right in, he is expecting you all."

"Good morning, Henry. How've you been? You are looking good as usual. One day you are going to have to give me your secret. I want to introduce you to Reggie Morton. He has agreed to work with you in developing an affirmative action plan," Gordon said in a more relaxed tone than when he was talking to Reggie.

"Good morning Reggie. I'm glad you've agreed to take on this project. It's very important to the agency," Henry said in a polite though serious manner as he reached to shake Reggie's hand.

"I'm glad to meet you Henry," Reggie said as he extended his hand to this man who looked and sounded a lot like the actor Glenn Ford. His spacious corner office with windows facing west and north was furnished traditionally with a totally uncluttered desk, four leatherback chairs, a leather couch and a round glass top coffee table.

"Take a seat you guys," he offered.

"I'm going to leave you guys to yourselves. I have to get back to my full inbox," Gordon said as he shuttled out of the office with a relieved mission accomplished look on his face.

"Of course," Henry said. "I'll talk to you later."

"Well Reggie I think we can do the agency a great service with not a lot of effort," Henry said with a slight frown on his face as if he were annoyed. "I understand the Department of Labor is not the best monitor of these things so if we put something together that's well-written without making any significant changes to our personnel system, we should be able to get them off our backs. I am sure we can come up with a well-worded Equal Opportunity Policy Statement. That's something they really focus on. I've had staff put together a package of materials about our various personnel policies and practices. You can go over them and get an idea of some of the things that will have to be addressed in the affirmative action plan. Included in that package is the Department of Labor's sample plan to guide you. Why don't I get Sandra to show you the office you will be using? I understand she has placed the materials I just mentioned there. Do you have any questions?"

"No." Reggie answered. However, he wanted to verify that he was on loan to the department for just thirty days. Asking that question, he concluded, might reveal the truth that he did not want to work on the project and he did not want to reveal that.

"My door is open if you have questions as you move along. Again, thanks for taking on the project." Henry said through a forced smile while patting Reggie on the shoulder.

"Well, I'm willing to give it my best shot. I am sure I will have questions as I move along. Gordon said the Department of Labor indicated they would be willing to meet with me to discuss the project. Do you have contact information for the person in charge there?" Reggie asked.

"Oh yes, I think that is part of the package you will find on your desk," Henry said as he rose from the chair next to Reggie and reached again to shake his hand and then led him out to Sandra.

"Sandra, have you been introduced to Mr. Morton?"

"No, not yet," she said looking up from her typewriter with a forced smile.

"Mr. Morton is on loan to us for the development of the agency's affirmative action plan. Could you get him settled in his office and with anything that he needs?" Sandra extended her hand to shake Reggie's and said," Glad to meet you, Mr. Morton."

"Please call me Reggie."

"Okay Reggie, follow me," Sandra said seeming to have broken through her Monday morning lethargy. Reggie followed her down the hall to his office. "This is it. Next to your phone, I have noted my extension and Henry's. That folder is the materials Henry asked that I put together for you and you will find supplies in your top draw. Welcome aboard and don't hesitate to come to me for questions you might have. If I don't have the answer, I know where to find it."

"Thanks, Sandra. I am sure I will be calling on you a lot."

As soon as Sandra left, Reggie plopped down in the chair behind his desk. He felt confused by all that had happened to him since arriving at work. After his initial reaction that developing an affirmative action plan could be an opportunity, he was no longer certain after detecting Henry's less than stellar enthusiasm for the project, especially since it would be his responsibility for its implementation. What kind of plan did he expect him to develop, Reggie wondered.

He began to feel anxious which was compounded by the realization of his surroundings. The office had no windows. It was half the size of his other office, with only one chair other than his and a file cabinet with two drawers. There was only overhead lighting. He felt like he had been demoted to a summer intern and given an assignment to test his abilities. He sat staring at the folder in front of him without opening it. He was certain, at the moment, he would not be able to concentrate on whatever was in it. He looked at his watch and decided he would take an early lunch although he was not hungry. He just needed some time out of this environment to try to get his head around the situation. He walked out of the building into winds that indicated fall was paving the way for winter's debut and started to walk with no particular destination in mind. He ended up in Central Park where he sat on a bench staring into the sky as if a guardian angel would soon arrive and wash away all his doubts. After a while, the winds began to sting and he decided to walk back to his office which, at least, was warm. On his way, he thought about calling Carol, but wasn't sure what to say to her about what had happened. He didn't want it to appear that he was in a situation that had overpowered him, but he concluded, he needed to share something with her. She might call the old number and find out I had moved which would at least cause her to ask why. He felt a bit nervous as her phone began to ring.

"Hello," she said in a soft quiet tone. Reggie immediately began to relax.

"Hello, love of my life," Reggie said in a seductive tone determine to project someone at ease.

"Reggie, what are you up to?" Carol asked in an enthusiastic tone.

"Thinking of you of course," he answered. "When will I see you again?" he asked.

"Maybe this weekend. I promised my parents I would try to come up Sunday. They are having some affair they want me to attend. I am not sure I will go, so I will let you know after I speak with them."

"I'll cross my fingers that your decision will be in my favor. Listen I want to give you my new telephone number here in the office. I moved today. The agency has asked me to take on a project of developing their first affirmative action plan so I will be on loan to the personnel office for the next thirty days working on it."

"Reggie! That's wonderful, what a great opportunity to have an impact. They must have a lot of faith in you to give you such a sensitive assignment. You must be proud," Carol said in a high- pitched, enthusiastic voice.

"I'm getting used to the idea. I have a lot to learn. I have never done anything like this before," he said trying to convey some reality about his feelings without revealing the depth of his doubts.

"I am sure you will do a wonderful job." Carol reassured him. "I have a meeting. I have to go. I am so proud of you," she said.

Reggie hung up the phone feeling encouraged and a bit energized. He immediately called Sandra and asked if she could order him a desk lamp. She responded emphatically "sure!" then asked if there was anything else he needed. The lamp arrived within the hour. Her very positive and prompt response energized Reggie even more. He reached for that folder in the center of his desk and began to thumb through the Department of Labor's guidelines. They seemed straightforward and easy to follow, but he felt it would be prudent to have a face- to-face meeting with their representative and get a feel for what they were expecting. He dialed the number and a woman in a sleepy voice answered, "Department of Labor. Mrs. Chance speaking."

"Mrs. Chance, I'm Reggie Morton from Benton, Barnes and Fowler. I will be developing the agency's affirmative action plan and I would like to meet with you to go over the requirements." Reggie said.

"Sure, Mr. Morton," she said with a bit more energy in her voice. "When are you available?"

"I want to get started as soon as possible considering the thirty-day deadline. If you are available, I would like to meet with you in your office tomorrow at your convenience," Reggie answered.

"Yes, Mr. Morton," she said with some hesitation in her voice. "Let me check my calendar." After about two minutes, she returned to the phone and said, "Why don't you come here at ten o'clock. Do you know where we are located?"

"Yes, I have your address."

"Then, I will see you tomorrow.

Reggie then began to tackle the part of the package that described the various personnel procedures that would have to be included in the plan. He was in deep concentration when there was a knock on the door. "Come in," he said. When he looked up and saw Jeff, his first reaction was embarrassment, but after some thought, he found something to give him a little happiness. He would not be on the same floors with either Harriett or Jeff and that would limit his contact with them, But at this moment, Jeff's appearance was welcomed.

"Hey man, what's up?" Jeff asked seemingly startled. "I went looking for you and was told you had been transferred to personnel. I was shocked. What the hell is this all about?" Jeff asked.

"Come on in man, this is a temporary assignment. I've been tapped to come up with the agency's first affirmative action plan. You know we got the Navy account and the government says if you are going to do business with us you have to have an affirmative action plan. So you can say I'm the Affirmative Action Man," Reggie said in an effort to convince Jeff that this was a positive move. Surely, he thought, Jeff would be pleased about having a plan and would probably congratulate him for being tapped to get it done.

"You will have to give me some time to digest all this news," Jeff said as he looked around checking out Reggie's office. "You okay with this?"

"Yes, it's a great opportunity."

"Are they going to let you do this or are they going to tell you what to do?" Jeff asked with a bit of sarcasm.

"I plan to give it my best shot and see what happens," Reggie responded, feeling he had not been successful in convincing Jeff that this was an opportunity. He was beginning to feel a little defensive.

"Well, I am anxious to see the outcome," Jeff said shaking his head in puzzlement. "How is life otherwise?" Jeff asked.

"Not bad," Reggie said glad to change the subject.

"How was your weekend?" Jeff asked with a smirk on his face.

"It was okay," Reggie said beginning to feel nervous.

"How was it?" Jeff asked raring back in his chair smiling.

"How was what?" Reggie asked looking perplexed and beginning to feel anxious.

"You know that good stuff you had Saturday night. I assume you got it," Jeff said.

"What the hell are you talking about, man?" Reggie responded feeling anger rising in him.

"Cool it man. Don't get excited. I'm cool with it. I saw you and your date getting off the subway at Seventy-Second Street Saturday night around ten-thirty," Jeff said in a more serious tone.

Reggie was stunned. He was speechless. He sat in silence for a moment feeling anger, embarrassment and somewhat relieved that it was now out in the open. "Yes, man that was me and we have been seeing each other for a few weeks. I met her on my flight here from Chicago. I'm really into her," Reggie said in a slow, sober, apologetic tone with his head dropped, looking away from Jeff while thinking I am guilty. So what.

Jeff leaned forward in his chair and looked toward Reggie and said in a very serious and quiet tone, "Hey man, if a white woman is what gets it up for you then that's your thing. That blood that rushes to your groin and arouses you and that adrenaline that flows through your veins making you fall in love gets its orders from what's deeply embedded in your brain and if that's what's there, that's what's there. But, before you go around getting serious, you might want to look into why it's embedded in your mind considering the world you live in."

"What the hell does that mean?" Reggie asked defensively.

"You said you were really into her. I'm just saying walk forward gently. The road you are on could have some major bumps in it. I'm not judging you man. I'm just offering a friend some friendly advice which I feel I have an obligation to do. You are okay with me," Jeff said as he reached across the desk to shake Reggie's hand.

"Was Harriett with you when you saw us?" Reggie asked sheepishly.

"She was with me, but she did not see you. When I saw you, I distracted her because I didn't want to hear her sermon about Black men dating white women. You heard her the other day at lunch. I think part of what she was doing was fishing for a reaction from you, but that taxi driver prevented you from biting. You will have to deal with her one day because she won't stop until she thinks you are interested in her or she knows why you are not. And if I thought the two of you were really into something and not just testing your powers, you would have to deal with me," Jeff said smiling.

"Well, I'll cross that bridge when I get to it-the bridge about me telling her about Carol of course, not about me and her," Reggie said smiling, but feeling nervous just thinking about Harriett finding out about Carol.

"I'll see you around, man. I have to go. Good luck with that affirmative action plan."

"Okay, man, I'll see you." Throughout the day he kept trying to absorb what was in those folders, but found himself reading the same paragraphs over and over without comprehending what was being said. The ups and downs of his emotions that day had drained him. He looked at his watch and saw it was nearly five. He called Sandra and gave her his plans for the next day and told her he was leaving. He fell asleep shortly after boarding the express bus and awoke just before it was time to get off. His muscles felt tight as he walked the rest of the way home. As soon as he entered the apartment, he went to the stero player flipped it on and began to sing along with Johnny Mathis, "A Time for Us" from the movie, "Romeo and Juliet."

CHAPTER 12

As Reggie walked up the steps to this drab office building, down the dimly lit hallways, and into an antiquated looking elevator, he wondered if the building was indicative of what he could expect to find in Mrs. Chance. When the elevator door opened he stepped into this hallway that looked deserted with no other human being to be seen. He marched down to Room 401, opened the door and faced, at the reception desk, a young Black man wearing a colorful dashiki and sporting a wide Afro that, at a distance. could be confused for a hat.

"My name is Reggie Morton and I have an appointment with Mrs. Chance."

The young man looked up and stared at Reggie's hair then shook his head seemingly in disgust before saying, "Go down the hall to your right. Her office is the third on your left." He then shook his head again and returned to something he was reading.

Who does the little ingrate nobody clerk think he is, looking like a baboon with a wig, Reggie wanted to say, but sucked it in.

"Mrs. Chance? I'm Reggie Morton."

"Yes. Come in Mr. Morton and have a seat," this stout white woman with hair just below her ears answered. Her office resembled his new one except hers was cluttered with stacks of folders and papers that didn't seem to have any particular order.

"How can I help you Mr. Morton?' she asked as she pushed aside a folder she had been reading.

"As I mentioned when we spoke, I am responsible for developing the affirmative action plan for Benton, Barnes and Fowler. I was hoping you would give me an idea of your expectations for the plan. You know, the kind of detail it should include."

"Did you get a copy of the guidelines I left with your office?"

"I did."

"Do you have any specific questions after reviewing them?"

"They were rather broad with very few specifics. Is that the kind of plan you are expecting?"

"We expect that you should address each section of the plan with your commitment for compliance or your procedures for compliance. And we would like for you to include your Equal Opportunity Policy Statement. If you do those things, you will be okay."

"What are your procedures for monitoring the plan?"

"We will, of course, review your plan and let you know if you need to make any changes to be in compliance and during the course of your contract we will make periodic reviews."

"Will those reviews be on-site?"

"They could be. But we will give you advance notice of any such reviews."

"What happens if we are not in compliance with the plan?"

"We will point out where we think you are not in compliance and work with you to remedy the situation. Of course ultimately your contract can be revoked if you refuse to comply, but that seldom happens. We believe in working with the contractor to get them in compliance," she said with a slight smile.

"After our plan is submitted, how long will it take for your office to inform us of your assessment?"

"We try to get back to you within a month, but that depends on our backlog. Is there anything else I can help you with, Mr. Morton?" She asked looking directly at Reggie without batting an eye and with slight irritation in her voice.

"I think not," Reggie said sensing her irritation.

"Well, you know how to contact me if you have other questions," she said with a tight smile.

"Thanks for your help," Reggie said as he extended his hand for a hand shake. Mrs. Chance gave him her hand and said, "You are welcome."

Reggie walked out of the drab building disappointed, but also somewhat relieved. He thought there is no support for this affirmative action plan. Henry doesn't seem to want it and it seems the only concern of Mrs. Chance is to get it done and off her to- do list. Why should I be concerned, he thought. Maybe I should just write something down and call it done. That way everyone will be pleased-everyone maybe except that little Black ingrate baboon.

Reggie sat at his desk wondering where to start. However, every time he started to read something, images of Jeff, his mother and the little baboon crept into his mind. He shook his head trying to clear those images when the telephone rang.

"Good afternoon. Is this the handsome, loveable Reggie Morton?" the voice on the other end asked.

"Yes, love of my life," Reggie said feeling a burst of joy consuming him. "It's good to hear form you. How's your day going?"

"Things are fine over here. What about you?"

"Well, I had a meeting this morning with a representative from the Department of Labor regarding the affirmative action plan. I got the impression they don't care much about what kind of plan you develop as long as you develop one. I'm not sure the people here feel any different. So I am not sure what kind of plan to develop."

"It's your project. You have to do what you think is best and defend it. Your responsibility is to develop a plan that assures that your company is in compliance with the law and in compliance with their own Equal Opportunity Policy Statement. What you do could provide many minorities and women the kind of opportunity that has been given to you. Give it your best shot and then defend it when necessary."

"You know you are going to make some man a good wife one day," Reggie said feeling ashamed of his doubts.

"Maybe," Carol said. "The reason I'm calling is about this weekend. I mentioned that my parents were expecting me home for an event. Well, they confirmed the event is a brunch on Sunday. They are hosting it for a group of local Peace Corps volunteers who are returning from a tour of duty in Africa. My mother asked me to invite you to join us. Will you be able to go up with me? We could take the train early Sunday morning and come back Sunday evening."

Reggie held the phone to his ear with his mouth open. He was caught totally off guard. He immediately realized he had no choice except to accept the invitation, but was nervous about actually going. He wondered what Carol had told them about him, especially if they knew he was Black or whether Carol was rebellious enough to show up and surprise them. Maybe since they are welcoming people back from Africa, they know I am Black and want to show me how liberal they are.

"Of course I will go with you. Just let me know what time the train leaves on Sunday," Reggie answered assertively through his fears, doubts and great anticipation.

"I'll check the schedule and get back to you on that."

"I'll wait for your call," Reggie said.

He hung up the phone and sat at his desk trying to sift through his feelings. Carol's advice about the affirmative action plan had given him the will to give the project his best shot. Her invitation to her parents' brunch had left him baffled about what it meant, but happy that she was willing to introduce him to them. He wanted to believe the invitation said a lot about what

Carol felt for him, but he also wondered if her parents wanted to meet him so they could shoo him away from their only child.

He shook his head in an effort to banish those thought invading his mind, thinking he needed to focus on the affirmative action plan for now. However, the thoughts had diminished his ability to concentrate on the plan. The work day was coming to an end anyway, so he closed shop and declared he would start fresh in the morning. During the evening his mind would not give him the respite he sought. The thought came haunting him- what if things went favorably with Carol's parents? She would probably expect him to do the same and he had no idea how he would handle that. Thank God they are many miles away.

Reggie arrived in the office early the next morning not as rested as he wanted to be but determined to begin work on the affirmative action plan. He decided to tackle the Equal Opportunity Policy Statement first. It would be the heart of the plan he concluded. He decided it would focus on the agency's commitment to developing each employee's full potential and to assuring that all its practices fell in line with that commitment.

At the end of the day, he had three drafts so he decided to put them aside and take a fresh look at another time. He spent the rest of the week going over the Department of Labor's guidelines and the different personnel procedures of the agency.

When Friday arrived, he could no longer give the project his undivided attention. His thoughts were on the trip to Ridgefield and what he needed to do to impress Carol's parents. They would certainly want to know about my background, he concluded. My preference would be to talk about my life in Chicago instead of what it was like growing up in Tennessee, especially since they are probably rich with no idea what life was like for Blacks who grew up in the South during the Forties and Fifties. If they did, they probably wouldn't want their only child involved with such a person. I need to know what Carol has already told them in order to develop a good strategy. I'll find a way to squeeze it out of her on the train, he decided.

Reggie was standing under the clock in Grand Central Station dressed in his navy blue suit, white shirt and blue and white poker dot tie, and carrying his trench coat on his arm when Carol arrived promptly at eight-thirty for the eight forty-five train.

"You are looking mighty handsome, Mr. Morton," Carol said as she approached Reggie in a light blue coat and with her hair in a ball.

"You are glowing like a burst of sun on a cloudy day," Reggie said, smiling as he reached for her hand. Hand in hand, like teenagers falling in love for the first time, they walked through the gate onto the train, made their way to two vacant seats and slid into them as Reggie let go of Carol's hand. Feeling a little embarrassed, Reggie sat in a stiff upright position to project a more business- like air. Carol looked at him, smiled and placed her hand over his. Reggie's business air began to melt and he managed a forced smile. He looked at Carol, trying to appear at ease, and said, "Thanks for letting me tag along with you today."

Carol looked directly at Reggie and in a casual and matter of fact tone said, "You are not tagging along. My mother thought you might be interested in meeting some people just returning from work in Africa. I wholeheartedly agreed with her. So here we are. Also, my parents are anxious to meet you. Ridgefield is a small, friendly New England town where people tend to know each other. Most are financially secure. It's a nice escape from the hustle of New York and yet still close enough to the city to have quick access to all its advantages. I think you will like it."

At that point, Reggie felt her parents knew he was Black. He didn't want to press her further about what else they knew about him for fear of exposing his anxiety about meeting them. It might make her uncomfortable about bringing him. He now had acquired more anxiety. First of all, what he knew about Africa would only fill up a thimble, so he wasn't sure what kind of conversation he could have with these people who had worked there. Second, Carol's revelation that most of the population of Ridgefield was rich made him more certain that he did not want to talk about growing up in a Black community in a Southern town during the period he grew up. And he worried that he would be the only Black at the brunch and would be expected to speak for the Black population, especially what was going on in the Civil Rights movement which he was embarrassed to say he had not kept up to date.

He felt a knot rise in his stomach. He shifted in his seat trying to get relief from the discomfort and quickly remembered he needed to keep cool so as not to cause Carol discomfort. So, he squeezed her hand and said. "Let me rephrase what I said, I'm glad to be escorting you to your parents' brunch honoring the Peace Corps volunteers. I'm sure I will be glad to meet them."

"That's better," Carol said as she rested her head on Reggie's shoulder and closed her eyes. Reggie looked out the window, searching for some thought that would calm his anticipation about this visit. Unable to escape, he finally turned and looked down at Carol's head and felt maybe the price was worth it.

"Branchville," the conductor called out.

"This is our stop," Carol said. Reggie stepped into the aisle and stood back making room for Carol to lead the way out. As they stepped off the train, this medium height, stocky man with thinning salt and pepper hair sporting a pipe clutched between his teeth walked over to Carol, hugged her and said, "Its good to see you baby."

"Father, I want you to meet Reggie Morton."

Reggie extended his hand. Mr. McKay, a man who apparently had spent a life time mastering the art of masquerading his innermost feelings, gave Reggie a very flimsy handshake without looking him in the eye then said "It's nice to meet you, young man."

"It is my pleasure, sir. Thanks for inviting me," Reggie said trying to project some enthusiasm. Mr. McKay made no response. He ushered them to his Volvo and opened the back door and pointed to Reggie. Reggie stepped in with mixed feeling. He expected he might be invited to the front seat so the two could talk easier and get to know each other. On the other hand, there was comfort in the back seat while he continued to size up the situation which, so far, had not given him much comfort.

Carol and her father engaged in conversation about her work as the car rolled through the country roads with stone fences that seemed to date back to colonial times and houses sitting on acres of land nestled behind clusters of trees. Reggie sat silently, determined not to interrupt the flow of conversation and bring attention to him and maybe embarrassing questions about his background. The more indicators of wealth he saw the more insecure he became about the whole situation.

The car turned onto a long graveled driveway and stopped in front of a two story brick house with a manicured lawn and sculptured hedges. Reggie stepped out of the car and Mr. McKay said, "Come, come young man," in a tone that implied Reggie might need careful directions. "My wife is waiting for us." Carol walked ahead of Reggie and her father into the house where she was greeted by an attractive, slim, middle aged woman with a smile as warm as Carol's.

"Mother, this is Reggie Morton," she said.

"Mr. Morton, welcome to our home. I am so glad you were able to come. Carol has told us so much about you so it's really great to finally meet you," she said with that warm gracious smile.

With a restrained smile spreading across his face provoked by curiosity about what Carol had told them about him, but feeling his insecurity ameliorated by the warmth of her smile, Reggie reached out to shake her hand and said, "It's my pleasure to meet you. Thanks for inviting me."

"Come in here and make yourself comfortable and I will get you something to drink. Would you like a Bloody Mary or a mimosa?"

"I'll take a Bloody Mary," Reggie answered thinking something heavy is what I need just now. Carol had disappeared with her father. Reggie sat in this library with ceiling high stuffed book shelves, a mahogany desk, high-backed leather chairs, Tiffany lamps and a leather couch. It looked like a room out of a movie, Reggie thought. At that moment he began to feel what his aunt used to call, "rubbing knuckles with the upper crust." Carol entered the room with his Bloody Mary and her mimosa.

"While mother and father are attending to last minute preparations, let's take a walk around the grounds."

"Sounds good to me," Reggie said as he took the first sip of his drink which seemed to raise his comfort level a notch higher. As they walked around the beautifully landscaped grounds with tall evergreens lining the pathway to the house, Carol began to talk about childhood memories growing up there.

"I remember on my eighth birthday, father and mother led me out here where a pony was saddled and tied to this beam. I jumped up screaming with joy and ran over and hugged the horse's leg. I had begged for one ever since my cousin got one for her birthday a year before. Father put me up on the horse and led it around the grounds for about an hour. I will never forget that day. After that, father and I would go horseback riding at least once a week. The horse was my favorite possession until I graduated from high school and father bought me a Mustang after sending me to driving school. He said he loved me too much to teach me himself," Carol said with a hearty laugh and a glow of nostalgic happiness.

"How did he react when you broke off your engagement to Nicholas?" Reggie asked looking out across the lawn.

"He was supportive. He said he was sure I would find the right man one day; still, I could tell he was very disappointed. He and Nicholas really got along and he and Nicholas's father had been friends."

"What about your mother?" Reggie asked.

"Mother is romantic. She is a real believer in chemistry. She said she wasn't sure Nicholas and I had the right blend. But he was a really nice guy who would make a good husband, so she would accept the union as one that would work if I wanted it. I think she sometimes has fantasies of someone other than father and she probably wants to live out those fantasies through me. Mother comes from one of those Newport, Rhode Island families with a more bohemian point of view about life. Father comes from a well-known family in Richmond with what I call a southern point of view- a point of view my mother has worked night and day to erase. I think they complement each other very well. We better go in. Guests are beginning to arrive" Carol said in a tone of pleasant satisfaction.

Reggie followed Carol through the spacious foyer into the large living room where a fire was crackling in the fireplace. The room filled up with guest, about twenty, seemingly all at the same time. Carol greeted several of those she seemed to know and introduced Reggie who greeted each with what seemed like a perpetual smile. Mr. McKay beckoned Carol and she dashed to him leaving Reggie standing alone. A young woman, dressed in colorful African garb with her long brown hair in one braid trailing down her back, walked up to Reggie with a quizzical, but friendly look on her face and introduced herself. Reggie reciprocated.

"Are you here representing the government of Gambia?" she asked.

"No," Reggie answered, feeling embarrassed but a bit proud of the perception.

"Where did you serve in the Peace Corps?"

"I didn't. I'm a guest of the family from New York," Reggie answered.

"Oh, I'm sorry," she said casually.

"No apology is necessary." Reggie said apologetically.

"I just thought," she said as the Latino waiter interrupted them with the offer of a drink. Reggie accepted another Bloody Mary and the woman took a mimosa. Reggie sipped his drink and immediately felt a buzz.

"My two years were spent teaching in Gambia," the woman continued. "It was a deeply gratifying experience. The impoverished kids were so grateful for the opportunity to learn. Some of them were really bright. It was so gratifying to see them grasp something I was trying to teach. I've kept in touch with a couple of them. I'm filled with joy when I receive a correspondence from them. One served as a guide to a group of us on a weekend trip to Dakar. While we were there we took a tour of Goree Island and saw what had to be the most horrible conditions for the number of slaves they packed into the small space while they waited to be shipped to America. It was hard to imagine how anyone survived there, especially considering the heat. Have you ever visited Africa?" she asked.

"Not yet," Reggie said. "I hope to make the journey one day."

"Oh, I am sure you will go one day," she said with much confidence.

"Hello ladies and gentlemen, may I have your attention for a moment?" Mr. McKay asked. " On behalf of the board of directors of the town's Youth Volunteers for America program, I want to welcome you all back from your tour in the Peace Corps and thank you for your wonderful work spreading our civilization to the darker, uncivilized parts of the world. I am sure your experiences in Africa gave you a deeper appreciation of your own culture and gave you a well-deserved sense of accomplishment for reaching out to those less fortunate than yourselves. We look forward to having each of you come and share your experiences with our youth. Thanks again and enjoy yourselves."

There was a round of applause following the speech. Reggie jumped right in. By that time, Carol had reappeared next to him. She looked at him and said, referring to her father, "Isn't he wonderful?" Reggie smiled and nodded his head in agreement feeling the effects of the Bloody Mary.

Mrs. McKay walked up to them, placed her hand on Reggie's shoulder and with a hearty smile asked, "How are you doing?"

With an equally hearty smile, Reggie said, "I am doing just fine."

"Carol, why don't you get Reggie some food?" she asked as she walked away.

"Yes, mother," Carol said as she led Reggie to the table where they loaded their plates with croissants, Swedish omelet and green salad. They then snuck off into the library and had their food. Carol, in a joyful mood, spoke about how much she admired the Peace Corps volunteers. Yet, it was not something she could do considering the sacrifices that were necessary to live and work in a strange environment. She told Reggie about her experience one Christmas when she joined a group collecting toys for under- privileged children in Stamford, Connecticut and going to deliver them. She said when it was over she cried because of the joy she felt. Reggie sat, with the food only slightly compromising the effects of the Blood Mary, staring at her in pure, unadulterated admiration. All the doubts and anticipation he felt leading up to that moment seemed to have been lost in his memory.

"We had better rejoin the crowd before mother come looking for us," Carol said with a slight bit of rush in her voice. They walked back into the crowd and were accosted by this tall lanky blond-haired guy wearing a tweed jacket that was holding onto a few wrinkles and a pair of blue jeans.

"Hello Carol. Where have you been hiding?" he asked flashing a mischievous grin.

"Hello Chester", Carol answered ignoring his question.

"Who do we have here?" Chester asked looking at Reggie.

"Oh, Chester, this is Reggie Morton, a friend of mine from New York. Reggie, this is Chester Rowland."

"Nice to meet you Reggie," he said maintaining his mischievous smile while extending his hand to shake Reggie's. "Are you a Peace Corps volunteer?"

"No, I work in advertising," Reggie answered wondering about the nature of this guy's relationship with Carol.

"Man! What is it like working in that industry?" Chester asked in a sarcastic tone.

"I find it a great job and a great opportunity in an important industry. Advertising plays an important role in our economy. It provides a service that educates the public about making choices that meet their particular needs," Reggie answered feeling proud of what he considered a quick, smart, articulate response.

"What Reggie meant was advertising makes us aware of what is out there so we can make decisions that we feel are in our favor," Carol interjected like a teacher clarifying to the class her student's answer while looking a bit apologetically at Chester. Reggie felt like he had just suffered a blow to his stomach but smiled at Carol to hide his hurt feelings.

"Well guy, I wish you the best in your career," Chester said, this time seeming to have substituted his sarcasms for a tone of sympathy.

"What are you going to do now that you tour in the Peace Corps is over?" Carol asked Chester with a friendly smile.

"Oh, I don't know, I'm exploring right now. If I can't find anything that I really like, I just might sign up for another tour. Maybe this time I will go to South America."

"Well, best wishes in your search. I am sure you will find something," Carol said as she patted his arm.

"Yes, best wishes," Reggie said extending his hand for a farewell shake. Carol then proceeded to satisfy the curiosity of just about every guest who at one time or another stared in the direction of Reggie. She very cordially introduced him to a select few as a friend of hers from New York who worked in the advertising industry. Reggie very politely shook their hands. As if she were trying to make as many introductions as possible, Carol would then move on to the next person without any further discussion, leaving many of them with the look of being unfulfilled. However, each of them seemed to return to discussing with each other their experiences in Africa. After she felt she had fulfilled her host responsibility, Carol led Reggie to the table for some pumpkin pie.

"Can you two stay for dinner?" Mrs. McKay asked Carol while dashing to some guest that was leaving, to say good-bye and tell them that she looked forward to their visit to the Youth Center.

"No mother, I'm sorry I have to get back to get some work done for a meeting tomorrow morning. We are going to have to leave shortly."

"Okay, but promise me you will bring Reggie back when we are not entertaining. Reggie, promise me you will come again."

"I promise to remind Carol that we owe you a visit. I had a great time and I would love to come back," Reggie said, feeling the invitation was legitimate.

"Father, at your first opportunity could you drive us to the station?" Carol asked.

"Yes, baby, your mother can continue entertaining. I'll be with you in a few minutes."

Mrs. McKay returned from saying good-bye to a guest and walked Carol and Reggie to the car and waved good-bye as the car rolled down the gravel driveway.

"Young man, Carol tells us you are responsible for developing an affirmation action plan for your company," Mr. McKay said startling Reggie. He was expecting to sit back and enjoy the scenery of the countryside while Mr. McKay ignored him as he had done earlier.

"Yes sir, that's my responsibility," Reggie said glad to be recognized, but hoping the conversation would end with his answer. This was the last thing he was expecting to be asked and had given no thought to how he would answer.

"Is that how you got your job?" Mr. McKay asked.

Reggie began to tense up. "The company did not have an affirmative action plan when I was hired," he answered.

"What the hell, do they need one for now?" Mr. McKay said in an emphatic tone.

"The agency has been awarded a contract to do advertising for the U.S Navy. As a result, the government requires companies with contracts the size of the one awarded by the Navy to have an affirmative action plan."

"So if you do business with the government, they want to tell you who to hire whether or not they know anything about your business, just so they can get minorities to vote for them."

"Sir, the affirmative action plan doesn't tell them who to hire. It merely establishes procedures to assure that minorities are given a fair chance to compete for jobs."

"Do you really believe that, young man?"

"Yes sir, I do."

"The government needs to step aside and let businesses run their businesses. They know how to get the best-qualified people for their jobs."

"Well, sir, those decisions in the past have not resulted in many opportunities for minorities and the government has a responsibility to spend taxpayers' money in a way that benefits all its citizens," Reggie said feeling anxious and irritated. He wasn't sure whether his feelings were because he felt under a personal attack or whether he was feeling the weight of the history of Black people in the country. In any event, he decided he needed to tame his emotions so as not to seem too defensive. So his response was slow and in a calm voice.

"Well, a company can't function without qualified employees," Mr. McKay said in a tone of frustration.

"An affirmation action plan takes that into consideration, sir."

"Father, there are a lot of women qualified for jobs and can't get them because they are women. Is that fair?" Carol asked.

"No baby it is not. But there are some jobs that women can't handle."

"Yes, father, I don't deny that, but what Reggie was trying to say is that the government has a responsibility to protect the rights of all its citizens."

Reggie cringed again thinking Carol had to clarify what he was saying because he was not articulate enough. However the conversation had awakened something in him. He thought about his answers to Mr. McKay and began to feel confident that it was his responsibility to put together a meaningful affirmative action plan.

"Well, here we are. When will we see you again, young lady?"

"I promise it won't be that long, but I can't say exactly when."

"Young man, it was nice meeting you," Mr. McKay said, this time giving Reggie a somewhat firmer handshake than the first one.

"Same here, sir," Reggie said without a smile.

"I am really glad you were able to come with me today and meet my parents. They like you. Don't be misled by father's conversation. He loves to debate." Carol said as she rested her head on Reggie's shoulder as the train pulled out of the station.

"No problem," Reggie said as calmly as he could considering the grilling and embarrassment he felt he had just experienced. He laid his head back against the cushioned seat, careful not to disturb Carol who looked at peace, as he tried to sift through the various experiences he had that day and to determine their meaning.

Unable to unravel the implications of everything, he looked down at Carol and smiled, thinking I am so lucky to have this beautiful woman in love with me. What more could I wish for. He closed his eyes listening to the monotonous shackling sound of the train rolling along the tracks. The sound helped him relax. He began to fantasize watching Carol walk down the aisle with her adoring, approving father and saying, "I do," receiving a kiss from her as he walks out of the apartment on his way to work, holding her hand as she gives birth and walking hand-in-hand with her in the park with their grandchild.

When the train arrived in Grand Central, Reggie kissed Carol on the head to awaken her. As they walked into the station, Reggie told her he had a great time and hugged her. She kissed him on the cheek and waved him good-bye as she headed for the subway and Reggie headed for Metro North to Riverdale.

CHAPTER 13

Reggie stepped into his office on Monday morning charged from the energy he had acquired on Sunday for developing an effective affirmative action plan. This, he declared, would be his contribution to the civil rights Movement and free him from any claims that he had done nothing but benefit from it. He picked up the three drafts of the policy statement he had left to be reviewed at another time and decided on one. He then pulled out all the material from the Department of Labor and the folder on the agency's personnel procedures.

After spending most of the day combing through and analyzing the data he had read the previous week, he decided on several points he considered basic to an effective affirmative action plan. They included: outreach to minority resources for recruiting, reviewing and revising job descriptions that overstated the required qualifications, developing a bank of minority and women applicants and employees with their qualifications that could be referred to when filling vacancies, conducting exit interviews with minorities who choose to leave the agency so as to detect obstacles to minority employment, and analyzing salary differences in jobs to detect patterns that favor non-minorities.

At the end of the day, he leaned back in his chair with his hands cupped together behind his head and said, "Well done." He immediately thought this is news his parents would love to hear, especially his mother. She would spread the word around town and the folks back home would really be proud of him.

After entering his apartment and shedding his coat, he picked up the phone and dialed his home.

"Hello," the tired and somewhat weary voice on the other end said.

"Hello mom. It's your younger son," Reggie said in his jovial tone.

"Oh, baby, it's good to hear your voice. How are you?"

"I'm fine. How are you and dad doing?"

"I'm okay, but your father is doing poorly. His breathing is more labored than it has been in a while and neither of us gets that much sleep at night. Sometimes I'm afraid he might just stop breathing. If things don't improve I am going to have to put him back in the hospital."

"What are the doctors saying about treating him?" Reggie asked, hoping for something positive that he could hang on to.

"They keep changing his medication, but none of it seems to be doing any good. When do you think you will get a chance to come home?"

"I don't know. I'm working on a project that has to be completed by the end of the month. The agency has asked me to develop an affirmative action plan that the federal government requires before awarding a big contract," Reggie said in a subdued tone.

"That's nice, son. I hope you hurry up and finish it and come home to visit us," she said, sounding tired and weary.

"I will do my best mom. You take care of yourself and give dad my regards," Reggie said with all the steam fizzled out of his enthusiasm for making the great announcement. It had been replaced by a feeling of guilt about what he could do to help his father and relieve the stress on his mother. He decided he would go home as soon as he felt secure about completing the Plan and before he returned to overseeing the Texas Oil campaign.

Reggie returned to work the next day determined to begin drafting language to achieve his objective in each of the areas he had identified for the Plan. By the end of the week, he had pulled together a rough draft of a plan and a policy statement that he felt would brand the agency as committed to opening up opportunities for minorities and women. He walked over to Sandra's desk and handed her the drafts and said smiling, "See what you can do with this."

Sandra looked at the package and then at Reggie a bit perplexed and said,
"I will do just that. Give it a number."

"How about number one?" Reggie answered, still smiling.

"In your dreams," she said, this time smiling.

Reggie decided it was time to reward himself for the week's accomplishment and he could think of no better way than spending time with Carol. He had heard somewhere that women like men who cook for them, so he made a date with Carol to come to his place Saturday night for dinner; however, at that point he had no idea what he would cook since there was no dish he had perfected. On the bus ride home he wondered what he could do to avoid a disaster that would ruin a romantic evening.

He walked into the grocery and started down the meats aisle and nervously decided on steak. After all, he declared what can you do to mess up a steak? He then headed for the frozen foods section and decided on some French cut string beans that should impress, he declared. Then he picked up a package of wild rice whose instructions said it only needed boiling with some butter. He walked back to the frozen food section and pulled out a quart of strawberry ice cream. On his way to the checkout counter, he passed the baked goods section and spotted a pound cake and grabbed it. He decided the meal would not reflect that much creativity, but maybe the effort is what would impress her. He rushed home and started laying out a plan for his maiden voyage in designing a romantic evening. Saturday found him rushing out to get those things he needed to help create a romantic atmosphere-wine and candles. When he returned to the apartment, he realized he wanted the evening to end with her in his bed, so he needed to make sure he had clean sheets and towels. There were none so he had to rush to the laundry room and wash some. When he finished the laundry, he realized he needed to make sure he had clean glasses, plates and silverware. He checked and he had them, but they were not all clean, so he washed everything.

Reggie decided to grill the steaks but he wanted to marinate them before, so he poured some wine over them. He had seen on some television program that when men were trying to impress a woman they always had fresh flowers on the table, so he ran out again and bought some. By this time, he was exhausted. He said to himself that he sure hoped she was impressed because he was never going to do this again. He looked at his watch and realized she was due there within the hour, so he jumped in the shower.

While in the shower, it occurred to him that he had not planned for one of the most important things to create a romantic evening-music. With the towel still trying to dry his hair, he rushed to his music collection and chose Johnny Mathis' "Wonderful" and Aretha Franklin's "Soft and Beautiful" albums and placed them on the turntable. As he dressed, he thought, I hope the hell I haven't forgotten anything else and if I have, the hell with it.

When the intercom rang and the sound of Carol's voice came through, his heart began to race. He turned on the stereo and waited for the doorbell to ring. With Johnny Mathis' "Chances Are" flowing through the room, Carol stepped into the apartment and Reggie greeted her with a hug and a light kiss on the lips.

"Reggie, you have a very spacious apartment. Your neighborhood seems quiet. It's like living in the suburbs of New York. Do you really like it?" Carol asked.

"It's not bad. Sometimes it feels like the great escape from the hustle and bustle of Manhattan, and other times it seems isolated from the rest of the world. The agency's real estate agent found the apartment. I guess she was looking for something reasonable." He didn't want to reveal his love for the Riverdale environment just now since Carol seemed to be in love with Manhattan and he did not want any discord to interfere with his romantic evening.

"This is for you," Carol said as she handed him a bottle of wine.

"Thanks baby. Let me take your coat and why don't you make yourself comfortable while I pop open the wine."

"I love Johnny Mathis. What album is that?" Carol asked as she sat down and began quietly singing along with the record.

"That's "Wonderful," one of his first," Reggie said as he handed Carol a glass of wine then dashed back into the kitchen and got everything started. He then returned and sat next to her while Johnny Mathis belted out, "The Twelfth of Never." He looked into Carol's eyes and sang along with the record emphasizing the part that said, *"You ask how much I love you. I'll tell you when until the twelfth of never and that's a long long time."* Carol stroked his faced while he sang. When the record ended, she decided to quiet things down a bit and asked, "What was your week like?" Reggie proudly announced that he completed the first draft of the affirmative action plan and turned it in for typing.

"Congratulations!" Carol blurted out. "That was quick. Are you pleased with what you wrote? Did you address all the areas required by the Department of Labor?"

"Yes! yes! yes," Reggie answered with great satisfaction.

"Well, I am proud of you, Mr. Morton," Carol said as she patted him on the shoulder.

"How are your parents doing?" Reggie asked, fishing for some word of their impression of him.

"They're fine. I spoke to mother a couple of time this week and she said she and father were debating whether we should go to aunt Melba's on Martha's Vineyard for Thanksgiving or stay home. I told her I voted for home. She said they would take that into consideration. Are you planning to go home for Thanksgiving?"

"I don't know. I spoke to mother this week and she said father is not doing too well. So, I might go to see him."

"What's wrong with your father?" Carol asked with a look of serious concern in her voice.

"He is suffering from the complications of a stroke," Reggie answered.

"Oh Reggie, that sounds serious."

"Yes, I know."

"Maybe you should consider going to see him as soon as possible. If you want me to I could probably rearrange my schedule and go with you. Let me know what you decide," Carol continued staring at Reggie with a look of sorrow in her eyes.

"I will let you know. I'll talk to mother again next week." He never expected Carol's offer to accompany him home. He was sorry the conversation had made a turn in that direction because he dreaded the thought of taking Carol to meet his parents and he was not sure how to explain that to her. In order to change the subject, he asked Carol if she needed her drink refreshed. She said yes and he disappeared into the kitchen, checked on the food and decided that everything needed about ten more minutes. He returned with more wine for Carol. She asked if there was anything she could do and he gave her the task of setting the table with all the dishes and silverware he had strewn across it. In about fifteen minutes, Reggie presented the food, lit the candles and beckoned Carol to join him.

"Well, Mr. Morton I am impressed. Did you do all of this yourself or did you buy it and bring it in?"

"You are witnessing the chef side of me," Reggie said pounding his chest. "Of course I probably should have waited until you tasted everything before I claimed ownership."

"I am sure everything is fine. However, I was looking for the fried chicken, collard greens, black eyed peas, potato salad and corn bread," Carol said in jest.

"Well you can find them down at Sylvia's restaurant in Harlem. I'll take you there one day and you can indulge yourself," Reggie said in a matter of fact tone.

"Never mind, that kind of food isn't really good for you," Carol said in a somewhat authoritarian tone.

"It may not be good for you, but it sure is good to you," Reggie bounced back in a somewhat authoritarian tone. They both then broke out in jovial laughter.

As Aretha Franklin serenaded them with "Friendly Persuasion," they consumed what Carol described as a tasty meal. Reggie basked in the compliment.

"Well, what do we have for dessert, master chef? Sweet Potato pie?" Carol asked with a burst of laughter.

"Well, my favorite critic, we are having ice cream and cake. I made the ice cream and baked the cake just for you. How about that?" Reggie said, looking adorably at Carol while trying to hold back laughter.

"Bring it on chef. I am honored," Carol said, lifting her wine glass.

Reggie cleared the table and served dessert which Carol, while laughing, declared it topped anything Sara Lee could come up with. Reggie hit his chest and said gallantly, "Thank you madam."

He then filled their glasses with wine and retired to the couch both sitting close to each other listening to Aretha singing "But Beautiful." When she burst into "I Wish I Didn't Love You So," Reggie pulled Carol to the floor and began to dance around the room. He continued the dance down the hall and into the bedroom.

When Reggie awoke the next morning and saw Carol next to him, he felt like Santa Claus had come and brought everything on his list. She looked like a princess waiting for the knight in shining armor to kiss her and bring her out of her dreams. Reggie resisted the temptation and slid out of the bed as quietly as possible and headed for the shower. While showering, he realized he had not prepared for a breakfast, so he decided they would go down to the International House of Pancakes on Broadway. When he returned to the room, Carol was wide awake, sitting up in the bed.

"Good morning sleepy head," Reggie said.

"Good morning, my favorite chef, where did I leave my purse?" Carol asked trying to hide her face.

"Everything is right here- your purse and some towels and the bathroom awaits your arrival. When you are ready, we will go to International House of Pancakes for breakfast. It's down on Broadway," Reggie said in a very jovial tone.

After a hearty breakfast, Carol dashed off to meet her friends at an art exhibit in the Village and Reggie, feeling exhilarated, walked the thirty blocks back home and settled down to the Sunday New York Times. Just as he curled up on the couch and reached for the paper, the telephone rang. He figured it was Carol so he picked it up and said, "yes" in a seductive tone.

"Son, it's your mother." Her voice sounded as if she were close to tears. "Your brother and I just came back from the hospital. Your father was admitted yesterday and he is not doing well. I was with him all night and just came home to change clothes. You might want to come see him."

"Yes, mom, I'll be there just as soon as I can. I'll notify the people at work tomorrow and hope to get out by tomorrow evening or early Tuesday morning. Were you able to get any sleep at the hospital? Try not to run yourself down and get sick."

"I'm all right son, but I will be glad when you get here."

Reggie put the phone down in a state of shock and confusion. He didn't know what to do at the moment. He began to pace the floor pounding his fist in his hand and shaking his head from side to side. He wondered if Carol may have stopped by her apartment before meeting her friends. He dialed her number, but got no answer. There would be no one in the office until tomorrow morning so he would have to wait to inform them and let them know how to contact him.

He finally decided to go ahead and call the airline and make a reservation for some time tomorrow afternoon. He made reservations for two o'clock, then started to pull together what clothes he wanted to take with him which was a challenge since he did not know how long he would be gone. He did not want to be away from work more than a week. He continued calling Carol throughout the evening, but got no answer. It occurred to him that she might suggest accompanying him which was a definite no, especially at a time like this. His father's condition was enough for the family to deal with. He wasn't sure how to handle such an offer without revealing his real motive. When she did not answer the phone at eleven o'clock, he figured he had his answer. He would call her at her office the next day after he had spoken to his office and he would tell her how he tried to get her the night before. Speaking to her with such a short notice before he was due to leave would make it too inconvenient for her to prepare to accompany him.

He went to bed but tossed and turned all night wondering what it would be like for his mother if his father passed; what would it be like being away from the job for a week when there was a deadline for submitting the affirmative action plan and what kind of art exhibit could keep Carol out until after eleven.

Promptly at nine-thirty, Reggie dialed Henry's number and explained what was happening. Henry told him to take as much time as he needed and asked for his mother's telephone number. Reggie then called Carol. His stress must have been apparent in his voice because as soon as she heard his voice she asked, "Is anything wrong?"

Reggie explained his situation and Carol continued to say, "I'm so sorry." When Reggie finished his story, she asked, "Is there anything I can do? How can I contact you there? I hope thing will turn out okay."

Reggie, feeling relieved that the subject of her going with him never came up, told her there was nothing she could do at the moment, but he would keep her informed and then gave her his mother's telephone number.

"Remember I am here for you." Carol said.

"I know. I know," Reggie responded.

CHAPTER 14

Reggie sat on the plane feeling tense. His mind began to wander as he tried to imagine what he would face at home. The call from his mother shattered any hopes that his father would survive and although her faith in God gave her a wealth of strength, she needed support of her two sons to help rebuild her life in case his father died, he concluded.

He thought about his brother and decided he wouldn't be that much help. He recounted his life after graduating from high school. After an honorable discharge from the Army, he had spent many years trying to find a decent paying job to help him make ends meet only to end up at the mattress factory alongside his father at what he considered a minimum wage, not always enough to pay the bills. He then turned to alcohol to escape his frustrations, which included a wife who needed the attention of many men. Reggie's thoughts then turned to his nephew. He wondered what impact his parents' behavior would have on him. His mind then jumped to how he would respond if or when he could no longer avoid the subject of Carol with his family. He closed his eyes and asked the Lord to save him from this confrontation at a time when the family was in a state of turmoil.

"Welcome to Memphis, ladies and gentlemen and thanks for flying Delta Airlines. We hope you had a pleasant trip and you will remember Delta for future flights. Please stay seated until the plane has come to a halt and the pilot has turned off the seat belt sign," the stewardess announced.

Reggie took a deep breath and exhaled, trying to calm his anxiety as he left the plane and headed down the long aisle to the baggage claim area and then to the car rental counter. After wanting to reach across the counter and choke this very slow moving talkative, but courteous clerk, he finally got his car and pulled out of the lot trying to remember the fastest route to the public hospital. It was the only one near Smoky Mountain where Black people had traditionally been admitted, which meant you were at their mercy for whatever treatment you received.

As he drove through the light traffic, pleasantly different from New York, he wondered what kind of treatment his father had received and what he could do if he detected questionable practices that could have worsened his father's predicament. After he parked the car and entered the hospital lobby, he was greeted by the antiseptic smell that made it clear you were in a hospital which usually brought on feelings of sadness. The friendly white nurse at the reception station gave him the room number for his father then directed him to the elevator that would take him to the fourth floor. He walked into the room with a heavy stale odor where four occupied beds were separated by an adjustable curtain.

His mother was leaning toward his father's bed which was next to a window with a view of the main street in front of the hospital. Her head was bowed and her eyes closed in silent prayer. His father's upper body was enclosed in an oxygen tent and his breathing was slow and his eyes were open wide as if he were looking at an unidentified flying object. Reggie touched his mother on the shoulder. She looked up and reached and grabbed him in a tight hug.

"Oh son, I am so glad you are here. Thank the Lord, thank the Lord," she repeated.

"How is he doing?" Reggie asked looking down at his father.

"Not good. Every now and then he is lucid. But those times are less and less frequent."

"What are the doctors saying?"

"They say it's a matter of time. It's in the hands of the Lord. Some times he responds to touch. Hold his hand and say something. If he understands, he will squeeze your hand."

Reggie took his hand and said, "Hey dad it's Reggie. Can you hear me?" Reggie felt the light squeeze. "We're going to do everything we can to get you well," he said holding back his tears so as not to add to his mother's obvious pain.

"Mom, have you been here all night?"

"Yes, son," she said as a team of nurses and orderlies came in to change his sheets and replace the intravenous fluids.

"Come on, while the nurses are here I'm going to take you down to the cafeteria and get you some food. You don't want to get sick," Reggie said.

"Okay, son."

Reggie placed his arm around her shoulder and led her out of the room and into the elevator. They walked in silence to the line in the cafeteria. Reggie ordered soup, sandwich and a Coke while his mother ordered only soup and a cup of coffee. They sat near a window where the bright sun was shining through and they could see people laughing, chatting and going about their business as if it were just another day. His mother looked out at them as tears began to roll down her cheeks. She stirred her coffee without looking at it. "It's so hard watching him suffer that way. He was never good at handling pain. I just want him out of that pain even though it might mean he will be gone for good," she said still stirring her coffee without taking a sip.

"Haven't they given him medication to ease the pain?" Reggie asked.

"Yes, but it seems to wear off fast," she said, still not even tasting the food before her. With the look of sudden anxiety and her hands shaking nervously, she looked at Reggie and noticed that he had just about finished his food and said, "I think we had better get back upstairs."

"But mom you haven't touched your soup. Can't you just try to eat it?" Reggie asked looking for some way to calm her sudden anxiety.

"I'm okay son, but I feel we need to be up there with him in case he asks for us."

As they walked to the elevator, she took Reggie's hand and squeezed it tightly. They walked out of the elevator and noticed a flurry of activity coming out of his father's room. She dropped Reggie's hand and rushed down the hall. A nurse stopped her at the door.

"What's happening? Is it my husband?" she asked frantically.

"Hold up here. The doctor will be with you in a minute," the nurse said holding her hand.

"Is it my father?" Reggie asked in a demanding tone while he hugged his mother.

"Sir, the doctor will be out in a minute. He is the only one who can answer your questions," the nurse, understanding their anxiety, said in as calm a voice she could muster.

"Mrs. Morton?" the soft voice from this man with black hair, tan skin-a look of Latin ancestry, asked.

"Yes, I'm Mrs. Morton," she said hoping that soft voice would not utter what she was expecting.

"We did everything we could but his heart had worn out. He showed no signs of pain as he passed. He just stopped breathing. A member of our staff will talk to you about your plans. You have my deepest sympathy."

Mrs. Morton buried her head into Reggie's chest and let the tears roll uninhibited. Reggie held her tightly holding back his tears. They walked into the room stood over the bed. The oxygen tent was gone. His eyes were now closed which gave him a look of sleeping peacefully. Mrs. Morton took his hand and said, "You are now with the Lord. It won't be long before I join you." Reggie embraced her and told the staff that he would be in touch with them regarding arrangements as soon as he got his mother settled.

After convincing his mother to try to take a nap, Reggie telephoned his sister-in-law, Doris, and asked her to break the news to Doug as soon as he came home and ask him to meet him at their mother's as soon as possible.

Doris, sounding surprised and at a loss for words, said, "I sure will as soon as I see him, but, it's no telling when that will be. I am sorry to hear the news, Reggie. I'll let Doug Junior know. He will want to come over with Doug."

About an hour later Doug and Doug Junior walked in the house. Doug had that pasty look of someone who had a long history of excessive alcohol abuse. The neat look he was so famous for in high school and the sharply dressed soldier who had served in Germany during the Korean War had disappeared and replaced by someone who seemed to dress with the sole purpose of covering their bodies. He hugged Reggie and asked, "What are the plans?"

"That's what I wanted to talk to you about," Reggie answered.

"Whatever you decide is okay with me. Mom and dad carried burial insurance didn't they?"

"I think so. I haven't spoken to mom about that yet," Reggie answered.

Doug Junior stood next to Reggie as if he had found an anchor. Reggie rubbed his head as he spoke to his father. Before Reggie could greet Doug Junior, he dashed into the bedroom where his grandmother was trying to sleep. She grabbed him and held him tightly and said, "Grandfather has gone to heaven to be with the Lord. He is happy there and now we must be happy for him."

"Can I talk to him grandmother?" He asked.

"Yes, you can talk to him, but you won't be able to hear him talk back to you, but he can hear you."

Doug Senior walked into the room and said in a non emotional tone, "How are you doing, mom?"

"I'm doing okay son," she answered without looking directly at him.

"Can I get you anything?" Doug asked, pacing the floor and looking as if he were trying to bolt himself from an awkward situation.

"No son, I'm all right thank you." He then walked back into the living room where Reggie was and began looking at family photos dating back to when he was a child. His eyes became glassy. He walked into the kitchen, opened the refrigerator door, took out a Royal Crown cola and walked back into the living room sipping it. "Whatever you think is best, brother, go ahead and do it and let me know what you want me to do," he said as he reached up to wipe his eyes.

"You might want to go with mom and me to the undertaker to pick out the casket. I could set up an appointment for us after you get off work," Reggie suggested, hoping that he would not be alone in this process and that Doug was serious about doing whatever was asked of him.

"No! no! brother," he answered emphatically. "You'll go ahead. I don't know what time I'll be getting off work," he said as he paced the floor sipping his drink.

"It's past Junior's bedtime so I had better get him home. I'll check in with you tomorrow after work. Junior, let's go. Mom, I will see you tomorrow," he called out.

After checking on his mother who had fallen asleep, Reggie noticed it was near midnight. He felt stiffness in his back and neck that told him that he needed to close his eyes. He found his way to bed, but sleep was not immediately forthcoming. He thought about how his brother looked and acted. The reality of seeing him was more daunting than he imagined and the longing he saw in his nephew's eyes for attention disturbed him. He couldn't imagine his brother being anything more than a burden to his mother at this tough time in her life.

Reggie thought that his mother's love for Doug Junior would fill some of the parental needs that he seemed to be lacking and that in turn could possibly help fill the emptiness in his mother's life left by his father's death. That scenario, he concluded, would be a great relief to him since he would be too far away to provide the daily support she might need. At that moment, he realized he had not called Carol and he did not feel comfortable calling at that hour. Maybe, he thought, it's a good thing since he hadn't given any thought to what he would say to her if she decided she wanted to come to the funeral. He turned in bed from side to side hoping sleep would come and give him some relief.

The sound of voices coming from the kitchen and the smell of salty country ham and freshly baked biscuits permeating his room brought Reggie out of sleep. He looked at the clock on the dresser and saw that it was nine o'clock. He couldn't believe that he had actually fallen asleep and slept for at least six hours, considering how stiff he still felt.

He slowly pulled himself out of the bed and searched for his robe. He was very anxious to see who the voices were coming from and was most inclined to follow the smell of the enticing food considering how little he had the previous day. He slowly strolled into the kitchen and was greeted by Mrs. Walker, the next door neighbor, standing over a pot of simmering grits.

"Good morning Reggie. Come on in here and have some breakfast," she said with a saddened face.

"Good morning Mrs. Walker. Thank you, just let me wash my face," Reggie said, yawning and wiping his eyes.

He returned and sat down at the table across from his mother who was picking over her plate of food and sipping her coffee. Mrs. Walker placed a plate with hearty portions of grits, ham, eggs and biscuits before Reggie. He dove into it like a refugee eating his first meal in many days. "Everything tastes great, Mrs. Walker. Thank you," Reggie said without looking up from his plate.

"What are you doing up there in big New York City?" Mrs. Walker asked, hoping to distract him and his mother from thoughts of their sorrow.

"I'm an account executive in advertising. Right now I am managing the agency's account for Texas Oil," Reggie answered proudly between bites of food.

"What about the work you are doing to develop the agency's first affirmative action plan you mentioned to me?" His mother asked proudly, showing, for the first time since getting the news of her husband's death, a reaction other than sorrow.

Reggie felt full even though he had only eaten half of what was on his plate. This question caught him off guard. The suddenness of his father's death had distracted him from coming up with a strategy to present himself to the people back home. He wanted them to be proud of his work in affirmative action, but he also wanted to make clear that was a special assignment he was tapped to do. His regular job was in managing accounts which was in the mainstream of the agency's business.

"Oh yes, the agency was awarded a contract with the Navy and one of the requirement of that contract is the recipient must have in place an Affirmative Action plan. I was asked if I'd mind taking on that job which should take about a month. I agreed and am in the process of getting that done before I return to my regular job." Reggie explained with some nervous tension in his voice.

"Reggie! That's wonderful. God knows we need someone like you telling those corporate executives what they need to do to give Black people a chance. Thank God they had good enough sense to select you to do it. I am going to pray that God guides you in this big responsibility. I know he will," Mrs. Walker said while patting Reggie on the shoulder.

"I'm going to give it my best," Reggie said in a high-pitched voice trying to convey some enthusiasm. However, he was feeling disappointed. She didn't acknowledge or seem to care about my job as an account executive, he was thinking. I am certain she will spread the word that I am the affirmative action officer for the agency and never mention my work as an account executive. That, he declared, was disturbing.

"Oh, Reggie," Mrs. Walker said, "speaking about your job, I think someone from your office called this morning. I peeped in your room and you were in a deep sleep and knowing how worn out you must have been I told them you were sleep and asked if they wanted to leave a message. It sounded like a white woman. She said to tell you that Carol McKay called and that you had her number. I assured her I would give you the message."

Reggie's emotions immediately jumped from being disturbed about Mrs. Walker description of his job to wanting to choke her for not waking him for Carol's call. At that point, the sliver of will he had to clean his plate had become a challenge. His appetite had vanished, but he didn't want to get up from the table at that moment and rush to the phone and leave food on his plate. He felt certain such a response would cause Mrs. Walker and his mother to raise questions about Carol that he did not want to answer.

"Thanks for the message. I'll get right on it," he said as he racked the last spoon of grits off his plate and swallowed the last pieces of ham and biscuit. With a cup of coffee in his hand, he rose from the table and headed down the hall for the telephone. He felt anxious as he dialed her number and listened to her phone ringing, hoping she would be in the office.

"Hello," the velvety, calming voice crept into his ear easing his anxiety, somewhat. Remembering he was about to deliver sad needs, he immediately suppressed his desire to flood her with romantic oratory.

"Hello, how are thing going with you this morning?" he asked in a very sober voice.

"I'm doing fine except I am anxious to know what is happening with you. How is your father?"

"He didn't make it. He passed shortly after I arrived at the hospital."

"Oh Reggie, I am so sorry. Did you get a chance to let him know you were there?"

"I think I did. He responded by squeezing my hand when I spoke to him."

"What are the plans for his funeral?"

"I will be working on that today."

"Let me know as soon as possible so I can make arrangement to be there."

"You don't have to do that. I am going to be so busy with everything. My mother is in no condition to do anything and my brother is working and doesn't have time, so everything falls to me. I wouldn't have much time to spend with you and that would bother me," Reggie said feeling proud that he was able to think fast and come up with a reasonable excuse for keeping her away.

"I understand. Just let me know where to send flowers." Carol said in a slow, sad tone.

"I will as soon as I get things finalized. I'll probably call you tonight at home."

"Are you sure you are going to be okay because maybe I could help you with some of the things you have to do?"

"Yes, I'm going to be fine. Thanks baby for the offer, but I think I can handle it."

"Well, if you change your mind, let me know. I love you," she said in a tone of condolence.

"I love you too, baby." Reggie hung up the phone and stood in his tracks with his hand resting on the phone while Carol's words continued to float in his ear, igniting a moment of relief. The sound of someone knocking on the door propelled him back into the reality of the moment. He opened the door and received one of many neighbors and friends stopping by over the next two days to extend their condolences and bring prepared food. Mrs. Walker remained with him to manage the flow of food, while his mother sat in the living room and received the guests.

Feeling comfortable that he had persuaded Carol not to come, although at the moment, he could think of nothing more pleasing than holding her in his arms, he proceeded to make the arrangement for the funeral. He would seek his mother's advice when needed while trying not to exacerbate her grief.

The final plans called for the wake to be held on Thursday from five to nine p.m. and the funeral and burial would take place on Friday morning beginning at eleven. He then decided that he would make reservations to fly back to New York on Sunday evening and back to work on Monday. With all the plans intact, Reggie called the job and Carol and gave them the information regarding the funeral. When he revealed his plans to his mother she asked if he could stay a little longer. He explained that he needed to get back to work, but he would call her every day to check on her. He was feeling anxious about being away from work any time longer considering the deadline for completing the affirmative action plan. In addition, he considered a longer absence would probably fit a stereotype of Black people that he did not want to project.

Doug, Doris, and Douglas Junior walked into the house, a half hour later than they had been instructed, to take the limousine to the funeral home for the wake. Doug's eyes looked sleepy, but Reggie was unable to detect a smell of liquor on his breath. His black suit hung a bit loose. His shoes were polished, but not shiny. He walked in as if he were right on time.

Doris, still maintaining a figure that always caused men to do a double take, followed Doug into the house, holding Doug Junior's hand. She positioned herself next to the door and stood in place without any kind of greeting to Reggie or his mother. Doug Junior pulled his hand away from hers and ran over to this grandmother and hugged her. Mrs. Morton held him tightly as tears rolled down her cheeks.

Reggie, irritated by Doug's cavalier attitude about his late arrival and Doris' insensitive manners, announced, in a haughty manner, that the other members of the family were in their limousines and their driver was waiting. Their ride to the funeral home was in silence. Reggie put one arm around his mother's shoulder and the other around Doug Junior, who had crawled into the front seat with them. Doug and Doris sat in the back seat as far apart as they could get.

The family marched into the packed room. It seemed the whole neighborhood had turned out to pay their respects. The open casket exposed Mr. Morton in his favorite brown suit. He looked as if powder had dried on his face. There was a forest of floral arrangements surrounding the casket. Organ music played softly in the background. Reggie walked up to the casket escorting his mother and nephew. Mrs. Morton leaned over and kissed Mr. Morton on the cheek and took a deep breath, holding back tears.

Doug Junior pulled on Reggie's leg until he got his attention. He said, "I can't see granddaddy." Reggie picked him up and he said, "Granddaddy can you hear me? There are a lot of people here to talk to you so I will talk to you again tomorrow, okay?" Mrs. Morton reached for his hand as they moved to their seats.

A long line of friends and neighbors began marching by to view the body and pay their respects. Every now and then someone would say to Reggie after extending their condolences that they were really proud that he was working in affirmative action and that they would pray that the Lord would guide him along the way, as they patted him on the shoulder. Each time someone said it he would thank them, but his thoughts turned to Mrs. Walker. He wanted to confront her and ask her to stop giving out incomplete information about him and to say to her as loudly as he possibly could, "I am an account executive, not an affirmative action officer! Can you get that through your skull?"

In an effort to calm his anger and focus on the moment, he asked himself, what do these people know about an account executive, except an impressive sounding name. The thought made him feel anxious to hurry back to New York and finish the affirmative action plan and return to his work on the Texas Oil account. While fantasizing his escape back to New York, Reggie looked up and there was Alfred, one of his best friends from high school. Reggie stood up and hugged him. The demands of arranging for the service had not left much time to contact old friends and now the line of mourners was too long to close the gap in their lives so they arranged to meet Saturday evening at their teenage gathering place, Harlem House.

Around eight-forty-five the line of mourners had scaled down to a dribble. Reggie decided to search the floral arrangements to find Carol's so he could speak intelligently about it when he saw her. It was a stand up spray with a sea of white roses. The card simply expressed her deep sympathy but it was signed, "Love Carol," which, of course, did not sound like someone from the office, especially since there was another spray from the office that said, Benton, Bowles and Fowler. When he thought no one was looking, Reggie removed the card and put it in his pocket. He was certain no one would notice since at the end of the burial, the undertakers would give the family a bundle of cards without any indication of the floral arrangement they represented.

After the last of the mourners left, Mrs. Morton walked up to the casket alone and kissed her husband and with tears in her eyes said, "Good night, honey. May you rest in the arms of our Savior Jesus Christ." Reggie then led her out to the limousine. Doug and his family were driven home by a friend. When Reggie and his mother walked in their house, Mrs. Walker had a buffet of food laid out from which they could choose. Seeing Mrs. Walker caused some anger to rise in Reggie. He bit his bottom lip in an effort to contain it. He realized the support Mrs. Walker was trying to give and that she would remain a help to his mother after he was back in New York. She insisted that they sit down and eat something and they both did. While eating the phone rang.

"I'll get it. You'll stay put," Mrs. Walker said. She walked back into the room and announced, "Reggie its Miss McKay, the woman from your job. Since she is calling from New York I figured you might want to take the call."

"Yes, I will take it, thanks." Reggie said as he bolted from the table and dashed down the hall. "Hello baby," he said quietly, determined to shade his conversation from the ears of Mrs. Walker who had lowered her voice as if she were trying to convey to the person on the phone that this was a house in quiet mourning.

"How are things going with you?" Reggie asked.

"I'm worried about how things are going with you." Carol said in a very serious tone. "How are you holding up? What about your mother?" she asked.

Very quietly, Reggie said, "So far things are going as planned. Mom is holding up pretty good and so am I. We just returned from the wake which was packed with people. I'm still on schedule for returning to New York Sunday night. Your flowers were really beautiful, thanks."

"I hope your family likes them. I wish I could be there with you. Be sure to extend my sympathy to your family, especially your mother."

"Hearing your voice is all I need right now to keep me going," Reggie said.

"I love you so much. I pray that things will go well for the funeral tomorrow," Carol said sounding as if she were near tears.

"I love you too and look forward to my return to you," Reggie said. In deference to his current circumstance, he felt he had to restrain his reaction to her words. Carol had never said she loved him in such a direct and emotional way.

"I will talk to you again tomorrow," Reggie said anxious to go to his room, close the door and bask in Carol's words.

As soon as he hung up the phone, Mrs. Walker called out, "Is everything okay?"

Reggie wondered if he had been successful in shading his conversation. He felt irritated at Mrs. Walker's intrusion. He took a deep breath and walked back into the kitchen and said, "Things are okay. They were just checking up on me and trying to show their sympathy."

"That's really nice," Mrs. Walker said in a slow, curious tone.

"I'm going to turn in," Reggie announced.

"Okay, son. Try to get a good night's sleep. Lord knows I am glad you are here," his mother said in a stronger tone than he had heard since he arrived.

Reggie lay in the bed trying to fall asleep. Carol's words about loving him kept replaying in his ears. He pictured holding her in his arms and kissing her. However, thoughts of leaving his mother so soon after the funeral, people's perception of him as an affirmative action officer, the pattern of behavior his brother had fallen into, and the apparent needs of his nephew kept interfering with his thoughts of Carol.

Doug and his family arrived promptly at ten o'clock, the designated time established by the undertakers. Doug looked more alert then he did the night before and this time his shoes were shining. Doris was dressed in a tight black dress flaunting her libido-igniting body. Doug Junior immediately dashed to find his grandmother. Seeing the improvement in Doug's appearance and his promptness was encouraging. Maybe, Reggie wished, he is not too far gone to assume some responsibility for his mother's well- being.

The funeral was being held in the hand laid brick and stone walled church that Reggie had known since he was a child. Marching down the newly carpeted center aisle with his family brought back memories of long sermons and choirs spewing out gospel music that was more loud than harmonized. He and

Doug used to whisper jokes to each other to pass the time until his mother detected what they were doing and gave them a look that immediately brought their behavior to a halt.

The organist played soft, sad-sounding music as they marched to their seats. Reggie, his mother, Doug, Doris and Doug Junior sat in the front row facing the closed casket that was covered with an arrangement of white lilies. As the last of the family took their seats, the music stopped and Rev. Bailey, who was famous for his long sermons, stepped up to the lectern and began a prayer that lasted about five minutes. Reggie wanted to look at Doug and see if he was having some of the memories he was having, but he didn't dare, sitting on the front row next to his mother.

The members of the choir who were there that day did not seem to be that much different from the choir when Reggie was last there. When the time came for speakers to provide remarks, it seemed they would never end. No one seemed to be conscious of time. From some of the remarks, he thought the speaker was talking about someone other than his father. By the time they finished, the service had gone on for more than hour. Reggie felt anxious and with no possibility of a physical escape, he began to think about what it would be like meeting Alfred the next day and how he would present the work he was doing, feeling sure Alfred had heard the rumor about his affirmative action job.

He wondered if Alfred could give him the latest news on Arnold since his black power militant days at Howard University and if he had been in contact with Beverly since she graduated from college in Minnesota and moved to San Francisco. Reggie was brought back to the present with the baritone voice of Rev. Bailey inviting the congregation to join him in prayer which lasted another five minutes. He then dove into his message for the day. He quickly put the deceased to rest by saying, "Mr. Morton has reached the end of his journey and his soul is now in the hands of our Heavenly Father. I want to say to our sister Morton and her family that they should be at peace because the Bible says this is a time to rejoice." He then went on for the next hour challenging the congregation to check their lives to see if they would be ready when death comes knocking at their doors and if they weren't, he scolded them that there was no better time than now to dedicate their lives to God because you don't know when your time will come.

Reggie felt he kept looking directly at him during the sermon which was very irritating. He decided he would pretend to be looking in every direction except at Rev. Bailey to convey that he was unmoved by his message. When the sermon finally came to an end, Reggie let out a sigh of relief which made his mother look up at him in disapproval. He pretended that he did not notice.

As the choir sang, "Soon I Will Be Done with the Troubles of The World," the undertakers rolled the casket down the aisle with the family marching behind to the burial ground behind the church. When everyone had gathered at the burial site, Rev. Bailey asked the crowd to join him in another prayer which lasted another five minutes. He then beckoned the undertakers to begin lowering the casket into the ground. At this point, Mrs. Morton's suppressed grief boiled over and a stream of tears rolled down her face as she began to reach for the casket calling her husband's name and asking, "Why did you leave me?" Reggie reached for her and his stoic exterior crumbled and he began to cry while holding his mother. Doug's grief was totally uninhibited. He stood up over the casket bellowing, "I'm sorry. I'm sorry please forgive me," over and over again. Doris stood up and pulled him back from the casket. Doug Junior grabbed his leg and said, "Don't cry daddy, granddaddy can hear you."

The family rode back to the house in silence and was greeted by a throng of friends. Mrs. Walker had set the table with the bounty of food that had been contributed. Reggie wanted to take his mother to some place quiet so they both could rest from the emotional morning. However, she seemed to relish the crowd and he realized it would be impolite for him to disappear so he walked around thanking people for their support and cringing every time someone would praise him for his work in affirmative action.

When they all finally left, he felt like he was the one who dug his father's grave. Doug had remained silent since the burial. He remained at the house until the last guest left. He then hugged his mother and trailed off with his family. Reggie then excused himself and left his mother and Mrs. Walker talking in the kitchen. He went to his room and closed the door. He felt like calling Carol just to hear her voice, but he fell asleep.

The sounds of a tree branch pelting his window awakened Reggie. The weather had turned winter- like with grey skies and occasional gusts of wind. After collecting his thoughts and realizing where he was, he listened for some sound of his mother. When there were none, he tiptoed to her room and peeped in. She lay in bed looking at the ceiling with her arm resting on her forehead.

"Are you all right, mom?" Reggie asked.

"Yes, son, I will be better in time. How are you doing?"

"I'm okay. Why don't I make some coffee and fix us some breakfast?"

"All I need is some coffee. I'll be there in a moment."

Reggie brewed the coffee and sliced a piece of ham and a slice of coconut cake that was left from the day before. Mrs. Morton walked in covered in her flannel housecoat looking as if she had not slept. Reggie put a cup of coffee in front of her and she began to add sugar and stir. Looking into space past Reggie she said, "You still leaving tomorrow?"

"Yes, tomorrow evening. I need to get back to work. I have a pressing project." He didn't want to say the words affirmative action again. "I can get started on finding all the papers you will need for the insurance. Do you think Mrs. Walker will be able to help you with anything that is left undone?" Reggie asked in a very serious sad tone.

"I'm sure she is willing, but I think I can manage things myself. I guess it's too close to Thanksgiving to expect you to come back for it. But will you be back for Christmas?" she asked with her sad eyes looking directly at him.

"I will do my best." Reggie said in an upbeat tone trying to hide his doubt.

"Well, you start working on it now so nothing will stand in the way of you getting here. It will be a sad Christmas for me if you can't make it."

"I will start working on it as you suggest."

"What time is your flight?"

"At six tomorrow evening."

"Well, you can go to church with me tomorrow."

"Yes, I can," Reggie said with much dread.

The conversation was interrupted by a knock on the door. It was Mrs. Walker coming to check on things. Reggie left the two of them sitting around the table while he went and called Carol.

"Good morning baby," he said.

"Reggie, I was just thinking about you and wondering how things went."

"Things went as well as could be expected. Mom is holding up and that is the most important thing," Reggie said in a firm tone.

"What flight are you returning on tomorrow and what time are you due to arrive?" Carol asked anxiously.

"I'll be flying in on Delta and should arrive around nine-forty-five."

"I'll meet you," Carol said.

"Don't worry about meeting me. It will be too late and who knows whether the flight will be on time. I'll call you once I'm home," Reggie said feeling satisfied just knowing that she wanted to meet him.

"Okay, you probably need as much rest as you can get before returning to work Monday, a disappointed Carol said.

After spending the day searching through his father's papers while Mrs. Walker was in and out of the house entertaining his mother, Reggie prepared to meet Alfred.

He strolled into the Harlem House anxious to be there one more time. It was the same except Mr. Snow, the owner who used to treat all the kids in the sundry as his own, was not there. Reggie's mother had told him that he had a massive heart attack that killed him and the sundry was sold to new owners. Reggie ordered his usual hot dog with cold slaw and a Nehi orange drink and made his way to one of the booths where he and his friends used to gather.

Sitting there waiting for Alfred and watching the noisy young kids horsing around, he began to drift back into memories of the days when he and his friends were the ones playing around in this same place. He remembered the day they gathered there and announced their plans for college. His friends had been critical of him for wanting to go to an integrated school as soon as the Supreme Court handed down its decision in the case of Brown V Board of Education. However, on that date, no one teased him about his choice of the recently integrated state university. He thought about the consequences of that decision-student rejection, prejudice professors, isolation from both Black and white students, abandonment by Mona, his high school sweetheart, and Betty, the white girl on campus that he fell for. He remembered how he made it through that part of his life with the help of Dr. Thorn, his favorite professors, and the friendship he developed with Harry, a white student who became his best friend and whose family encouraged and supported him in developing some of his life's goals. He took a sip of his drink, sat back in the booth and declared he had taken it and made it, just as Rev. Bailey advised at his high school baccalaureate service.

"Hey buddy," Alfred said as he plopped down all the adipose tissue he had acquired since leaving high school. He was sporting a bushy Afro. He reached across the table and shook Reggie's hand with what seemed like an embarrassing smile.

"You look great man, haven't gained a pound. How the hell do you do it?"

"Having no one to cook for me is my biggest reason," Reggie said jokingly and immediately regretted that answer since it would likely lead to a discussion he was not anxious to broach.

"Well, how long is it going to take to get a good cook in your kitchen?" Alfred asked looking Reggie in the eyes with a mischievous smile.

"I'm working on it," Reggie said trying to keep up a jovial conversation.

"Come on, man. This is Alfred talking to you. What's up? A man with all your qualities living in New York must have them lined up knocking at your door and you haven't found one who can cook. Or maybe you are keeping them all waiting in the wings. That wouldn't be a bad thing," Alfred teased, but obviously wanted more information than Reggie had given.

"I work too hard and don't have the time to have them lined up. Right now, I'm focusing on just one." Reggie said sheepishly.

"Well, don't stop there," Alfred said leaning over the table looking hungry for some details.

"She's somebody I met since I've been in New York. We've only been dating for a couple of months. I'll see how things work out," Reggie said trying to diminish the importance of the relationship and bring the conversation to a close.

"What's she like?" Alfred asked.

"She is a human resources consultant who travels a lot," Reggie said with his head looking down at the table.

"Sounds like she is breaking barriers just like you are. By the way, I heard you were working in affirmative action at this advertising agency. What's that like?"

"Well, that's not the whole truth. I am an account executive and right now I am in charge of the agency's Texas Oil account. The agency got a contract with the Navy and that requires them to have an affirmative action plan. They asked if I'd mind developing the plan and I agreed. I expect to have that project completed in a month," Reggie carefully explained.

"Who's going to monitor it when you return to your regular job?" Alfred asked, sounding very serious.

"I assume the office of personnel. It will not be part of my job," Reggie answered proudly.

"Well, I hope you write it so they will have to be accountable for seeing that something is done," Alfred said leaning back in his seat with his hands cupped on the table.

"The U. S. Department of Labor has the responsibility of seeing that the plan is implemented. So it will be monitored," Reggie tried to say with confidence.

"What's happening with you?" Reggie asked trying to push the conversation in another direction.

"I'm tied down with a wife and two kids who drive me out of my mind sometimes, but it could be worse, I guess. My son, Junior, is smart as a whip. He was saying his ABC's as soon as he started walking. My daughter is the oldest and her teachers say she is one of the smartest ones in her class, but needs to learn how to stop talking so much," Alfred answered with a big smile and with great pride in his eyes and voice. "I'm doing pretty good at Mid- South Insurance. I was made a senior manager last year. There's this secretary at the company who wants a piece of me and every now and then I have to be merciful and give her a piece and that seems to be enough for her. So all and all, I guess things are going fairly well with me," Alfred said looking into the air and leaning back in his seat like a man who just realized how good he has it.

"I would agree with you, Reggie said, glad he had succeeded in redirecting the conversation away from him. "What do you hear about our old friend Arnold? The last thing I heard was he had been arrested after some Black Power demonstration in Washington. Did he ever graduate from Howard?" Reggie asked.

"He was here about a year ago with his long hair and beard. I think I remember him saying he was still a member of the Black Panther party. I don't think he ever graduated from Howard. He never spoke about how he was making a living. I heard his mother was still sending him money to live off. I ran into him at the shopping center with his mother and we spoke briefly while she went grocery shopping. What I remember most was he showed me a picture of a child that he said was his. Man, that child was as white as rice and I was certain the mother was white. I asked if he had a picture of his wife and he said that he had never been married. He promised to call and set up a time to get together, but he never did. He did say he was still in Washington," Alfred said, looking disgusted. Reggie wasn't sure the source of the disgust-whether it was his feelings about the white child or what he perceived as a tragic life of his once good friend.

"What about Beverly? Have you heard anything from her?" Reggie asked feeling empowered by the speculation that the black power militant, Arnold, had been in a relationship with a white woman.

"She called me a month ago. She was in town but was about to leave. She had come to see her mother who was ill. It seems she moves around a lot. She had been teaching high school in San Francisco; but had moved back east and was teaching at Wellesley College and enrolled in a Ph.D program at Harvard. I asked her when she was getting married. She said 'when hell freezes over and the devil goes ice skating.' I said, that soon, and we both laughed. She promised to keep in touch. I think I have her address and telephone somewhere. If I can find it, do you want it?"

"Yes, call and give it to me. My flight is tomorrow evening at six. By the way does anyone know whatever happened to our favorite teacher, Miss Wright?"

"Oh yes, Beverly said her mother told her that several years after she retired, she had a stroke and was losing her sight and moved to St. Louis to live with a relative. That was the last anyone heard of her."

"I would have loved to get her take on what integration has done to Black children. If you remember, she was not optimistic that white schools would move with all deliberate speed to desegregate as the justices instructed when they handed down the Brown decision. Neither was she convinced that integration would benefit Black children if they suddenly began to have all white teachers as she was sure would be the case with desegregation. Remember, we all said she was just trying to protect her job. She sent me a really nice letter when I graduated from college. I paid her a visit once on one of my trips back home after graduating. She still seemed to be less than optimistic about the impact of the court's decision or what I was doing at the time," Reggie said with a sad tone of regret.

"If I happen to hear something about her I will pass it on to you. Well, my man, I have to run. I promised to take my wife to the Delta's dance tonight. Why don't you come?"

"Thanks for the invitation, but I need to stay close to home tonight with mom since I'm leaving tomorrow. I'm really glad to see you. We have to keep in touch," Reggie said as he stood up and shook Alfred's hand.

Reggie sat at the table for a while after Alfred left reflecting on their conversation and thinking how each of his friends' lives had gone in different directions, especially that hypocrite Arnold. He remembered the last time they ran into each other. Arnold, with a bit of self righteousness, insinuated that he had made a mistake by going to an integrated school. And now Arnold was in the bed with the so-called enemy and had produced a mixed-race child while still waving the Black Panther flag. Reggie felt some vindication about his relationship with Carol. It occurred to him that people in the community probably knew about Arnold's arrest and his militant look and actions and probably attribute his behavior to being a little crazy. However, he had a feeling his relationship with a white woman would be viewed as a betrayal since he seemed to be in control of all his faculties.

Reggie was awakened Sunday morning by his mother, much to his surprise. It was good to see her doing routine things. The smell of perked coffee permeated the house. She had baked a "ho cake," fried some of her homemade sage sausages, scrambled some eggs and placed a jar of Sorghum molasses on the table. Reggie hauled out of bed and into the shower. When he came out, his mother served him the hot breakfast while she went into the shower. Reggie devoured the food knowing he would not get that kind of breakfast for a long time. He felt like going back to bed after the hearty breakfast, but his mother called out.

"You don't want to be late for service so don't sit around that table and forget the time." With that command, Reggie headed to his room and pulled out some Sunday clothes appropriate for a New Yorker. A New Yorker would not wear the same clothes to Sunday service that he wore to the wake and funeral. So this time, he took out a blue blazer and a blue and white striped shirt and a solid blue tie and gray trousers.

Reggie held his mother's arm as they march into church. He wanted her to stop at a row toward the back but she strode down the center aisle three rows from the front. As they sat down, several people in the pew reached over and greeted them with sad but encouraging gestures. Mrs. Morton held each of their hands and quietly said, "thank you," while Reggie sat looking straight ahead as if he did not notice anyone surrounding him. The full choir, as opposed to those that sang at the funeral, began to sing and Reggie began to tune them out by fantasizing what it would be like when he was back in the arms of Carol.

After they finished singing in unison, "The Lord is the Strength of My Life and My Salvation," Reggie began to feel guilty that he was thinking such thoughts in God's house and tried to focus more on the service. After the weekly announcements, Rev. Bailey walked up to the podium and began addressing the congregation. He first recognized all visitors and then he said, "Thank the Lord for our dear sister Morton and her son Reggie who are with us today. You and your family will remain in our prayers, Sister Morton. Brother

Morton we are glad to see you here with your mother in this time of trials and tribulation. The Lord will bless you. I might mention folks that Brother Morton is the affirmative action officer of a big advertising agency in New York. I want you to know we are proud of you for the work you are doing to help your people. We need our young people to step up to the plate and move us forward. Let's give our brother Morton a hand." The clapping of hands and roar of "amen" swelled through the church. Reggie stood up determined to contain the frustration he was feeling. He took a bow and forced a smile while both hands were cupped into a fist pounding his leg.

Rev. Bailey launched into his seemingly endless doomsday sermon that was punctuated occasionally with, "I'm going to let you dears go" which turned out to be just a tease. Reggie shifted in his seat, crossed his legs then uncrossed them, folded his arms then unfolded them, looked up at Rev. Bailey like he was really into the message of the sermon, then looked down at his hands. Under his breath, he said to himself, if he says I'm going to let you dears go one more time I am going to get up and leave. When the sermon finally ended and Reggie and his mother were trying to leave the church, they were constantly stopped by concerned people expressing their condolences and congratulating Reggie. As he finally got his mother into the car and closed the door, Reggie could only think of escaping back to his life in New York which he did on that six o'clock flight to LaGuardia. However, when the plane landed he began to feel relieved but guilty and then exhausted. As he entered the terminal all those feeling evaporated when his eyes landed on the jovial, smiling face of Carol standing with her arms open to greet him.

"How are you? I've been so worried about you," Carol said into Reggie's ear as he held her tightly.

"I'm fine now that I can see and hold you."

"How did you leave your family?"

"As well as could be expected this soon after the funeral."

"I just had to come see you. You must be exhausted. Do you plan to go to work tomorrow? You really need some time to wind down."

"I'm going in tomorrow. I really need to get the affirmative action plan going so that I can get back to the Texas Oil account. I will be all right."

"Well, you need to go home and get as much rest as possible," Carol said as she pulled away from his arms.

Reggie reluctantly agreed, but he really wanted her to go with him. He kissed her and they took separate taxis away from the airport. He felt tired but exhilarated. As his taxi sped across the Triborough Bridge, the chilled night air swept through the cracked window and brushed his face. He looked out into the dark autumn sky and noticed a few stars and a full moon hovering over the glistening East River. "She is mine," he mumbled. "What more could I want?"

As the taxi rolled up in front of his building, he began to feel the comfort that had eluded him the past week. He looked forward to a good night's rest. He called home to report that he had arrived safely and to check on his mother. She told him she was okay and thanked the Lord for his safe trip and reminded him not to forget to call her. He rolled into bed, pulled up the covers, hugged his pillow and began to imagine Louis Armstrong singing, "What a Wonderful World." With the sound of the wind teasing the trees outside his window, the muscles in his back and neck began to relax and he sailed into a deep sleep.

CHAPTER 15

Reggie walked out of his building into blustering winds. Summer had truly kissed the city good bye. He began to whistle "Autumn in New York" as he took note of the bright yellow, red and rust colored leaves on the trees along the route to the bus stop. He imagined a carriage ride through Central Park with the love he envisioned holding on to the rest of his life.

During the bus ride into Manhattan, he planned his day. He was sure by now Sandra would have typed the draft of the affirmative action agreement and all he had to do was proofread it and turn it over to Henry for his review. He couldn't wait to complete the project and return to his work with Texas Oil and put affirmative action behind him. However, in deference to all the exuberance back home about the importance of his work in that area, he wanted to make the agreement as strong and as effective as possible. He decided he needed to comb through it to make sure there was nothing that needed to be added.

When Reggie opened the door to his office he expected to see the draft of the agreement on his desk; however his desk was just he left it. After resting his coat and sipping his coffee, he walked over to Sandra's desk.

"Reggie, welcome back. How are you? How did you leave your family?" Sandra asked.

"Thanks Sandra. Everybody is doing as well as could be expected. Thanks for the flowers. They were beautiful."

"You are welcome. Did they arrive on time?" Sandra asked.

"Yes, they were there for the wake."

"I am so sorry about your father's death. Was he around when you were growing up?" Sandra asked with a deep look of concern on her face.

"Yes, he was." Reggie answered wondering what kind of a question was that.

"Is Henry in?" Reggie asked.

"Yes, go right in."

"Reggie it's good to see you. How are you?" Henry asked.

"I'm okay."

"Well, we are glad to have you back."

"Thanks for the flowers," Reggie said.

"You are welcome. How is your mother doing?"

"I think she is handling it well so far, but I don't know now that all the ceremony is over and people have scattered. I will be constantly in touch with her for a while to see how thing are going."

"Well, when you get yourself settled back in, we can go over your draft of the affirmative action agreement. I have it here."

Reggie was stunned. He at least wanted to proofread it before handing it over to Henry and now whatever changes he may have wanted to include to strengthen it would have to be justified to Henry.

"May I see it?" Reggie asked.

"Yes, why don't you take a look at it and we can discuss it tomorrow morning. My calendar is pretty filled up today. I made a few edits. But I want to say you did a great job, especially the policy statement," Henry said with a forced smile as he handed the agreement over to Reggie. "Tell Sandra to put you on my calendar for tomorrow morning. Again, welcome back."

"Thanks," Reggie said trying to disguise his distress. After setting up a ten o'clock meeting with Henry, he walked slowly back to his office with the affirmative action agreement swinging in his hand. He dropped it on his desk and plopped down in his chair wondering what he was in for. He decided to first look at the policy statement. His language extolling the agency's commitment to providing opportunities to all, regardless of race, color, gender, religion or national origin and creating an environment where all employees are encouraged to realize their full potential, was just as he had written it. He leaned back in his chair with the statement in one hand and the other cupped behind his head feeling relief and satisfaction. He then leaned back over his desk and began reading the agreement. As he plowed through it his feeling of satisfaction turned to hurt, anger and bafflement. The language he had put in regarding the agency's commitment to reviewing all job description to determine their relevance to the actual job requirements had been deleted. It had been replaced by the statement: "The agency's job requirements will always reflect the actual job to be performed."

His language stating the agency would post all job vacancies with recruitment sources specializing in the placement of minorities and or women had been replaced. It now read: "All recruitment sources would be notified at the time of posting that the agency is an equal opportunity employer." His language laying out a system whereby the agency would develop a job bank of minority and women employees and applicants had been eliminated. It had been replaced by the statement that, at the discretion of the agency certain job vacancies would be posted. His language requiring the agency to conduct exit interviews with minority employees terminated had been removed with no substitute language.

Reggie pushed the agreement to the side of his desk and rested his face into the palm of his two hands. He wondered if the agency actually expected him to read their lack of commitment to substantive changes in its operations and develop a generic agreement just enough to get by the requirement. He wondered what the people back home would think of him if they ever found out this was the kind of agreement he put together. He wondered how to approach Henry about the changes without being viewed as a closeted member of the Black Panther Party. Out of frustration, he picked up the agreement and slammed it onto the desk. At that moment there was a knock on his door which frightened him. He thought it might be either Henry or Sandra, neither of whom he was in a mood to speak to. "Come in," he said with a slight tremble in his voice. In walks Harriett looking very concerned.

"How are you doing, Reggie? I heard about your father and I am so sorry," she said as she sat down and pulled the chair closer to the desk eliminating some space between them.

"I'm okay. Thanks for stopping by." Reggie said hoping to end the visit as soon as possible. He was in no more of a mood to speak to her than he was to Henry and Sandra although for a different reason. Her presence reminded him how much he wanted to avoid revealing his relationship with Carol so seeing her sent the guilt demon parading through his psyche.

"How are things coming with the affirmative action plan?" she asked.

"I was just going over my draft and looking at some of the changes Henry made." He immediately felt angry with himself. He did not want to talk about his disappointment with those changes until he had had a chance to discuss them with Henry, but the words had just rolled out.

"I bet he tried to strip it of anything that meant the agency would actually do something to improve opportunities for minorities," she said. You realize the only reason they are doing this is because they want that big contract with the Navy. They can also say to organizations like the NAACP and Urban League that have been critical of advertising, 'hey look what we are doing' and then go right on saying they can't find qualified minority candidates for our jobs and then point to you as a positive result of their exhausted efforts." Harriett said with a stern look and anger in her voice.

It made Reggie very uncomfortable. He felt Harriett was right; however if it turned out to be a weak agreement, he would probably be accused of being a consensual partner in the charade. He felt anger toward Harriett for confronting him with that truth, but realized if he tried to defend the changes Harriett would feel that he was already a consensual partner. She could spread that word and who knows how far that impression could reach.

"We have a meeting tomorrow and I will see what he has to say," Reggie said in a tone that portrayed dissatisfaction.

"What are you doing for lunch?" Harriett asked in a tone of sincere concern.

"I have plans," Reggie said although he did not.

"Well, maybe later this week we can get together for lunch. Call and let me know when you are available," Harriett said as she stood up and reached across the desk and took Reggie's hand in hers and said, "Hang in there."

"Thanks again for stopping by," Reggie said as his hand slipped out of hers. As soon as the door closed behind her, he picked up the phone to turn his lie into a truth. He called Carol and they agreed to have lunch.

"Are you all right?" Carol asked as she hugged Reggie.

"I'm always all right as long as I can be with you," Reggie whispered into her ear. Carol pulled away from him and smiled as they were ushered to a table in the Chinese restaurant where they had their first date. Reggie wondered if this was the ideal moment to pop the question.

"What's it like back at the office?" Carol asked, looking very concerned.

Without any thought of how to answer the question, words began to roll out of his mouth. "I took a hit out of left field this morning. The draft of the affirmative action agreement I submitted for typing before I left and that I was expecting to finalize today was handed back to me by the head of personnel. He had already read it and made some changes that stripped it of any teeth."

"What were the changes he made?"

Reggie threw his hands into the air and began ranting- "Posting job vacancies with recruitment agencies serving affected minorities and women, reviewing job descriptions, developing a jobs bank for qualified minorities and women and conducting exit interviews."

"Did he substitute other language in those places?" Carol asked, seeming unperturbed.

"In most instances, he just declared that they were an equal opportunity employer and would treat all employees the same and that they would convey that fact to all recruitment sources. He provided no substitution for conducting exit interviews."

"What's wrong with that, if they committed themselves to really adhere to an equal opportunity policy?" Carol asked in a very confident manner.

"According to the guidelines provided by the Department of Labor, what he has done makes it an equal opportunity agreement and not an affirmative action agreement. An affirmative action agreement reaches out to the protected classes in an effort to reverse past practices that have excluded them from the workforce."

"Well, if the agreement commits them to treat minorities like all other applicants and employees, isn't that reaching out to them?" Carol asked seeming perplexed.

"The assumption is that companies with affirmative action agreements have some catching –up to do before they can declare themselves as just an equal opportunity employer," Reggie said, feeling a bit impatient with Carol's lack of understanding of the principle.

"Well, doesn't the Department of Labor have the responsibility to approve and monitor the agreement?" Carol asked in a somewhat condescending tone.

"Yes, it is their responsibility and maybe I should wait and see what they have to say about it," Reggie said, anxious to drop the subject. "What have you been up to while I was away?" he asked.

"Besides worrying about you, not much," she answered as she reached across the table and squeezed his hand. The gesture made Reggie forget the affirmative action agreement for the moment. He thought about how much he missed her and how much he wanted to hold her in his arms and pop the question.

"I lost the battle over Thanksgiving. We are going to Aunt Melba's and mother wants you to come. She thinks it will be good for you to be with us considering the recent loss of your father. I thoroughly agreed with her. You will love Martha's Vineyard and Aunt Melba is a great cook who believes in tradition, which means she will have all the traditional dishes for the holiday-turkey, sage stuffing, cranberry sauce, mashed potatoes, pumpkin pie, etc. Also, I wouldn't think of celebrating the holiday without you. I didn't think you would be returning home so soon. What do you say? Will you join us?"

Reggie also couldn't imagine being alone in New York for the holiday. There was no question whether he would accept the invitation, but, the situation presented some daunting apprehensions. First of all, he wondered if Aunt Melba was the sister of Carol's mother of father. If she were the father's sister would she be like him? Could he spend four days with the family without talking about growing-up in the South and revealing his humble beginnings? What kind of neighborhood did Aunt Melba live in? Who else would be coming besides Carol's family and what would they be like? He tried to diffuse his concerns by reflecting on that Thanksgiving he spent in Chicago with Harry, his white college classmate, and his family. Those four days produced great memories that changed his life. Maybe, just maybe, this Thanksgiving could be just as rewarding, he rationalized.

"Of course, baby. I wouldn't miss this opportunity to be with you," Reggie said having mustered up a gleam in his eyes.

"Great, we plan to drive up next Wednesday afternoon in time to get the six o'clock ferry. Would you be able to get a train around noon to my parents?" Carol asked with exuberant satisfaction in her voice and a wide smile on her face.

"That should not be a problem. I understand that everybody at the agency has cleared out around noon that day," Reggie said in a very confident manner in an effort to disguise his concerns.

During lunch, Carol spoke enthusiastically about the summers she spent on Martha's Vineyard when she was a child- the carousel rides, the trips to the ice cream parlor, bike riding along roads through forests and night parties on the beaches. She said they could take a bike ride around the island if the weather permitted. Her enthusiasm sparked Reggie's curiosity about the island. He fantasized riding a bike into an exotic spot along a lonely road or standing on the beach looking out over the ocean with the wind blowing a mild breeze over their bodies and falling on his knees and popping the question. They would return to Aunt Melba's and make the announcement and everybody would raise their glasses of champagne and toast them. His mind couldn't hold on to that part of the fantasy so he imagined they would make the announcement and Carol's father would escort him to the ferry without Carol and bid him farewell.

As Reggie said good bye to Carol and began his walk back to the office, he realized he was not as tense about the affirmative action agreement as he was before lunch. The trip to Martha's Vineyard had overtaken his tensions. He decided he would question Henry about his changes, but would leave it to the Department of Labor to challenge them. Hopefully, they would require a more proactive agreement that he could tell people back home was his idea. He also thought if he were to get into a debate with Henry about the changes they would probably end up going back and forth with drafts. That would take too much time which could prevent them from meeting the deadline for submission of the agreement and probably delay his return to the Texas Oil account. Feeling he had come up with a strategy for dealing with the dilemma, he returned to the office and jotted down the questions he wanted to ask Henry.

As Reggie sat at his table that evening nibbling on a pizza with Walter Cronkite in the background still speculating about what Nixon's election would mean for the Viet Nam War, he tuned him out. He returned to thoughts of how and when to pop the question. He wondered what it would be like if he did it before Thanksgiving or during that weekend while they were with her family. He discarded both alternatives. He wasn't sure what to expect from this extended family. News of his engagement to their daughter, niece or cousin would possibly cause hurricane-type damage to the weekend or he could be chased into the ocean. In any event, he thought the first step is to buy a ring and he would begin shopping for it immediately.

Reggie arrived promptly at ten o'clock for his meeting with Henry. When he walked into the office, Henry stood up, shook Reggie's hand and said,

"I want to thank you again for the wonderful work you did in developing the affirmative action agreement. Let me explain why I made some of the changes. These agreements are usually negotiated so the changes I made would give us some room to negotiate. It's hard to tell where we will end up but we need a comfortable place to start out. When the Department of Labor responds to our submission you and I will sit down and decide our next position and we will go back and forth until we reach an agreement. What I would like to do now is have Sandra put it in final and have you hand deliver it to the Department of Labor. I would like to have you stay with the department until we have a final agreement if that is okay with you."

Henry's explanation disarmed Reggie. All he could say was "okay." He assumed Henry was well versed in how the Department of Labor operated and that they would end up with a respectable agreement that would make the folks back home proud of him. He marched out of the office, walked back to his, laid down his pad and headed out to the jewelry district to shop for a ring.

Reggie's first stop was a shop about five blocks from the office. A very savvy saleslady pulled out a tray of rings and picked up the most expensive one and said, "She will love this one and it will be a great statement of your commitment to her." Reggie took it into his hand and began to examine it when there was a tap on his shoulder. He turned around and almost wet his pants.

"Is this for me?" Harriett asked with a forced smile plastered across her face. Reggie was dumbfounded. Blood rushed from his face and his hands began to shake. "What are you doing here?" he asked through a slight stutter.

"The question is what are you doing here with a diamond ring resting in your hand." she asked nervously, but in a "got you" manner.

"Well, obviously I'm looking at rings," he said this time defensively.

"Did you renew your love when you were back home?" Harriett asked with a bit of sarcasm.

He felt cornered with nowhere to escape. "No, I don't have a love back home," he said, this time with an added bit of defiance trying to obliterate his defensiveness. "As a matter of fact I am considering proposing," he said still defiant, but looking away from Harriett.

"Well, who is the luck lady?" Harriet asked, seemingly with all her might to hide her disappointment.

"Her name is Carol McKay," Reggie answered as his hand began to shake.

Harriett hesitated for a moment then repeated the name twice as if she were trying to remember if they had met previously. She then looked Reggie directly in the eyes and, with contempt and resentment in her voice, said, "Congratulations, Mr. Morton.

I hope you find happiness in your world. What a waste," then walked out of the store.

The saleslady stood looking down at the counter as if she were not aware of what was going on. "What do you think, sir?" She asked.

The experience dampened his spirit. Reggie turned the ring over in his hand but was unable to concentrate on it. He handed it back to the saleslady and said, "Let me look around. I might be back." He then walked out of the store and slowly back to the office.

The encounter had shaken him. He really didn't want to lose Harriett as an ally. But, he concluded, he still had Jeff on his side. He knew he loved Carol and wanted to marry her and that the truth would inevitably come out. However, it just jumped out before he could plan it. He felt angry that he had to even consider such matters.

When Reggie returned to his office the affirmative action agreement was on his desk with a note from Sandra asking him to review it before she put it in final. Reggie sat down at his desk and began to thumb through it. He was in no mood to concentrate. Anyway typos were the only things he felt he could point out that needed change. He started reading, but couldn't remember what was in the previous paragraph. There was a knock on the door. He sat up in his chair trying to portray an alert conscientious employee. He figured it was Sandra asking about the agreement. "Come in," he said in a commanding in charge voice.

"Hey man, what's up?" Jeff asked with a mischievous smile covering his face. "Hey, I'm sorry about your father, man," he said wiping the smile off his face.

"Thanks," Reggie said relieved for this moment of distraction.

"Are you going to be all right?" Jeff asked.

"Yes, I'm okay," Reggie said as he leaned back in his chair.

The mischievous smile returned to Jeff's face as he said, "I heard you were 'outed' today."

Reggie leaned over the desk and looked directly at Jeff and said in a hostile defensive tone, "What the hell does that mean?"

"Hey, wait a minute brother, cool down." Jeff said, extending his hands gesturing for Reggie to sit back in his chair.

"I'm sorry man. There's a lot going on here," Reggie said leaning back in his chair.

"You remember we talked about how Harriett would react. Weren't you ready for her? But when she told me you were actually considering proposing, I was as surprised as she was. Was that one of those quick decisions? Is this the same 'chick' I saw you with?" Jeff asked this time leaning forward in his chair and looking into Reggie's eyes.

"Yes, she's the one," Reggie answered in a quiet, calm tone looking down at his desk.

"As I recall you haven't known her that long. Have you met her family, her friends?" Jeff asked with a quizzical, serious look.

"Yes, I met some of her friends and her family," Reggie said showing a bit more confidence in his voice.

"What were they like?" Jeff asked, still leaning over Reggie's desk.

"Her friends were friendly and, as a matter of fact, one of them, I think Carol said she was from Jamaica," Reggie answered exerting more confidence.

"What was the girl from Jamaica like?" Jeff asked leaning back in his chair.

"We all went bike riding in Central Park. As I remember she had very little to say to me."

"Did you see her interact with or talk about any other Black person?" Jeff asked with a smirk on his face.

"What do you mean? The girl from Jamaica is Black." Reggie asked, looking confused.

"Well, all Jamaicans are not like Marcus Garvey," Jeff said in a condescending tone.

"Now what does that mean?" Reggie asked, still looking confused.

"Well, some West Indians ain't that comfortable with Black Americans." Jeff said, crossing his legs. "What about her family?" Jeff asked again leaning forward in his chair.

"I went home with her to Connecticut. Her mother invited me to a brunch they were hosting. She was very friendly. Her father was a little stiff. He had some problems with affirmative action." Reggie said in a manner to convey he saw no real problems with the family.

"What did he say about affirmative action?" Jeff asked in a very forceful voice.

"He just didn't think it was necessary."

"He didn't, huh." Jeff said as he shook his head. "Man, have you thought this thing through? Marriage is a serious step. Are you sure you haven't been duped by a good rump in the bed?"

"Carol loves me," Reggie answered as if he were trying to convince himself.

"Yes, but does her love take into consideration your history as a Black man growing up in a segregated society? I doubt it seriously," Jeff responded, leaning over the desk and pointing his finger at Reggie.

"I expect there will be some things we will have to work out. What are we talking about anyway? I haven't proposed and she hasn't accepted," Reggie shot back, trying to shift the conversation away from a subject that was causing his irritation to rise.

"I'm just trying to help open your eyes, man, that's all," Jeff responded as he threw his hands into the air and shook his head from side to side.

"I appreciate your concern man," Reggie said as he exhaled to keep from saying something defensive.

Jeff sensed Reggie's discomfort and moved to change the subject. "Hey, Harriett told me that Henry messed with the affirmative action agreement you developed." Jeff said with fury in his eyes. "What did that 'cracker' do?"

"He did change some of the things I put in, but he explained in a discussion I had with him this morning that he was trying to establish a negotiation position. He said these agreements are always negotiated. That sounded reasonable," Reggie answered as he looked at Jeff for some word of approval.

"I guarantee you he has spoken to every company he could find that has one of these agreements and he has come up with a strategy to agree to as little as he can. What he said might sound reasonable, but I wouldn't trust him any further than I can spit. If you are the one doing the face to face negotiations with the Department of Labor, I suggest you find a way to get some serious provisions in that agreement that's going to hold their asses to the fire."

"I'll see how things go," Reggie responded, thinking Jeff would blame him for a weak agreement.

"Are you all set for Thanksgiving?" Jeff asked as he stood up to leave the office.

"Yes, Carol's mother invited me to spend it with them on Martha's Vineyard," Reggie answered almost apologetically.

"Well, go for it brother," Jeff said sounding like a big brother disgusted with a little brother who refused to understand what he was trying to tell him. "Let's get together for lunch after Thanksgiving."

"Okay," Reggie said as he raised his fingers in the peace sign.

As the door closed, Reggie leaned back in his chair pushing aside that cold cup of coffee from the morning and picked up the agreement then slammed it down. He was in no mood to review it. He sat there looking at the ceiling for a few minutes then suddenly remembered he only needed to proofread it since he had decided to buy into Henry's plan for dealing with the Department of Labor. At the end of the day, he returned the agreement to Sandra. Although he had completed the proofreading much earlier, he thought it might look good if he delayed the return to give the impression that he had done a serious, conscientious review.

"It looks fine to me," Reggie said with a very serious look on his face as he handed the agreement to Sandra.

"If you could draft a cover letter for Henry's signature tomorrow morning, I'll put it all together for you to hand deliver," Sandra said looking at Reggie as if she wanted to apologize for what had been done to his draft.

"I'll get it to you first thing in the morning," Reggie answered, sensing some kind of empathy from Sandra and wondering where it was coming from.

He walked out of the building into a chilly, drizzling rain- just what he needed, he thought. It matched his mood. It was good that Carol was in Chicago because it might be difficult to hide his mood if they were together and he was certain he could not share with her what was driving his mood.

As the bus maneuvered its way through the slower than usual traffic brought on by the rain, he tried to close his eyes and think of something pleasant, but no such thoughts would come. He kept thinking of what he considered harsh reactions from Harriett and Jeff regarding his relationship with Carol. Whereas he rationalized that he didn't really need their approval, their reactions gnawed at him. That realization made him angry and he began to justify his relationship. First of all, he loved Carol and she loved him and from everything he had ever heard, love conquers all. Also, all he had ever heard was that no matter how much two people loved each other, there are always things that they have to work out. Anyway it's inevitable that when the races begin to integrate, they are bound to get into relationships. Jeff and Harriett probably haven't had the opportunity to develop relationships with white people like he had while in college and afterwards, he told himself. Harriett and Jeff be damned, he declared.

As he walked through the chilly rain towards his apartment, he found himself humming the lyrics to the love song from Romeo and Juliet. *"A time for us someday there will be when chains are torn by courage born of a love that's free. A time when dreams so long denied can flourish, as we unveil the love we now must hide. A time for us, at last to see a life worthwhile for you and me. And with our love through tears and thrones, we will endure as we pass surely through every storm. A time for us, some day there'll be a new world, a world of shining hope for you and me."*

He decided he would resume his search for a ring and have it ready for the right moment.

At the top of Reggie's agenda the next morning was drafting the cover letter for Henry's signature. He completed it and left it on Sandra's desk. A couple of hours later she arrived at his office with a large sealed envelope addressed to the Department of Labor. "It's all ready for delivery," Sandra said in an upbeat tone that seemed contrived. "I called Mrs. Chance, our contact person. You met her, right? I told her you would be bringing it and so she is expecting you."

"Yes, I met with her. Okay, I'm on my way," Reggie answered trying to mimic Sandra's contrived, upbeat tone.

Reggie expected to be greeted again by the Afro sporting, rude kid when he entered the Department of Labor's office; however, this time a pleasant middle-aged white woman invited him to have a seat while she announced his arrival. Reggie decided that Mr. Afro was probably out that day pretending he was sick. Typical. Reggie concluded.

"Good morning Mr. Morton," Mrs. Chance said, beating back a yawn as she shifted in her chair trying to find comfort for her full figure in a chair that refused to yield. "Please have a seat."

"Thank you. I have our affirmative action plan for you this morning." Reggie said trying to portray satisfaction with its contents. "Could you tell me how long it will be before you've had a chance to review it and respond to us? I would like to set up a plan for its implementation and I would especially like to know if there are things you would change or add before I move forward."

Mrs. Chance pointed to the pile of documents on the radiator behind her desk and said, "I will get to it as fast as I can; however, if you have complied with the guidelines given you, I suggest you go ahead and begin developing a plan for implementation."

That was a strange response, Reggie thought. Maybe I need to put it in more specific terms. "Since this is our first time developing such a document, it would be very helpful to me to know what you think of what we have done, especially if there are thing you wish to add," Reggie again emphasized trying to give her a hint. However, Mrs. Chance seemed to ignore his plea.

"I'll do my best, Mr. Morton. Thanks for delivering it," she said as she reached for her cup of coffee and placed the agreement on top of the pile behind her desk.

Reggie walked out of her office feeling his reputation was in the hands of someone who couldn't care less about who might throw stones at him. He tried unsuccessfully to think of a believable explanation that he could give to people like Jeff and those back home, if the agreement remained weak. At least, he thought, he might redeem himself by excelling in his work as an account executive. He then remembered Henry had asked him to remain in personnel until the agreement had been approved and if it takes a long time to get a response from Mrs. Chance, he could be stuck in personnel starring at the walls. He walked out of the building trying to think of something pleasant to ease his mind. "The ring, the ring," he said.

He walked back into the jewelry district, avoiding the store where Harriett had confronted him. After visiting three stores, he finally found the ring that he considered just right for Carol and made the purchase. He felt nervous but uplifted. As he walked back to this office, he pondered when would be the right moment to pop the question.

CHAPTER 16

"Hello Reggie, I'm just getting back. My flight was a bit late. How was your week?" Carol asked with a rush in her voice.

"My week was the best to be expected without you around," Reggie answered.

"Well I'm back now. How's that? Listen, there has been a slight change in the plans for leaving on Wednesday. Father has some business in Boston on Monday and Tuesday so he and mother are leaving Sunday night and will go to the Vineyard from Boston. He is bringing down the VW tomorrow for us to drive up. That means we should try to leave around eleven in order to get the six o'clock ferry."

"That's okay with me. Will we be able to get together before then?"

"I don't know. I have a lot to do before Wednesday. Let's see how things work out."

"Well, go to bed and get some rest. I'll call you tomorrow." He was intrigued by the thought of them driving to the Vineyard alone. Maybe the moment will present itself. "No, no," he said, thinking of the family's possible reaction. Maybe I need to wait and see what things are like. Who knows, he decided.

Saturday turned to Sunday, Sunday into Monday and Monday into Tuesday while Reggie nervously pondered what his behavior would be from the time he and Carol left Manhattan to the time they returned. He finally decided on a strategy. He would keep the ring close at hand to be retrieved on a moment's notice. He would do his best to avoid talking about what it was like growing up in the segregated South if quizzed about his past by any of the family members. He would try as much as possible to guide the conversations to his time with the biracial and white families that mentored him in Chicago and the positive things that happened to him while attending the recently integrated Davis University.

Feeling comfortable that he had a plan, his thoughts turned to other concerns. He wondered what the sleeping arrangements would be since he was sure Carol's father would shoot him if he got caught anywhere near her bed. He gasped at the thought of sharing a bedroom with her father. He would probably never sleep, expecting her father at any moment to press a pillow over his face until he was certain he could no longer breathe.

"Hello Reggie, why don't you meet me here at eleven?" Carol asked. "The car is parked in the parking lot in front of my building."

"I will be there with bells on."

"Okay, Santa Claus," Carol said laughing.

Reggie, with his bag swinging from his shoulder, walked promptly into the lobby of Carol's building at eleven. She was there waiting for him.

"I don't hear any bells," Carol said, laughing.

"They are in my heart, ringing loudly crying out Carol, Carol, my love," Reggie said as he hugged her.

"Come, come now, let's hit the road. We don't want to miss the ferry,"
Carol whispered into his ear.

"Shall I drive?" Reggie asked.

"We can share the driving. Right now let me get us out of New York City traffic. I'm probably more used to it than you."

They rolled off the parking lot and made a couple of short turns and landed on the West Side Highway where traffic flowed freely. Carol, looking a bit tense, gave her undivided attention to the movement of traffic around her. Reggie sat quietly, careful not to do anything to distract her. They arrived at the exit to the Cross Bronx Expressway and it lived up to its reputation of forever congested and slow to move. Carol seemed more tense. Reggie wanted to take over the wheel but didn't want to convey any discomfort with her driving. In any event, the flow of traffic provided no opportunity to stop and exchange drivers. So, he sat there quietly wondering how long the situation would prevail and thinking the mood for proposing certainly couldn't rise out of a situation like this. As the Cross Bronx turned into Interstate 95, the traffic began to flow smoother, but still congested with travelers heading to join loved ones for a traditional gathering. The stress on Carol's face began to dissipate. Without uttering a word, she turned on the radio to WPAT an easy listening station, and soft music began to flow through the car.

"Are you still with me?" Carol asked without taking her eye off the road.

"Yes, baby, I am with you and ready to relieve you whenever you are ready."

"We will make a stop after we pass New Haven and then you can take over. Okay?"

"Whatever you say," Reggie said as he stroked her head. The music seemed to relax Carol. Reggie silently exhaled. Maybe, he thought, we can engage in a conversation now.

"And what is Thanksgiving like in New England? Do you go out and find a Native American to invite to dinner? Does someone take their rifle and go out and hunt a wild turkey?" Reggie asked in jest.

"Well smarty pants, we celebrate like the rest of the country. We forget there are Native Americans and we go to the store and buy a frozen turkey. Is that any different from how they do it in Tennessee?" Carol shot back, also in jest.

"Well, I guess I won't be able to write home and tell my family that I went hunting with guys with feathered crowns and we sat around an open fire gnawing on wild turkey reminiscing about the day you all landed offering beads for land," Reggie said with a smirk on his face.

"Well, I guess you won't. You will have to tell them you dined on store bought turkey, mashed potatoes, pumpkin pie with a family that didn't know one Native American. And that you enjoyed every minute of it," Carol snapped as she lightly slapped Reggie on the cheek.

"You forgot to include that I sat at the dinner table next to the most beautiful woman in the world."

"Well, you can include that too," Carol said, smiling.

The sun burst out from behind the clouds taking some chill off the winds as they pulled into the rest stop. They both exhaled and stretched as they stepped from the car and looked into the blue sky. "Great day for traveling," Reggie said as he anticipated taking over the wheel. He touched his pocket to reassure himself that the ring was still there.

The restaurant was crowded with holiday travelers. There was a line for the restrooms and the concession stands. Reggie took his place in the line for food while Carol went to freshen-up. After an unnerving wait in line with customers complaining about wrong orders and changing orders after the waiter had placed theirs and noisy children making all kinds of demands of their parents, Reggie finally got his two cheeseburgers, French fries and cokes. Carol was sitting quietly at a table she had captured.

"Are you ready to release the wheel into the hands of an aspiring Indianapolis 500 driver?" Reggie asked while devouring his burger.

"Yes, I'm ready to turn it over to someone with no opportunity to satisfy his fantasy in this traffic."

"Okay, okay, now what is the route from here to the ferry?"

"Continue to follow New England Highway until you approach New Bedford where you will pick up Route 6 which will take you to Woods Hole where we will get the ferry. You may want to turn the wheel back over to me when you reach Route 6 where traffic will be slower because it is not a divided highway like the New England Highway."

"I don't know about that." Reggie said feeling his pocket to make sure the ring was still there.

As Reggie pulled out of the parking lot and headed north, Carol leaned back in her seat and closed her eyes. The rush of the past few days preparing to leave and the stress of maneuvering through the congested traffic had caught up with her. The muscles in her face relaxed and Reggie knew she had fallen asleep. He reached over and, in a stroke of affection, brushed her hair. He turned on the radio and found a station with soft jazz and shifted in his seat to find the best position for comfort. The highway was congested, but it was dry. The sun was shining brightly and the traffic was flowing smoothly except for an occasional back-up.

A jazz rendition of "A Canadian Sunset" came on the radio and Reggie began to hum along. He began to fantasize flying away on a honeymoon to a tropical island with white sandy beaches and tropical breezes brushing across Carol's and his bodies as they watched the sun give way to the gulping horizon. He glanced at Carol again and felt a rush of euphoria. "She's mine," he said. The traffic suddenly slowed down to a crawl as rubbernecks watched a driver who had been pulled over by the Highway Patrol.

The interruption gave the demon of doubt a chance to declare equal time. Reggie began to visualize his mother racing to the altar to ask the Lord to deliver him from the tragedy he was about to march into or to relieve her of the pain of watching it. He wondered what it would be like for her when the folks back home discovered he had married a white woman. He cringed at the thought that Carol's family would be just as opposed to the thought as the folks back home. What if Carol turned him down? What would he do then? He looked up ahead and saw that he was about to approach the exit to Route 6 to Cape Cod. He slowed down so that he would not miss it. Carol turned, but did not open her eyes.

Seeing the Cape Cod sign reminded Reggie of Frank Sinatra singing "Old Cape Code," He wondered how much of Old Cape Cod he would be able to witness on his way to Martha's Vineyard. As he approached New Bedford the smell of the salty ocean crept into the car. He took a deep breath to capture it.

When he approached the town of Mattapoissett, a name he thought was curious, he noticed the weathered shingles on houses, a trade make of the Cape. Just about all the shops along the way advertised salt water taffy and fudge. The restaurants advertised their fish and chips and "frappes." Reggie felt he was wandering into a world favored by the rich and famous. He wondered if he would pass through Hyannis where the Kennedy family lived.

He began to think that maybe he was venturing too far from the vine and that neither he nor the people in this circle would be comfortable with each other. Also, what could he add to the life of a rich girl like Carol, except his undying love? Maybe he should let that ring stay in his pocket until he found some nice Black woman to give it to. Maybe Jeff had a point that he was heading for danger that he had not anticipated. Can love really conquer all, as they say. He thought about driving the car to the nearest Greyhound bus station and giving the keys to Carol as he headed back to New York and to a Harlem restaurant for Thanksgiving dinner. He felt beads of sweat forming on his forehead.

"Where are we?' Carol asked brushing hair off her face and wiping her eyes.

"We are a few miles from Bourne Bridge," Reggie answered feeling proud he had come so far without disturbing her sleep. He also felt his doubts begin to fade as she reached over and began rubbing the back of his neck, sending an erotic charge racing to his crotch.

"You poor guy why didn't you wake me so I could relieve you? I didn't intend for you to do this much driving."

"I'm doing just fine. I like watching you sleep."

"I guess I was really worn out. You are a sweetheart," she said as she pinched his neck. "We can stop for gas just after we cross the bridge and I can take over the driving."

"No need, I'm enjoying the driving and taking in the scenery," he said, seeming to have escaped the grip of the demon of doubt.

"Well, we only have about another hour and a half before we reach Woods Hole. It's three-thirty. We've made good time, considering the kind of traffic you find on Thanksgiving. We should be in plenty of time for the six o'clock ferry."

There was bumper to bumper traffic crossing the bridge, around the rotary and into the gas station where they stopped. They took their place in line for fill-ups and stepped out of the car into brisk chilly winds. Reggie wrapped his arms around Carol as she shivered a bit before heading for the ladies room. The line was moving so slow Reggie did not wait for her return before he took his nature break. When he returned, Carol was waiting for him with a Coca Cola and suggested they wait in the car for their turn at the pump.

"I'm wide awake now and can at least keep you company. I wanted to point out places along the way. Maybe on our way back. I hope you will forgive me for abandoning you."

"If I thought you had abandoned me, I would have driven to the nearest river and jumped in," Reggie said, reaching over to kiss her forehead.

"You are a true charmer," Carol said, looking at Reggie with affection gleaming in her eyes.

Their turn finally came for a fill-up. The young attendant in oil-stained overalls and a baseball cap came to the driver's side, looked askance at the two of them and said slowly, "What can I do for you?"

"Fill it up," Reggie said aggressively. After the attendant filled it up, he came around to Carol's side and said, "That will be eight dollars." As Carol reached for her purse to search for her charge card, Reggie reached across her and handed the attendant the eight dollars and said as cool as he could considering the insults, "Have a good day, my man."

"You didn't have to do that. I usually use my credit care to keep track," Carol said without any acknowledgement of the dynamics of what had just occurred.

"No problem," Reggie said without any further comment. He pretended to be totally focused on the heavy traffic coming around the rotary as he waited his turn to pull into it.

"There's a lot of merging traffic here. Things should smooth out shortly. Are you sure all this congested traffic is not wearing you out?"

"No, driving relaxes me," Reggie said without looking at Carol as he pulled into the rotary.

"How are things going with you at the office? We haven't had a chance to talk since discussing the changes Henry made to the affirmative action plan." Carol asked as she shifted in her seat to face Reggie.

"Henry and I discussed his changes and he said that the ones he made were designed to establish a negotiating position. If the Department of Labor comes back with more stringent requirements, the agency would be in a position to maybe meet them half way."

"Oh, that sounds like a good strategy. Have you had any response from the Department of Labor?"

"No, I delivered the agreement to them and their representative indicated that she would review it as soon as she could. She had a stack of documents lined up on her radiator. So, I don't know how long this process will go on. Henry asked me to remain in his office until the agreement has been signed. So for now, I feel like I am in limbo since I don't know what I will be doing while the Department of Labor is reviewing the agreement."

"I am sure Henry has a list of things he needs you to help him get ready for implementation of the plan. He would be a poor manager if he didn't. So, I doubt you will be idle while the Department of Labor figures out what they want."

"I guess so," Reggie said very soberly.

"How is your mother doing?" Carol asked still facing Reggie.

"She is doing okay. If your parents don't mind, I would like to call her tomorrow."

"Absolutely," Carol said as she shifted back in her seat where she was facing forward. The traffic began to thin out and speeds picked up. Carol searched for a radio station that would come through clearly. She found some rock and roll and leaned back in her seat listening to the Beatles singing, "I Wanna Hold Your Hand."

Reggie kept up with the flow of traffic as he headed down the highway for Woods Hole. He felt his pocket to assure himself that the ring was still there, then began to doubt an opportunity would present itself this weekend so he sent up a prayer that he would not lose it. Around five fifteen he pulled into the parking lot at the ferry dock and claimed his space in the line of cars for the six o'clock ferry.

"Here with plenty of time to spare," he said as he exhaled.

"Well, you can be my driver any day," Carol said patting Reggie on the head.

He almost responded with, what about being your husband but caught himself and said, grinning. "You've got my number just call when you need my services."

Fog was beginning to roll in, seemingly shoved by the autumn winds and peppered with the smell of the salty ocean. Reggie took a deep breath as if to internalize the moment that seemed like an eerie scene from a mystery movie. It made him feel he was a long way from home and about to experience something mystical. He reached for Carol's hand to reassure himself that things would be okay. They then walked into the terminal for a cup of hot chocolate.

"You must be starving," Carol said. "I understand dinner will be served around seven-thirty. Father will be irritated if it isn't. So I am pretty sure it will be."

"I am hungry, but I won't starve before seven-thirty."

"We should be docking close to seven so dinner should be ready when we arrive," Carol said rubbing Reggie's hand.

They headed back to the car with their hot chocolate and cars began to roll onto the ferry. Reggie heeded the signals of the attendant directing him to line up in the belly of the ferry. Carol suggested they leave the car and go sit in the waiting area. As Reggie stepped into the room, he began to feel the toll of the long drive finally weighing down on him. He could not remember ever driving that far for that long. The adrenaline that kept him going was beginning to evaporate.

The area was filled with passengers flaunting skin care that implied wealth. Very few were Black and those who were resemble the light skinned well-to-do pillars of the community in the segregated South where he grew up. There was a lot of animated conversation among some who seemed familiar with each other. Young children were all over the place in wild pursuit of each other. Teenagers were huddle together in corners as if they were plotting some mischief. There were no biracial couples in sight. Reggie felt conspicuous. He couldn't remember whether he and Carol had been in that kind of situation before and how he might have felt if they had. Thoughts of spending Thanksgiving on Martha's Vineyard with the McKay family were becoming unsettling. He felt he wanted to escape the situation when, out of the fog, came the sound of the whistle announcing the ramp was up and the boat was leaving shore. At that moment he felt trapped.

"Would you like to go up on the deck for a while? In this weather, it's probably not as crowded as down here." Carol asked. Reggie jumped at the opportunity.

"Yes, that's a good idea," he said thinking the night air might rescue him from another grip of the demon of doubt. The dimly lit deck appeared ominous. The creeping fog intermittingly passing by and revealing a black sky with a full moon and dots of stars lingering far in the vast universe; the sloshing sound of the ocean waters yielding to the ferry's robust throttle; and the haunting invisible winds stroking their bodies were things Reggie thought might sooth him, but they turned out to be no match for the demon of doubt. He felt vulnerable.

"I hope you will enjoy this holiday with us. Aunt Melba is a lot like mother, very outgoing, comfortable with herself. She loves cooking and always insists on everyone stuffing themselves. Uncle Jack loves to talk. He has an opinion on just about every subject that comes up. He and Aunt Melba often disagree. She teases him about being bound by old school Portuguese thinking. He's Cape Verdean. Aunt Beatrice, father's sister, and my two cousins will also be there. Aunt Beatrice is a widow. Uncle Ted died of cancer several years ago. Her house is about a mile from Aunt Melba and about two miles from ours. Jacqueline and Melissa, my cousins are around my age. The both live in Boston. Aunt Beatrice is like an old school mom. She believes in doing things by the book. That's probably why Jacqueline and Melissa couldn't wait to graduate from college and move to Boston after Uncle Ted died. Jacqueline can be a little wild. She is known for her free spirit. She drives Aunt Beatrice crazy at times. Melissa is the level-headed one. Both are fun to be around. I think you will like them."

"So we will be staying at your family's house? I thought we would be staying with your aunt," Reggie asked.

"Oh, I'm sorry I just forgot to explain. Aunt Melba is the host for the dinner. That's why I said we were going to Aunt Melba's. We have a house there, too. Aunt Melba and Aunt Beatrice live there year-round." Carol said.

After listening to Carol's description of her family, Reggie was glad he did not have to face them all that night especially in the mood that had overtaken him. He began to wonder if fatigue was causing his apprehensions and, if he could get a good night's rest, he might be okay. He looked out into the night and through the fog he glimpsed some dim lights in the distance.

"That's the Vineyard where you see the lights. We should be arriving in about a half hour. We can make our way back to the car," Carol said with excitement in her voice. Her excitement penetrated Reggie's sober mood, sending a spark into his adrenaline reserve bank which released a shot of energetic anticipation as he and Carol followed the other drivers to their cars.

Shortly after they made their way through the crowd and into their car, the ferry was preparing to dock, car engines started up and attendants began to organize themselves for directing traffic off. Reggie was cautiously paying attention to instructions of the attendants as he drove off the ferry. He then carefully followed Carol's directions through Vineyard Haven to the house just off the street and facing a tributary of the ocean. As they pulled into the driveway, lights illuminating the driveway popped on and out came Mrs. McKay. She walked around to the driver's side and as soon as Reggie stepped out of the car she embraced him and said. "I am so glad you all made it okay. Did Carol make you drive all the way?"

"No, we shared the driving. The area of the country is all new to me so I enjoyed the driving."

"Hello mom, I'm here too." Carol said as she took out her bags.

"Yes, dear and how are you?" she asked as she hugged Carol.

"I'm rested. Reggie drove most of the way and I was naughty. I slept a great deal of it. So I am sure he is more tired than he admits."

"Well, why don't you all come in? Your father and I have been waiting for you to have dinner."

"Hello Dad," Carol said as she walked over to the chair where he was sitting with a glass of gin and tonic in his hand watching Walter Cronkite still talking about Nixon's victory and speculating what that would mean for the country.

"Hello baby," he said as she leaned over to hug him.

"Good evening, Mr. McKay," Reggie said as he walked over and shook his hand.

"Good evening young man," he said as he immediately released his hand from Reggie's.

"Carol why don't you show Reggie his room while I set the table?" Mrs. McKay said as she looked askance at her husband.

Carol directed Reggie to a bedroom on the main floor just off the kitchen facing the tributary with a door leading to a deck. The room was small and cozy with a queen size bed that was stuffed with pillows. The only lighting was a table lamp beside the bed. There was a private bathroom. Reggie felt like jumping into the bed at that moment and taking a long nap.

"You can unpack your things and I will get you a drink. What would you like?" Carol asked.

"What's everybody drinking?"

"Father is drinking gin and tonic. Mother is having white wine."

"I'll have a gin and tonic."

Carol closed the door as she walked out and Reggie fell into the fluffy pillows on the bed. It felt like an angel had come to tell him "fret no more everything is going to be alright." He didn't want Carol to catch him in that position so he got up and began to take some things out of his bag. Carol knocked on the door.

"Come in."

"I hope it is not too strong."

"I am sure I can handle it.," Reggie said as he took a sip.

"Dinner will be ready in fifteen minutes," Carol said as she kissed him on the cheek.

"Okay." He began to feel a modicum of relaxation. About halfway through his drink, Mrs. McKay called out that dinner was ready. Reggie walked out of his room and into the unpretentious living room. There were wicker chairs; a blue and white striped, cushioned couch with an oil painting of a sunset over Cape Cod on the wall behind it; the La-Z- Boy chair hosting Mr. McKay and an entertainment center with pieces of Oriental sculpture. The dining area was off the living room with a window facing the water and a door leading to a sun room. It was not as grand as Reggie anticipated. He handed Mrs. McKay a bottle of wine he had brought.

"Oh, Reggie, thank you so much. It's very thoughtful of you. Why don't you take this seat?" Mrs. McKay said. It was facing the window. Carol was seated across from him. The table had been set with a green salad, grilled sirloin steaks, boiled potatoes, steamed zucchini and a bottle of red wine.

"Now, help yourself Reggie. You must be starved after that all day drive," Mrs. McKay said.

"I'll admit I do have an appetite "

"Well, go ahead and satisfy it."

Carol poured wine in each glass. Reggie had brought his drink to the table and for a moment, wondered if he should have until he noticed that Mr. McKay had done the same. He was already feeling the effects of his drink and wondered how much wine he could consume before becoming too relaxed.

Food began to be passed around, without a word of grace. When he began to chew his food, Reggie noticed that except for the dressing on the salad, the only seasonings he could detect were salt and pepper. He was, however, too hungry to care, although he did wonder if daughter was like mother in the kitchen.

"Well, young man, how is your affirmative action work coming?" Mr. McKay asked with a sober look on his face.

"We have submitted a plan to the Department of Labor and they are in the process of reviewing it," Reggie answered while continuing to slice his steak.

"Well you just might be waiting for a long time. I don't think President Nixon will tolerate any affirmative action plans. I think his election will bring to an end this so called civil rights movement. Everybody is going to have to make it on his own without government hand-outs. Anyway there isn't another person around trying to change the country like Martin Luther King. It's time for you people to know that America is a country of equal opportunity, not special opportunities. I'm tired of hearing this crap about being held back because of discrimination. The Irish were discriminated against when they came to this country and look at them today. John Kennedy was Irish."

Reggie cringed in his seat thinking someone should tell Mr. McKay that the South lost the Civil War.

"Honey, Nixon is a loser, a liar. How long do you think it will take for those who voted for him to realize that? He's bound to be exposed in due time. Anti-discrimination laws in employment and housing have been passed by Congress. Do you really think he can cause those laws to be revoked? Come now, honey, the country has moved forward. There is no going back now, Martin Luther King or no Martin Luther King," Mrs. McKay said in a calm voice with a look of embarrassment on her face.

Reggie wanted to clap for her response. It gave him time to come up with a diplomatic response. He felt he needed to demonstrate some level of intelligence while, at the same time, taking into consideration Carol's relationship with her father and the fact that he was trapped in his house on this island for a few days. Also, he did not want to be identified as a drum major for affirmative action or an opponent or a member of the Black Panther Party.

"I think affirmative action is a mechanism the government can use to provide opportunities to people who have been underprivileged for a long time. It is also a good business decision. People who have jobs are not qualified for government assistance and they pay taxes and taxes keep the government working. Tax money that would have gone to support people needing public assistance, but now have jobs, can be used for other needs of the country that benefits all. So affirmative action is actually a good investment for our country."

"If you have been underprivileged, what qualifications do you have for any job?" Mr. McKay asked as he leaned back in his chair with a smirk on his face seeming proud that he had rebutted Reggie's response.

"What Reggie meant, father, is that while affirmative action helps to level the playing field, it's also good for the whole country," Carol said.

Reggie cringed again. He thought he had made a clear and articulate response. Did Carol think differently?

"How is your mother doing, Reggie?" Mrs. McKay interjected.

"She seems to be coming along fairly well. If you don't mind I would like to telephone her tomorrow," Reggie answered.

"By all means," Mrs. McKay said.

After dinner, Mrs. McKay offered everybody vanilla ice cream and chocolate cake she had purchased at the supermarket. Reggie and Carol took her up on the offer. Mr. McKay did not. He got up from the table, returned to his La-Z Boy, turned on the television and worked on finishing his gin and tonic.

As soon as Reggie finished his dessert, he found it hard to keep his eyes open. However, he offered to help with the cleanup. Carol interjected and suggested he turn in. He didn't hesitate. He closed his door and wasted no time getting into that comfortable bed. He was too tired to concentrate on any of the disturbing thoughts that haunted him that day, especially the diatribe from the bigoted Mr. McKay. He slept through the night and was awakened the next morning by a tap on the door. Before he was awake enough to respond, Carol opened the door and stuck her head in and said,

"Good morning sleepy head. Did you rest well?"

"I must have. I didn't wake up once during the night. This bed is like a cradle rocking you to sleep."

"Well, when you are ready, you can come to breakfast. I'm in charge this morning."

"I can hardly wait. I've never had a meal prepared by you," Reggie said smiling.

"Well after this morning, you still won't."

After his shower and subjecting his Magic Shave sensitive-skin to a razor, Reggie stepped into the kitchen. He didn't smell anything except coffee.

"In here," Carol called out. Reggie walked into the dining area and on the table he found cereal, blue berry muffins, orange juice and coffee.

"I warned you," Carol said with a smirk on her face.

Reggie hugged her and said, "This breakfast is all I need. Where are your parents?"

"Mother went over to give Aunt Melba a hand and father is still in bed. I am going to take some breakfast up to him and then take my shower. So make yourself at home. Would you like to do what is an American tradition on Thanksgiving morning- watching the Macy's Thanksgiving Day parade?"

"Well, never let it be said that I broke an American tradition." Reggie said with a bit of sarcasm.

He felt good that the disciple of George Wallace was not joining them for breakfast. How will I ever get used to dealing with him, Reggie wondered. Am I supposed to pretend to like him? Am I supposed to try to find a way to get through to him? People say there is always some good in everybody. Could there be any under that tough skin? Should I be satisfied having Mrs. McKay on my side? But Carol adores her father and they seem to be very close. Some family members often cause conflict in marriages so why should mine be any different, he concluded. He smiled, thinking that Mr. McKay and his mother would probably see eye to eye on their marriage-totally opposed. He tried to imagine them in a conversation. It would probably look like George Wallace and Martin Luther King hugging each other. The thought reminded him that he promised to call his mother.

Carol turned on the television, kissed Reggie on the cheek, filled a tray and headed up the stairs. Reggie noticed there were two bedrooms up there, but he didn't dare venture up to satisfy his curiosity about the layout. Mr. McKay might walk out of his room covered in a white sheet and carrying a double barrel shotgun.

As Carol disappeared behind her father's bedroom door, Reggie picked-up the telephone and called home.

"Hello mom, how are you doing?" Reggie asked in as jovial a voice as he could muster.

"I'm doing okay, considering, son. What are you doing for dinner today?"

"I'm having dinner with the family of a friend here on Martha's Vineyard."

"Where is that?"

"It's on Cape Cod."

"Is it up there where the Kennedy family lives?"

"Yes, it's near there. It's an island off the coast of Massachusetts. Jackie Kennedy has a home here."

"That sound like a place for rich folks."

"Some like Jackie Kennedy are rich, but there are also some Indians here and a group of Black people who have been here for many years."

"Is your friend someone you met at work?"

"Not really, we met on my way to work," Reggie said trying to dodge any more revealing questions about Carol.

"Well, I hope you enjoy it and I hope you are planning to come home for Christmas."

"I'm going to try."

"Well, I want you to try hard."

"I promise. What are you doing for dinner today?"

"I've agreed to go over to Doug's. He's trying to be as helpful as possible. Doug Junior kept asking me if I would come. So, I'm going. I don't know what kind of Thanksgiving dinner Doris is capable of fixing. I just hope she and Doug don't explode while I am there. I promised to bake a sweet potato pie and I had better get up and get started."

"Okay mom, I will talk to you later. Give my regards to Doug and all."

"Okay, son."

Reggie took his coffee out to the sun room. He could see the TV and the ocean from there. It was a sunny day. The sway of the branches on the trees foretold of vigorous winds. Still, the rays of the invading sun brought some warmth to the chilly room. Reggie sat there gazing at the ocean. The night's rest had made him feel more confident about facing the rest of the family. Hopefully, they would not all be clones of Mr. McKay. Regardless, he said, "She loves me. She loves me," as he watched the quivering waves from the ocean stroking the stoical shore.

The sound of crowds in exhilaration on the TV distracted him. An acrobatic marching band followed by high-flying balloons of cartoon characters and creatively decorated floats with celebrities rolled into Herald Square. Reggie became engrossed in the spectacle. He had heard of the Macy's Thanksgiving Day parade, but had never witnessed it. It reminded him of the parades he participates in when he was a kid, only they were much less spectacular, but every bit as energized.

Remembering that period in his life brought back the memory of his first love, Mona, who married that white guy who got her pregnant. He wondered how her marriage worked out and how she handled the mixed marriage issue when she visited home. He remembered his mother saying Mona's parents were very upset about the marriage; but she wasn't sure whether they were angry about the marriage, the pregnancy or both. He leaned back in his seat with his arms folded and a smile on his face thinking how he had finally found love with this beautiful, intelligent woman who returned his love.

"And what are you smiling about?" Carol asked, shocking Reggie with her sudden appearance.

"This parade is really interesting. It takes me back to when I was growing up and the parades we used to have. We never had parades in the winter. Ours were always in the spring. So it's interesting to see those majorettes in those short skirts marching in that wind. I'm as excited as the kids waiting to see Santa's roll into Herald Square."

"Well, one Thanksgiving we will have to go down to Herald Square to watch it in person."

"I would like that." Maybe, he thought, we could take our kid down there.

Carol sat on the love seat next to Reggie. He wanted to reach for her hand, but quickly discarded that idea. It occurred to him that her father might come down those stairs any minute and see that and there's no telling what he might do. So, he kept his eyes on the television just as Carol was doing. They sat there throughout the parade, exchanging views on the various floats, bands, celebrity performances and clapping when Santa Claus's float rolled in.

"What are you two clapping about?" Mr. McKay asked as he stepped off the last step of the stairs wrapped in a robe carrying his breakfast tray. He shocked Reggie who suddenly felt nervous.

"We were welcoming Santa Claus as he made his way into Herald Square, officially launching the beginning of the Christmas season," Carol said.

"It will be here before you know it", he said as he walked into the kitchen and deposited his tray. When he walked back into the living room he asked. "Did you get a good night's sleep young man?"

"Yes sir I did," Reggie responded, immediately feeling uplifted for the civil greeting. "What about you sir? Was your night restful?" Reggie asked trying to strike up a non-political dialogue.

"Oh yes, I usually sleep well in this house. The sounds here are so different from the ones around the house in Ridgefield-a little more soothing."

"They are drastically different from the ones in the city. You really don't realize how noisy it is until you get away from it. I enjoy hearing the ocean batting against the shore. It's very calming," Reggie said feeling he was finally making a non-political connection with Mr. McKay

"Where do you live in New York?" Mr. McKay asked.

"I live in Riverdale," Reggie said proudly.

"That's very Jewish isn't it?" He asked, looking askance at Reggie.

"Yes, sir it is," Reggie answered wondering if Mr. McKay considered that a negative for him or whether Jews were another target of his bigotry. Well, for now at least, he is not riding me about affirmative action. Reggie concluded.

Mr. McKay looked away from Reggie and toward Carol and asked, "What time did your mother say we need to be at Melba's?"

"Around two."

"Well, I guess we have about an hour. I'm going back upstairs and get dressed," he said.

Reggie looked at Carol and said, "I guess I will do the same" and headed for his room and took out the outfit that he had brought for the occasion and the bottle of wine the guy at the liquor store told him would be appropriate for a Thanksgiving dinner. He put on his favorite brown slacks and a pale yellow dress shirt and his suede jacket. There was only a mirror on the dresser so he could not get a full look at himself, but he had done that several time at home, so he looked to see if his hair was in shape.

He walked out into the living room with the car keys swinging in one hand and a bottle of wine in the other. Carol descended the stairs in a jump suit that made her look so tempting Reggie felt an electric rush through his body. She looked at the keys swinging in his hand and shook her head and whispered, "Father will drive the Lincoln."

Reggie leaned toward her, pinched her on the hip and whispered, "Okay" and handed her the keys.

From the top of the stairs Mr. McKay asked, "Are we all ready to go?"

"Yes, we are, Carol said as she jumped away from Reggie.

When they approached the car, Reggie opened the front door for Carol then took a seat in the back remembering the seat arrangement the last time they were all in the same car. The distance from Mr. McKay was also comforting. The car rolled out of the driveway onto the street that seemed to wind around and was dotted with unpretentious houses with the weather-beaten shingles. At the end of the street, the open ocean burst before them and the car took a right turn and began traveling along the ocean. This street was lined with two-story houses with porches, some of which had swings. On one of the porches Reggie saw two Black men smoking pipes and seemingly relaxing in spite of the cold winds coming off the ocean. He wanted to ask if this was the area where he heard Blacks dating back to the 1800s lived. But he hesitated, trying to avoid a bigoted diatribe from Mr. McKay that would spoil the civil conversation that started their day.

Reggie noticed a large sign on the side of the street that said Oak Bluff. It sounded like the name of the Black settlement. Could Aunt Melba live in this town, he wondered. This could get interesting. About a half mile down the street, the car pulled into a driveway. Reggie got excited. It was a spacious house with a picture window facing the ocean. To the left of the driveway, there was a pond. The car came to a stop and Mr. McKay and Carol hauled out so Reggie concluded they had reached their destination which heightened his curiosity.

"Hello. Anybody home?" Mr. McKay called out as the three of them entered the living room which looked like some room out of Architectural Digest. The off-white couch and chairs were sitting on a light blue rug. Hanging over the couch was a water color painting of a lighthouse with doves on a beach and a silhouette of a couple standing on the shore.

"We are out here." A male voice emerged from the back of the house. As they walked toward the voice, they passed through a dining room with a view of the pond. The table was set for nine. They walked into a spacious family room with comfortable, modern furniture and a bar with stools. Behind the bar was a man with a skin tone as dark as Reggie's, but with straight hair. Reggie's curiosity moved up a notch. He declared this man was Black. What was Carol talking about a Cape Verdean? What the hell is a Cape Verdean, he asserted in his mind. Why are they living on this part of the island? Was his family one of those early Black settlers, he wondered.

"Hello Jack," Mr. McKay said reaching across the bar to shake his hand.

"How have you been, Bob?" Jack asked.

Reggie noticed there was no apparent accent which supported his perception.

"Things are good," Mr. McKay answered. "Jack, I want you to meet Reggie Morton, a friend of Carol's from New York."

Reggie reached across the bar to shake his hand and before he could say, glad to meet you, Uncle Jack made a fast eye contact and barely touched Reggie's hand. And with a burst of excitement, he reached over and kissed Carol on the forehead and asked. "How's my girl doing down in the Big Apple?"

"I'm doing fine, Uncle Jack," Carol said seemingly oblivious to her uncle's reaction to Reggie.

Reggie began to wonder if Jack and Mr. McKay were hatched from the same egg. He decided not to hand over the bottle of wine he brought. He placed it on the coffee table.

"What can I get for you all?" Jack asked.

"I'll take a scotch and water," Mr. McKay said.

"I'll have white wine," Carol said.

Jack, looking at Reggie and with a devilish smile said, "I'm fresh out of corn whiskey. What can I get for you?

Carol and Mr. McKay laughed. Reggie did not. He looked directly at Jack and said, "I'll take a gin and tonic." Jack continued smiling as he handed Reggie his drink.

"Isn't anyone going to introduce me to our guest?" This tall, slim brunette with a disarming smile that was almost identical to Mrs. McKay's asked as she walked into the room in front of Mrs. McKay. Before Carol could speak, Mrs. McKay said, "Melba, this is Reggie Morton visiting us from New York."

Reggie reached out to shake her hand. She grabbed his hand and hugged him and said, "I'm so glad to meet you. I'm glad you were able to join us for Thanksgiving. I hope you will enjoy our New England version of the celebration, that is our food."

"From those aromas I'm detecting, I am sure I will. New England is the place where it all started, so I'm anxious to have the experience," Reggie said, feeling the warmth of her welcome. He handed her the bottle of wine.

"Where is everybody?" a voice from the living room asked.

"You know where to find us," Aunt Melba said just as this around five feet- five, vivacious attractive blond walked into the room with her mother and sister trailing and said. "A good afternoon to all of you and how are we doing?"

She looked at Reggie and asked, "Who is this handsome young man?" Before anyone could say anything she swayed over and extended her hand to Reggie and said, "I'm Jacqueline."

"I'm Reggie," he said almost giddy, thinking this day might not turn out so bad after all.

"Hi Reggie, I'm Melissa, Jacqueline's sister, and this is our mother Beatrice." Melissa was a bit on the heavy side with glasses. She resembled her mother more than Jacqueline. She didn't seem to be impressed one way or the other by Reggie. Her mother was cordial toward him, but not warm.

"It's a pleasure to meet you all," Reggie said shaking each of their hands.

"Your bartender is waiting to take your orders," Jack said as Mrs. McKay brought in a tray of celery sticks, carrots, radishes and a dip. Reggie eyed the tray that everyone immediately dove into, and decided that so far the New England tradition was not saying much.

Mrs. McKay and Aunt Melba headed back to the kitchen. Mr. McKay and Aunt Beatrice occupied the stools at the bar and joined in a conversation with Jack about their hero, Richard Nixon. Melissa and Carol sat on a couch and seemed to be involved in conversations about their work. Jacqueline cornered Reggie by the window quizzing him about his work, where he met Carol and how long he had known her. Reggie began to relax. His drink, the reactions of Aunt Melba and Jacqueline to him boosted his confidence. He decided that there were some warm spots in this family and he just might be able to fit in.

"Okay everybody come in here and let me seat you," Aunt Melba called out. Bob, Beatrice, Melissa, and sister sit over there. Carol, Reggie and Jacqueline sit here, Jack at the head and I am at the other end. Now how is that? Beatrice would you like to say grace?"

"Yes, why don't we all join hands and bow our heads. We thank you Lord for all the wonderful blessings you bestow on us each day and for bringing us together this Thanksgiving and for the food we are about to receive. Bless those who prepared it. These and other blessings we ask in your name amen."

"Amen," they all said and Jacqueline let go of Reggie's hand she was squeezing. Reggie didn't know what to do. It was a bit erotic, but also a bit nerve-racking.

The golden brown turkey sat near Jack who began to carve and ask for specific requests. He looked at Reggie with a mischievous smile and asked, "White meat?"

"No sir, dark meat," Reggie said without returning the smile. No one seemed to notice the subtlety, except Reggie. He tried to dismiss it by concentrating on the other food that was coming his way. There was stuffing with chestnuts, whole berry cranberry sauce, mashed potatoes seasoned with garlic, green beans with almonds and yellow squash. After tasting everything, Reggie declared Aunt Melba was indeed a good cook. It wasn't a southern Thanksgiving dinner, but it was good.

"I understand you are from Tennessee. What do you think of living in the hustle and bustle of New York?" Aunt Beatrice asked Reggie.

"I find it invigorating. There are more job opportunities in New York than in Tennessee. So it really works for me," Reggie said.

"You have family back in Tennessee?" she asked.

"My mother and brother are still there. My father passed away a few weeks ago."

"Oh, I am so sorry."

"How is your mother?"

"She is doing okay. I spoke to her this morning and she is having dinner with my brother, his wife and son."

"What does your mother think of Richard Nixon's election?" Mr. McKay asked. Before Reggie could answer, Mrs. McKay interrupted. "She is probably as disillusioned as I am and I am sure before long you will be too."

"I disagree with you as always when it comes to politics," he responded.

Between sending a mouthful down his digestive tack and piercing his fork into the next load, Mr. McKay asked, "Well, Reggie what do Black folks have up their sleeves now that Martin Luther King is dead and Nixon is in the White House?"

Reggie suddenly felt full. He swallowed and said, a bit nervous, "I can't say that I know. I assume there will still be efforts to continue the work of Dr. King."

Mr. McKay, resting the fork between his plate and mouth with a stern look on his face and in a calm voice asked, "How will they do that? Nixon said police can shoot folks demonstrating in the streets. I can't believe those folks who demonstrate are willing to be shot."

Putting down the fork on his plate that was holding a piece of turkey, Reggie said, feeling a slight lump in his throat, "You are probably right, but there are other ways of working for equal rights than street demonstrations. Working with legislators is always a good strategy. Legislators have responded by passing equal employment, anti discrimination in housing and voting rights laws. So, getting people registered to vote and getting them out to vote will probably be a high priority in furthering Martin Luther King's legacy."

Carol leaned forward and in a calm voice said, "What Reggie was trying to say is that he can't speak for all Black people and there have been different strategies used in the civil rights movement."

Reggie was embarrassed. He felt like a kid just learning to speak. He tried to rethink what he had said and wondered if he had said something different from what he was thinking or was he inarticulate in his delivery. He couldn't think of anything that might have caused Carol to feel the need to clear it up except maybe her desire to protect him.

Uncle Jack asked in an aggressive tone. "How do you fit into the civil rights movement? Have you joined the Black Panther Party?"

Reggie wanted to say, yes I am a member and why don't you step outside and let me show you some of their tactics, but instead he said, No I am not a member of the Black Panther Party. The work that I do fits into the movement. It paves the way for others to enter the field." He decided it would be masochistic to bring up the affirmative action agreement he was working on since he was sure Mr. McKay would come out of his anti-affirmative action bag and add fuel to Jack's obvious attack.

Aunt Melba tuned in with, "Reggie, is this your first trip to Martha's Vineyard?"

"Yes, it is," Reggie said, thankful for the relief from the grilling of the disciples of George Wallace.

"Well, you must take a tour around the island. It's really a beautiful place and once you see it, I am sure you will come again."

"I like what I have seen already," Reggie said.

"Good," Aunt Melba said with a big smile on her face.

Reggie looked down at that piece of turkey clinging to his fork and pulled it up to his mouth hoping to escape other questions or attacks. Although he had now lost his appetite, he realized he had no choice except to clean his plate.

"Well, what do you think of our New England Thanksgiving dinner?" Aunt Melba asked Reggie.

"I think you have done the tradition well. I loved everything and can't wait to tell my mother what Thanksgiving is like in New England or should I say on Martha's Vineyard?"

"Well, I'm glad you enjoyed it," she said.

"Now who is going to help me clear the table for dessert?" Aunt Melba asked. Melissa and Carol volunteered. While they were waiting for dessert, Reggie felt Jacqueline's foot rubbing against his leg. He moved it away, but she followed and rested her foot against his. He decided it might become obvious if he kept moving so he let it stand. It sent erotic thoughts through his mind but his rattled nerves curbed any resulting feelings.

Carol soon walked in with a tray of pumpkin pie and whipped cream. Jacqueline moved her foot back into her shoe. Reggie exhaled. He looked up at Carol with a nervous smile then recognized what was on the tray. Oh no! not that fake sweet potato pie, he thought. However, it turned out that Aunt Melba could even turn a pumpkin into an inviting dish.

As the family sat silently around the table consuming their pie, the sun escaped from behind the clouds and a burst of its rays invaded the window in the dining room lighting it up like the arrival of a long-anticipated guest.

"Reggie would you like to take a walk and see some of Oak Bluff? It has an interesting history," Carol asked.

"Absolutely," Reggie responded. He was more than happy to get out of the house and a safe distance from Jacqueline, Jack and Mr. McKay.

The sun was out but not enough to warm those chilly winds coming in off the ocean. As soon as they were out of sight of the house, Reggie reached for Carol's hand and she reached over and kissed him on the cheek as they walked hand-in-hand along the street overlooking the ocean. The tension and embarrassment Reggie had felt at dinner from what he perceived as attacks seemed to melt away with that kiss. It felt like the ideal moment to pop the question; but he imagined if they were to announce an engagement, he might have to get off the island as quickly as possible and Woods Hole was too far away to swim. Anyway, the water was too cold for swimming.

"Isn't Oak Bluff the part of the island where Black people settled?" Reggie asked.

"Blacks live all over the island, but yes, this is the area where several generations of Blacks have owned property," Carol said in a very confident manner without looking at Reggie.

Fishing to satisfy his curiosity, Reggie asked, "Does your Uncle Jack's family have property here?"

"Not to my knowledge. I think I mentioned Uncle Jack is Cape Verdean. His ancestors came to this country from the Cape Verde Islands off the coast of Africa which had been occupied by the Portuguese during the era of slave-trading. They do not identify as Black Americans," Carol said in nonchalant manner.

"Oh, I see," Reggie said feeling he had gotten the scoop on Uncle Jack who might feel the need to go out of his way to distinguish himself from Blacks and a Black person's presence in his house might have exacerbated those feelings.

"Uncle Jack likes to joke a lot. He can be a lot of fun. He and Aunt Melba make a great couple. They complement each other. Father sometimes says that I inherited too much of Aunt Melba and not enough of him. One summer Uncle Jack's nephew, Carlton, was working here on the island at the tennis club. Uncle Jack introduced me to him and we dated that summer and corresponded for several months after. I think he fell in love with the girl he married last year. He never told me he had found someone else. He just began to write less and less. I got the message and stopped writing. Uncle Jack pretended he didn't know what happened and I pretended we mutually agreed it didn't work," Carol said as she looked away from Reggie and toward the ground.

"Were you in love with him?" Reggie nervously asked.

"I thought I was, but as I look back I decided it was merely infatuation. He didn't move me like you do," Carol said smiling.

Reggie pulled her close to him and said, "I'm glad."

They walked in silence, swaying in the wind that was becoming more vigorous, until they were approaching a two story-shingled, house with a wraparound porch. Carol said, "That house is one that is owned by a Black family." It was the one where Reggie saw the two Black men when they were driving in.

"There, ahead of us, is the dock where the ferry stops in the summer. Now let me show you one of my favorite spots when I was growing up. This is the famous Merry Go Round. Father used to bring me here for a ride and then we would walk up the street to the ice cream parlor and have a cone of strawberry ice cream. That was always my reward for doing something that made him and mother proud," she said with a bounce in her steps and a wide smile on her face.

"And what did they do when you were naughty?" Reggie asked with a mischievous smile on his face.

"I was never naughty," Carol said, poking her face into his.

The sun began to slide toward the horizon and the winds began to assert their full effect. Reggie put his arm around Carol's shoulder and pulled her close and said. "As much as I am enjoying having you to myself, I think I had better get you back to the family gathering before your father sends out a posse with your Uncle Jack leading the pack yelling Nixon's orders, 'shoot to kill.'"

"My father would never do that and Uncle Jack would never yell in public," Carol said in a burst of laughter.

Reggie's hand dropped off Carol's shoulders and he asked through a forced smile. "What's so funny about that?"

"I was imaging Uncle Jack running down the street yelling. It was such an absurd idea. He is such a proud man who wouldn't be caught dead embarrassing himself in public."

Reggie again reached for Carol's hand and said with a perfunctory smile, "Well, I still think we had better head back just in case he reveals a new side of himself."

Carol again leaned over and kissed Reggie on the cheek as they walked down the deserted street. The wind was whipping his face, but the kiss softened its blow and sent a rush of warmth charging through him. As they were about to come in view of the picture window of the house, Reggie let go of Carol's hand and placed his hands in his pockets as if he needed to warm them. Carol had no reaction.

"Carol, we were just about to go. I'm glad you are back so we can have a chance to say goodbye to Reggie," Aunt Beatrice said. "I promised to take the girls by some friends of ours for an after dinner drink."

"Okay Aunt Bee," Carol said as she hugged her, Melissa and Jacqueline and then headed for the bathroom.

"Reggie, it was nice meeting you. You are welcome to visit us anytime," Aunt Beatrice said in a very perfunctory way as she shook his hand. She was followed by Melissa extending a hand shake. Then Jacqueline came along and hugged Reggie, scratched the palm of his hand and whispered, "I hope you will take mother up on her invitation. There are clubs here where we can go dancing and have a good time."

"I really enjoyed sharing Thanksgiving with you all," Reggie said as he let go of Jacqueline's hand.

Carol returned to the living room and handed Reggie a glass of Harvey's Bristol Cream. They sat there sipping their drinks and looking out the window over the ocean watching the sun glide into the horizon and darkness began to blanket the island. The adults were in the family room watching some National Geographic show.

"Melba, I think I had better round up my troops and take them home and put Bob to bed. He needs all the rest he can get before retuning to work on Monday," Mrs. McKay said, rising up out of her chair.

"Well, come and get some of this food to take with you. Jack will have a fit if he has to eat turkey more than two consecutive days."

Aunt Melba and Uncle Jack walked to the car with Mrs. McKay and her troops. Aunt Melba hugged Reggie and said, "It was really great having you join us for Thanksgiving dinner and I truly hope that you will visit us again. Promise me you will."

"I promise."

"I made sure they put some white meat in those leftovers just for you Reggie. Now you enjoy it without us watching," Jack said with a mischievous smile on his face. Reggie wanted to tell him to kiss him where the good Lord split him, but made no comment. He just shook his hand and got into the car.

"Bye, bye Uncle Jack," Carol said waving her hand through the car's window.

After arriving home, Mr. and Mrs. McKay watched television until they began to nod. They then headed upstairs for bed. Reggie and Carol walked out to the edge of the tide. Night had fallen and the full moon, unobstructed by clouds, and the stars radiated the sky. Reggie put his hands around Carol's waist and pulled her close. She rested her head on his chest. This kind of moment may never come again. It's perfect. I should do it now and let the chips fall where they may, he was thinking.

Carol raised her head and said, "Our reservation for the ferry is ten o'clock Saturday morning. We will trail mother and father to the train station in New Haven. Mother will take the car there and we can get the train back to New York. Keeping a car in New York is too much trouble and you really don't need it."

"No problem," Reggie said, feeling the interruption had killed the mood.

"It's getting cold. Let's go in," Carol said. They sat watching television as their digestive systems asserted top priority for the blood flow, causing them to fall asleep. Carol was first to awaken. She kissed Reggie on the cheek and said good night.

Reggie lay across his bed trying to recapture the events of the day. Thoughts of those moments when he was used as target practice jumped up, but he couldn't hold on to them. His thoughts gravitated to the warm reception by Aunt Melba, the flirtation of Jacqueline and those intimate moments with Carol. He felt reassured he never wanted to let her go. He pulled out the ring, kissed it then drifted off to sleep.

Reggie was awakened the next morning by the smell of bacon frying. It was a welcome aroma. He fantasized it would be accompanied by hot biscuits, scrambled eggs with cheese and simmering grits. His mouth watered just thinking about it. He rolled out of bed and headed to the shower. While showering there was a knock on the door and a voice that said, "Breakfast will be ready in twenty minutes."

"Okay,, Reggie yelled back.

Mrs. McKay had prepared breakfast and Carol had set the table which contained a platter of that bacon he smelled surrounded by plain scrambled eggs. There was a stack of white bread toast on the side and a jar of strawberry jam. One out of three ain't bad, Reggie concluded.

Breakfast was somewhat quiet. Mr. McKay did not come down. Everybody around the table seemed to be waiting for the caffeine to kick in. After breakfast, Carol decided it was too windy to take out the bikes, so she decided they would go driving around the island. Although it was windy, the sun was out, adding some warmth to the atmosphere.

They stopped at a flee market which was a new experience for Reggie. It reminded him of the truck farmers who used to bring their produce into the city, park their trucks on the street and yell out to the residents what they had to sell. Housewives with their aprons around their waists and scarves wrapped around their heads would line up and inspect the collard greens, smell the peaches and thump the watermelons. Reggie bought some jam that reminded him of the ones his mother used to can in the fall and breads that the vendors claimed were baked that morning.

They stopped at the Native American Village and then drove on to Gay Head, the outlook at a peak in the island where an ambitious vendor left over from the summer had set up shop to sell tuna and lobster rolls. They drove to Edgartown and Carol showed him Walter Cronkite's house. Reggie was awed. He fell in love with the island and vowed to return regardless.

That evening Carol and Reggie had a lobster dinner in a romantic setting around a rustic table with a lantern lit with a candle at the famous Black Dog restaurant. When Reggie finally went to bed that night, he was exhausted but invigorated. He fell asleep listening to the ocean splashing against the shore. In the middle of the night he was awakened again by that haunting dream. He lay there in the dark wondering why does this damn dream keep popping up. He rolled into the fetal position and tried to go back to sleep, but sleep would not come.

Around seven o'clock, he heard movement in the house. He got up, went to the shower, then packed his bag for the trip back to New York. Before they left the house they had orange juice, coffee and blue-berry muffins. Reggie didn't feel hungry, but he didn't want to bring attention to his tired body, so he ate. Carol took the wheel as they headed for the ferry. Reggie didn't mind since he was tired. The ride to New Haven was mostly quiet. Carol turned on the radio as soon as the car landed in Woods Hole. Her choice of music was soft. Reggie continued to doze off. Carol would look over at him and smile. They finally pulled into the train station in New Haven and said their good byes to the McKays. Once on the train, they both fell asleep until the train pulled into Grand Central Station. Carol kissed Reggie on the cheek and said, "Go home and get some rest. I will talk to you tomorrow.

Reggie hugged her and said. That was a wonderful Thanksgiving. Thanks for the invitation."

"I love you." Carol said squeezing his hand.

CHAPTER 17

Reggie returned to work Monday morning unsure what to expect. He felt certain the Department of Labor had not taken any action on the affirmative action plan; therefore, as far as he could see, there was nothing to do. He wondered what Henry had in mind to fill his time. He sat at his clean desk with a cup of coffee and a muffin. He took a bite out of the muffin and raised the coffee to his lips. Noticing his hand around the coffee cup, he thought about the ring that was resting on his dresser. He began to try to come up with a strategy for getting it off the dresser and onto Carol's finger.

He began to evaluate some scenarios: Should I pop the question and invite Carol to go home with me for Christmas and surprise mom? A brazen stupid idea. Should I go alone and tell mom I am dating a white woman and intending to propose to her and give mom a chance to adjust to the idea? A Christmas killer. Or should I stay in New York and call mom and tell her to start making plans to come to the wedding? Just plain dumb.

He sat back in his seat and placed his feet on the desk and looked toward the ceiling, hoping the incubation process in his brain would quickly produce the ideal solution. It suddenly occurred to him he might be putting the cart before the horse. Carol had not said yes yet and he needed to make sure she would. In the meantime, he remembered he had not checked in with his mother since returning from the Vineyard. He decided to try out his phone and see if you could really call long distance. He had heard employees do it all the time. He dialed the number and it indeed went through and his mother answered.

"Hello mom. How did Thanksgiving turn out at Doug's?"

"Hello son. It's good to hear from you. Where are you?"

"I'm at work."

"Is everything all right?"

"Yes, things are fine. I can call you from here every once and a while."

"Oh, okay, things went okay at Doug's. Some of Doris's folks were there so they were all on good behavior. How was yours?"

"I really had a great time. Martha's Vineyard is a beautiful place and the people were nice."

"I assume they were white."

"Yes, they were."

"Was the person who invited you a man of a woman?"

"It was a woman."

"I hope you aren't getting into any mess with a white woman."

Feeling caught off guard, Reggie responded, "Don't worry about me. I can take care of myself."

"Well, I sure hope so. When will you be arriving for Christmas? I'm really looking forward to having you here. I plan to prepare the dinner the way I used to. It would mean a lot to me to have all of us together the first Christmas after losing your father."

"I haven't come up with a date yet, but I'll keep you informed," Reggie said now feeling rattled about how to proceed with his plans.

"It will be here before you know it so you had better start making your plans. Don't wait until the last minute and find out you can't get a reservation."

"I won't. I've got to go now. I promise to keep you informed."

Reggie hung up the phone and looked down at the crumbling muffin and steam-less coffee with no desire to finish them. His mother's response was not a surprise, but at the moment, it felt like he had swallowed a stone that landed in the bottom of his stomach. It was quite clear now that he would not invite Carol to accompany him home; however, he had to go. All that was left now was when to pop the question.

He pounded his fist on the desk and walked around the office asking himself why something that's usually a happy occasion must produce such anxiety. He began to have flashbacks of those insulting, awkward moments on Martha's Vineyard and began to have doubts about getting along with the men in that family. He pounded his fist into his hand and said to himself if she wants me I am going through with it. I have found love and I am not going to let it go and that is all there is to it.

When Reggie left the building for lunch, he walked over to Fifth Avenue. The Salvation Army Santa Clauses were ringing their bells hailing the arrival of Christmas and the needs of the less fortunate. Scaffolding surrounded the Rockefeller Center Christmas tree which was scheduled to be lit on Wednesday and Saks Fifth Avenue department store was in the process of decorating its windows. The scene brought back happy memories of Christmas when he believed in Santa Claus and was rushed off to bed on Christmas Eve to avoid having Santa put ashes in his stocking if he were caught awake.

After dropping coins into the Salvation Army bucket, he looked down across the Rockefeller Center skating rink at the workmen placing lights on the Christmas tree. He felt the onset of the Christmas spirit and decided the time was right. I will do it Wednesday during the lighting ceremony and work out the rest later. When he returned to the office he made a date with Carol to watch the ceremony.

Carol met Reggie at the corner of Fifth Avenue and Fifth Street. The enthusiastic crowd had already filled just about every space in Rockefeller Center and it was an hour before the ceremony was to begin. Reggie and Carol maneuvered their way as close as they could to the banner over the skating rink. The crowd provided a shield against the chill that had settled over the city. Reggie put his arm around Carol's waist and pulled her close as if to protect her from the elements and so that he would not lose her in the crowd. The jubilation in the crowd was contagious and kindled a celebratory spirit in Carol and Reggie. They swayed with the crowd and sang as the performers leading up to the lighting revved up the audience. As the time rolled toward the lighting, Reggie's confidence grew. He rubbed his pocket to make sure the ring was still there.

"Ladies and gentlemen the time has come. The mayor will join us in hitting the switch," the master of ceremony announced. The crowd began the count down: "ten, nine, eight, seven, six, five, four, three, two, one." The lights exploded into a burst of colors bringing life to the tree and a festive illumination to Rockefeller Center. "Merry Christmas" could be heard throughout the crowd. Reggie whispered, "Merry Christmas" into Carol's ear, kissed her on the cheek and squeezed the box with the ring in her hand.

"It's not Christmas yet," Carol said nervously. She slowly opened the box with her hand shaking. She was caught totally off guard and could not immediately speak. Her mind shifted to a Betty Friedan message in 'The Feminine Mystique'. Women had the right to break out of stereotype and choose lives more suited to their desires. Furthermore, Carol was thinking, this was a time of a sexual revolution when sex was not viewed as sacred and could be seen as casual (one night stands) without prolonged commitments. She had a career she liked, good friends to share, many of the advantages of living in New York, and a comfortable apartment in the culturally diverse Upper West Side. However, she thought of her feelings for Reggie as being strong and not casual and he was someone she wanted in her life. She felt a bit irritated that she was being forced into this predicament at this point in their relationship. She wasn't sure what was the right answer to give him.

"Oh, Reggie it's beautiful. I truly love you. You are full of surprises. But do you think we are ready for this?"

"I am," Reggie said feeling a lump in his throat.

"Well, I ask that you give me a chance to breathe and absorb the shock. Do you think your family will like me?"

"They will love you," Reggie answered, wondering if starting off a relationship with a lie was the right thing to do.

"How much time do you need to breathe and absorb the shock?" Reggie asked in a jovial tone trying to bring some lightness to the conversation and also to hide his disappointment.

"Not long I assure you," Carol said looking directly into Reggie's eyes.

They walked hand in hand out of the crowd to the subway and into the packed car. Carol kissed him on the cheek when the train reached her stop. Reggie squeezed her hand. Although he was disappointed that he did not get an immediate yes from Carol, he felt relieved that he had finally done it and some comfort in her immediate response that she really loved him. As he prepared for bed that night, without realizing it he began to hum Cole Porter's *"What is this thing called love this funny thing called love just who can solve its mystery why should it make a fool of me............."*

Carol, on the other hand, tossed and turned through the night. Her thoughts vacillated between joy of the proposal and questions about how she wanted to move forward with her life. Marriage was no longer the overpowering option for women. Many had shed their aprons for a career. But, she wondered, would a career be enough to make her happy. Living together without marriage had become a popular cultural change. Could that be an option, she wondered? It could provide a psychological liberation. However, such an arrangement would probably break her father's heart, she decided.

Her mind kept drifting back to the proposal and how Reggie made her feel. It was a feeling that had not surfaced before in her relationships. Surely, she thought, this is the way you would want to feel about someone you would want to be with the rest of your life. It just so happened that this person was Black, but overcoming cultural differences is something that many bicultural marriages work through, whether they are Asian and white or Polish and British. She dismissed the idea that race could be a game changer in their marriage. The power of love would smooth all the edges that they would encounter, she declared. And she felt certain that she and Reggie loved each other. She decided that her mother would embrace Reggie and her father would eventually come around since he said he only wanted her to be happy.

Shortly after Reggie arrived in his office the next morning the telephone rang. He assumed it was either Sandra or Henry with some busy work to keep him engaged while waiting for word from the Department of Labor. He answered in a very business tone.

"Good morning Don Juan. How are you this morning?" The soft voice asked.

Reggie's heart began to race. Determined to mask those feelings, he paused, took a sip of coffee and said, "I am doing fine just checking my list to see how many I charmed the day before. May I add you to the list of successes?"

"We will have to see about that. May I be so bold to ask if I can squeeze into your schedule for dinner today?" Carol asked.

"Let me check my schedule. I think I can manage that. How about five-thirty at the Cattlemen Club?"

"Whatever you say, sir," Carol answered.

Reggie hung up the phone trying to figure what her answer would be. Was the referenced to Don Juan a play up or down of his proposal? Whatever will be, will be, he declared while the lyrics to "What Is This Thing Called Love" rang in his mind again as he was reminded of the two times his love had been rejected.

Carol approached the table where he was already sitting patiently waiting for her. She seemed tired, but managed to smile. She kissed him on the cheek before sitting down. He responded with, "hey baby". He began to melt. He wanted to let go of any restraint and grab her and say, you mean the world to me. Don't let me down.

Carol looked across the table and into his eyes, reached for his hands and said, "my answer is yes."

Reggie leaped out of his chair and grabbed her and said, "I will do everything in my power to make you happy. I love you with all my heart."

"I know you will and I will do the same because I love you, too."

They returned to their seats and Carol said, "There are a lot of things we need to talk about to turn this into reality. For now, let's celebrate with our own engagement dinner."

The waiter arrived and Reggie said with watering eyes, "We would like to start with champagne."

After they dined on steak, baked potatoes, green salad and apple pie a la mode, the waiter brought coffee and Reggie sat back in his seat and asked, "When can we get this show on the road? I don't need a long engagement."

"Well, I don't need a big wedding and I pray my parents won't insist on one. I will be meeting them this Saturday morning. They are going on a cruise that leaves from the pier at Forty Fifth Street and I am going to meet them there before they sail. I will break the news to them then and tell them I am thinking about something small with just a few family members and friends. That will be enough news for them to digest at one time so I will hold off trying to discuss any details until they return. What about you? when will you break the news to your family?" Carol asked.

"Well, I don't have much choice. I'll have to call mom and tell her," Reggie said in a sobering tone that contrasted his earlier jovial mood.

"I am sure she will just be happy for you even if you are not next to her," Carol said, reaching across the table and squeezing Reggie's hand.

"She will be glad that I am not in New York alone as she likes to say," Reggie said trying to hide from Carol his doubts about his mother's reaction.

The previous sleepless night had begun to take its toll on Carol and Reggie recognized her eyes were growing heavy.

"You have spread enough joy for one day, my love. Why don't I get you home for a good night's rest?"

"Yes, I am beginning to feel tired and I have a ten o'clock flight to Washington tomorrow morning. I'll be back on Friday. Why don't we get together Saturday night? We can compare note on our families' reactions to the news and begin making plans."

"Sounds good to me, why don't I try my hand again at cooking and we can have a quiet dinner at my place while we compare notes," Reggie said while wondering what he would be able to say about his mother's reaction.

"Okay," until then, Carol said.

When Reggie arrived home he was overpowered with the desire to share the news with someone, but with whom he pondered. "Harry, Harry" he said. He will be surprised to hear from me and to hear the news. I'll ask him to return the favor and be my best man as I was his. It would be good for Carol and her family to meet him since he is white. Reggie picked up the phone and dialed his number.

"Hey buddy. What's happening in the Windy City?"

"Reggie, what the hell are you up to? What's going on in the Big Apple?"

"I'm glad you asked. I'm about to march down the aisle."

"Congratulations! Now tell me more. You've only been in New York a few months and have already found your dream. I guess New York isn't as bad as they say. Who is she and when did you meet her?"

"Her name is Carol McKay and I met her on the flight to New York. She's wonderful. I can't wait for you to meet her. As a matter of fact I want you to be my best man."

"I would be honored. When is the wedding?"

"She just accepted my proposal tonight so we haven't gotten that far. I will keep you informed."

"I'll tell mother. She will be excited and look forward to coming to the wedding."

"I'll be back in touch as things develop."

"I'm happy for you. I'll look forward to hearing the details."

Reggie hung up the phone and turned up the volume on the radio that was playing, Johnny Mathis' "The Look of Love." He sang along and popped his fingers in rhythm. He basked in the thought of how happy he would be with this beautiful, intelligent, loving woman, how proud he would be having her at his side and how lucky he was to have someone like her to love him.

The song ended and he began to prepare to go to bed when the demon of doubt crept into the room. He began to feel tired, then weary-haunted by thoughts of his mother's reaction to his decision and when and how he would break the news to her. Telling her on the telephone would be the easiest way to do it. He could walk away once it was done. But it was not a very brave or sensitive way, he concluded. He then remembered his mother's plea for him to come home for Christmas and his reluctant agreement that he would. Waiting until Christmas to tell her might be too long, depending on the plans he and Carol might make for the wedding. Inviting Carol to go home with him was an idea he had already declared as absolutely stupid. And now that was even more apparent considering how much his mother was looking forward to having the family together the first Christmas after his father's death. Carol's presence and a wedding announcement would be like a stink bomb falling down the chimney.

He walked around the room, slapping one hand into the other and shaking his head from side to side unable to escape the thought that if he did not come up soon with a clever strategy to resolve this conflict both Carol and his mother could become victims of his indecisiveness.

Fatigue set in and he was forced to go to bed but, he continued to wake up during the night, causing him to feel he had not slept at all. The next morning he felt tired and weary. Life would have been simpler if I had waited until after Christmas to propose, he mulled. The one thing he was glad for at the moment was that Carol would be away for a few days. It would give him time to come up with a plan without her noticing his stress.

He went into the office and checked with Sandra and was told there was no word from the Department of Labor and Henry was out of town for the rest of the week. He decided he would try to clear his mind by getting a head start on Christmas shopping. He walked down to Herald Square and browsed through Macy's and Gimbels, touching items but making no purchases. He thought if he walked incubation in his brain would take place and a solution to his dilemma would be revealed. So, he walked up to Columbus Circle, entered Central Park and began to track through the park, crushing the autumn leaves that had fallen to the ground meeting their destiny. He stopped along the way and sat on a bench. As he sat there watching the squirrels searching through the leaves for food and listening to the birds chirping from the barren branches of the trees, a thought as clear as the sun entered his mind. He would go home alone and the day after Christmas he would make the announcement. It was the right thing to do. He would have to find a way to make that decision palatable to Carol without making her feel she would be rejected by his family.

While he was having dinner sitting at his table that evening, the telephone rang. It was Carol checking to see how he was doing. Reggie jumped into a jovial tone and said.

"Hey baby, how is the future Mrs. Morton doing in our nation's capital this evening?"

"I am doing fine, Mr. Morton. How was your day?" Carol asked. "Have you had a chance to speak with your mother yet?"

Reggie immediately felt nervous. He paused then said in a forced jovial tone. "No, I decided to make the news a part of my Christmas surprise."

"Oh no! Mother and I had planned to invite you to have Christmas with us in Ridgefield. Can't you surprise her over the telephone?" Carol asked in a tone of great disappointment.

"Baby, she has been planning on me coming for Christmas since my father passed. This is going to be a tough Christmas for all of us. I think I need to be there."

"You are right. I'll have to explain the situation to mother and tell her that I am going with you. Under these circumstances, she will be disappointed but will understand."

"Why don't we avoid disappointing either of them? Christmas is such a special time for families. So, I can imagine how disappointed your parents would be not having you with them at that time. So why don't I spend Christmas with my family and you spend it with yours and we meet up in Ridgefield for New Year's. How does that sound?" Reggie asked, thinking he had found the perfect solution that would do the least amount of damage to all parties involved.

"I guess that would be fair. Mother will be disappointed but I think I can sell that idea to her," Carol said, although she was very disappointed she would not have this opportunity to meet his mother.

"Okay, have a good night's rest. I will talk to you when I get back into town."

"Good night, baby, I'm counting the minutes until you are in my arms again," Reggie said as he kissed the phone.

Reggie hung up the phone and exhaled. He felt great relief that issue had been resolved in the way it had been. He knew he would sleep well that night and, indeed, he did. The next day he called his mother and confirmed that he would be coming home for Christmas and would try to get there by Christmas Eve depending on what was going on at work.

" Thank the Lord, I'm really looking forward to having you home, son."

Carol was standing at the pier when the limousine drove up. The driver opened the door for the passengers to exit and her father stepped out and embraced her. She threw her arms over his shoulders just as her mother was stepping out. Her mother was wearing dark shades which made her unsure, but she thought she glimpsed a ring on Carol's finger that was not there before. She felt flustered as she hugged Carol, but made no effort to clarify what she felt she had seen. Her father led the way to their cabin. Carol followed, holding a bottle of champagne close to her chest protecting her secret until the appropriate time. The outside cabin had sliding doors that lead to a terrace. They all walked out on the terrace and marveled at the Manhattan skyline under clear blue skies.

"I brought this champagne to wish you happy sailing and to celebrate. Father, will you do the honor of popping the cork and mother will you get us some glasses."

As her mother stepped inside to fetch the glasses, Carol handed her father the bottle with her right hand and let her left hand drop to her side against her jacket. Her father poured the champagne and they raised their glasses, Carol's in her right hand. She then said, "Happy sailing" then raised her left hand and turned it so they could see the ring.

Her mother and father froze watching her hand. Her mother's hand began to shake as she realized she was not seeing things when they arrived.

"Not that Nigger!" her father blurted out.

"Robert!" her mother shouted.

"Don't Robert me. This is my baby. I won't stand for her falling into the gutter with some social climbing ghetto thug."

"Robert, watch your mouth!" her mother shouted.

"Do you have any idea Carol about what you are doing? Do you know what you are up against married to a Black man? Are you prepared to handle the ostracism? Do you realize what your mother and I will look like if we go along with this disaster? Come to your senses young lady," He said as he sat down and lowered his head into his cupped hands.

"Shame on you Robert. You have met Reggie and you know he is not anything like a ghetto thug. He is a responsible young man with a promising career. He grew up in a segregated society, so he knows what he's getting into marrying a white woman and our daughter has been in relationships, so she can make a wise decision about what makes her happy. The world is changing Robert and it's time you get on board," Mrs. McKay said with a stern look on her face and her hand shaking.

Carol walked over to her father and put her arm around his shoulder and said, "You and mother have always told me that all marriages have ups and downs and that love is the only thing that sustains them through these times. Reggie and I love each other and are willing to face our problems together. I have never met anyone who makes me feel the way he makes me feel. He is an honest, decent and responsible man. He deserves your respect and I need to know that you support me in my decision."

Her father stood up, grabbed her and held her tight as tears began to roll down his face. "Baby you are all I got and I only want the best for you. It would break my heart if I thought you were being subjected to the kind of hatred people feel for people like Reggie. I will do my best to see him as you see him because I love you. But promise me you will try to look past how he makes you feel and consider how well you are prepared to withstand people constantly looking at you and your children with disapproval in their eyes."

"I promise father," Carol said feeling a bit relieved thinking she had softened his unanticipated strong resistance which had been unsettling for her.

Her mother, trying to regain some composure and minimize the impact of some of her husband's remarks, took a sip of her champagne then walked over to them as her husband was letting go of Carol. She hugged Carol and said, "You are going to be just fine, my dear. You and Reggie are going to make a fine couple. You represent the future. We old folks have to get used to the change in our society. It's high time. Have you all come up with any details yet?"

"No, we plan to get together tonight and begin that discussion."

"I hope you will wait until we get back and let us be a part of the discussion of time and place."

"I promise."

There was a call for all visitors to leave the ship. Carol hugged her parents and again wished them a happy trip and apologized for injecting a rocky start. As she walked toward the subway, she scoured for composure. The angry eyes of her father with tears meandering the lines that had been formed on his face flashed before her. In her search for some solace, she remembered her father saying he would try to see Reggie the way she did. She knew he loved her and believed that he would eventually. She knew Reggie would be waiting to hear from her about the outcome, but she needed some time to digest what had happened so that she could give him the best accounting. Instead of going shopping as she had planned, she decided to return to her apartment and do some long-needed cleaning and laundry, busy work that would distract her. She wasn't due at Reggie's until seven. By then, she decided, her thinking would be clearer.

Reggie spent his day trying to perfect his culinary skills. He wondered what had happened with Carol and her parents, but was too worried about how his smothered pork chops would turn out; whether his mashed potatoes would have lumps; or his shrimp would boil too long, to dwell on how shocked the McKays may have been.

Reggie was cursing himself for forgetting to buy napkins as he sat the table and laid out his bachelor napkins (folded paper towels) when the intercom rang announcing Carol. He gave everything a once over, including himself and declared that except for the damn napkins he had done a good job. Feeling a bit exhausted, he greeted Carol with a casual hug. She held tight, burying her head in his chest.

When she let go after the prolonged embrace, she asked, "Do you really love me?"

"As Johnny Mathis would say, 'Until the Twelfth of Never,'" Reggie said. He interpreted the question and hug as absence making the heart grow fonder and declared the night was going to be a very fruitful evening.

"Let me give you a glass of wine before you tell me how things went with your parents. Did you tell them?"

"Yes, I did."

"Well, have a sip of this and let me have it," Reggie said feeling a bit anxious. They sat down on the couch next to each other and Carol began.

"They didn't in the least expect it. They stood in silence when I first showed them the ring. Once it sunk in mother was excited. She asked that we don't finalize plans for the wedding until they return from the trip."

"And what about your father?" Reggie asked nervously.

"I think he is still trying to grasp the idea that his little girl has grown up. I don't think he ever really thought of me being married, so it will take a little time to adjust to the idea. That's probably like most fathers, especially with their only child. They seem to have a need to be their child's hero throughout their lives," Carol said as casually as she could, hoping her tailored account would be convincing.

"Did you have a chance to talk about our plans for Christmas?" Reggie asked.

"No, the engagement consumed us until there was a call for visitors to leave the ship. I'm sure what we agreed to will be fine with mother. After all, she now has something else to focus on beside Christmas," Carol answered, relieved that Reggie had not pushed her for more details of her father's response.

"Well then, can you and I at least come up with a tentative time for the wedding? I would like to be able to give some indication when I break the news to mom," Reggie said.

"Oh, yes we can do that. What are you thinking? I remember you saying you didn't need a long engagement."

"How about right after Christmas?"

"You can't be serious. That wouldn't be enough time to even have it at City Hall."

"Well, you said you didn't need a big wedding. So how long does it take to plan a small intimate wedding?"

"More than a month I assure you. How about at Valentine? That seems appropriate. Maybe that could be arranged. But let's give mother a stab at it to see what her schedule would permit. After all, a lot of the occasion is for parents' memories as well as ours. They will be back next Friday, okay?"

"Okay."

"Now my princess, let me feed you," Reggie said proudly. He brought out the first course-boiled shrimp with his homemade cocktail sauce. It was the same recipe used by the caterer he worked for when he was in high school.

"Well, don't tell me I lucked out and am getting a husband with a stamp of approval from Craig Claiborne. If that is the case, we should get married tomorrow," Carol teased.

"Well, Craig and I have traded recipes every now and them," Reggie joked. "However, you haven't tasted my premier dish for the evening."

"I can't wait," Carol said as she dipped her shrimp into the cocktail sauce. "This is really delicious."

Reggie returned to the kitchen and brought out his pork chops smothered in onion gravy, his lump- free garlic mashed potatoes, English peas and warm rolls he had bought at the store.

After Carol tasted everything, she said, "When we get married I am going to be ashamed to prepare you a meal. I can't compete with this."

"All I need from you is your love," Reggie said as he looked across the table feeling proud.

After they had devoured the main course and the table had been cleared, Reggie said, "Now you don't think I would have you over for dinner and not give you a dessert." Carol sat wondering what more embarrassment she would have to endure when Reggie walked in and placed this pie on the table.

"Don't tell me you also baked this pumpkin pie." Carol said.

"No baby, I bought the sweet potato pie at a bakery in Harlem. I think you will be able to tell the difference."

"Oh," Carol said looking very inquisitive as she dug her fork into it. "Indeed I can tell the difference. It's sweeter with a slightly different texture. It's delicious." Reggie leaned back in his chair with a smile on his face.

During the night as they made love Carol squeezed Reggie tighter than usual. He was flattered. She headed for home early the next morning. She had to prepare a briefing regarding her trip to Washington. Reggie spent the day reading his New York Times, napping and reflecting on the night before. He wondered if things had gone as well with her parents as Carol had described, especially with her father. He wondered if she was engaging in half-truths as he was.

Monday morning was cloudy, a temperature hovering around freezing with twenty mile an hour winds. Radio stations had begun to play Christmas music. Reggie walked out of his building and was greeted by a gust of wind. He took a deep breath and decided that he could feel Christmas in the air. He was reminded of the days when his mother would begin baking weeks before Christmas, filling the house with the sweet aroma of nutmeg, vanilla extract, pecans, raisins and coconut. She would be humming Christmas carols as she worked. He and his brother would begin the game of guessing how many of their requests Santa would leave in their shoe boxes on Christmas Eve. Each day leading up to Christmas, Reggie would walk by the Rexall Drugs store window and admire the display of gifts he wished he could buy. He wanted to bring back as much of that spirit of Christmas for his mother. He certainly could buy the gifts he wanted. He hoped he would get home in time to help decorate the tree and go with her to visit neighbors as they used to. But, at some point, he was going to have to break the news which was bound to put a damper on things. He wished he could avoid it. He needed some reason to justify his actions. He rationalized that life had changed for everyone over the past fourteen years since the Supreme Court's decision in the Brown case.

Blacks had been assimilated into previously all-white domains of the society resulting in close contact between the races and the inevitable development of intimate relationships. His relationship, he declared, was one of the byproducts of that decision in spite of the Black Power movement. Also, he had heard rumors that some of the leaders of the Movement were in relationships with white women. Surely, he declared, his mother would understand his relationship with Carol after he pointed out how the country was on the threshold of a cultural change and that his marriage was part of that change. She could say the same thing to any of her friends or neighbors who were clinging to old ideas.

Reggie stepped into his office ready to begin whatever project Henry had for him, but his desk was still empty and Sandra said Henry was overwhelmed with priorities associated with the execution of the Navy contract. She told Reggie that Henry would meet with him as soon as possible. Reggie decided he would focus on matters at hand-Christmas shopping and wedding planning until he was given some direction from Henry or was allowed to return to the Texas Oil account for the lack of something to do.

Reggie informed Sandra he was taking an early lunch and headed for Macy's. As he passed St. Patrick's Cathedral, a limousine pulled up and a bride got out and started up the steps. Reggie noticed about six men stepping out of another car in their long-tail tuxedos. It suddenly occurred to him he only had Harry and his brother as groomsmen for a wedding. He wondered what was Carol's definition of a small wedding and who could he possibly ask if her number of bridesmaids exceeded two. The question haunted him until he walked into Macy's which was decorated to assure that you could only think of Christmas after you crossed its threshold.

There were huge ropes of garland decorated with colorful bulbs, artificial fruit and holly berry branches hanging from the ceiling across the aisles. Christmas music was playing in the background. It captured Reggie and sent him roaming through the store. A middle aged saleslady with her hair pinned on top of her head collared him as soon as he stepped off the escalator onto the floor for women's attire. She pleasantly offered her services. He explained he was shopping for his mother. She gave him a once- over and offered him a seat. She disappeared and returned with a cream colored "Sunday go to meeting" dress she assured him his mother would love. He agreed. She disappeared again and returned with a pair of shoes and a leather purse she assured him would be the perfect accessories. Reggie gave her his mother's sizes and she gleefully returned with everything all boxed. He went on and bought a sweater for his brother and a silk scarf for his sister-in-law. He wanted to give his nephew a bicycle which he would ask his mother to shop for if he were not able to get home in time. He felt good he had accomplished all this in one day. Now, he wondered, what could he do for an encore for Carol after giving her the ring so close to Christmas. He decided to leave that decision for another day.

Reggie returned to the office and immediately checked with Sandra to see if Henry had set up a time to see him. He had not and Sandra said, "Don't worry about seeing Henry. He is going to be occupied with the new contract at least until the New Year. Anyway, from now until Christmas, office parties and the arrival of gifts from clients and would-be-clients will become the activities of the day. So if your liver is not already trained to handle onslaughts of liquor, I suggest you start training it because the liquor will flow," Sandra said smiling with excitement in her eyes.

"I don't think I need to do much training," Reggie said, wondering how much of Sandra's description was exaggerated. If Gordon's drinking habit is the standard, he concluded he would indeed have to do some training.

"You can bring your girlfriend to the president's party. A lot of people will bring their spouses. I think the president is concerned about a proper decorum at his party. He wants to promote this thing about us being one big family. From what I can tell, he is the only one here who sees us that way. But we all put on a show for him, after all it's part of the spirit of Christmas, Sandra said as she winked at Reggie."

"Thanks for the heads-up," Reggie said, wondering what people would think if they saw Carol on his arm. Well, they certainly had no authority to harass her like the authorities did the white woman in that play, "The Great White Hope." Nor could they expel her the way they did the white girl in his freshman class at Davis who was openly dating a Black student. The only power they have is over him, he suddenly realized. He felt anxious and thought about Jeff and Harriett's reactions to him walking into the party with Carol. He walked back to his office feeling a loss of the Christmas spirit.

Sitting in front of the television that evening watching all the bad news of the day, the telephone rang. It was Carol.

"Hello," Reggie answered.

"What's the matter?" Carol asked. "You sound tired."

"Oh, Carol, it's you. I'm fine. I was just sitting here watching the news. What's happening with you?"

"I got a call from mother this morning. She has decided to invite us to lunch on Saturday when they return to talk about arrangements for the wedding. She will take a train home later. Father is having some problem with his stomach, so he is going to head back. Is that okay with you?"

"That would be fine. How did your presentation go?"

"Oh, it went fine. I'm thankful I don't have any further trips before the New Year, especially with Christmas so close and the short time we have before the time we are thinking about for the wedding."

"I'm glad you don't' either so I can see you more often," Reggie said in jest.

"Okay lover boy, why don't we meet at my place around twelve Saturday. Mother wants to go to her favorite Jamaican restaurant so we can meet her there around one."

"I will see you at twelve Saturday," Reggie said. As soon as he hung up the phone, he began to wonder if Carol's father knew how his stomach would feel on Saturday a week ago.

When Reggie awoke on Saturday morning, his room was still dark even though it was seven-thirty. He could hear the pelting of raindrops on the leaves that had collected outside his window. He pulled the sheet up over his shoulders and stared at the ceiling. A feeling of melancholy crept in. He wasn't sure the source for it. His thoughts turned to his mother's possible reaction to his news and then to Carol's father's possible struggle to accept him as his son-in-law and then the fact that he only knew two people he felt comfortable asking to be in his wedding.

He rolled out of bed in an effort to erase those thoughts and headed for the shower. As he began to apply the magic shave to his skin, it suddenly occurred to him how repulsive the smell would be to Carol when they were living together. He couldn't imagine how he would deal with that. Would he have to endure ingrown hairs and a ruddy complexion or reveal an embarrassing ethnic practice that had worked for Black men for some time? He lingered in the shower letting the water pulsate over his body, hoping the sensation would wash away the thoughts that were haunting him.

Reggie arrived at Carol's promptly at twelve on Saturday. On their way to the restaurant, they agreed they would tell Carol's mother that they wanted a small wedding in the near future. They arrived at the restaurant before Mrs. McKay and claimed the reservation and ordered Bloody Marys.

Carol's smiled at Reggie across the table and asked, "Do you remember our first time here?"

Her smile swept away those melancholy thoughts that had been haunting him and he responded, with a very seductive look on his face, "Like it was yesterday," then threw her a kiss across the table.

"Hello you two. How are the Bloody Marys?" Mrs. McKay asked as she stood over the table with a forced smile plastered on her face.

"Oh mother, you look great," Carol said as Reggie stood up and pulled the chair for her to sit.

Mrs. McKay hugged Reggie and said, "It's really good to see you again."

"The same here," Reggie said feeling a bit anxious.

The waiter came and Mrs. McKay ordered a Bloody Mary and commented how the restaurant looked as it did the last time she was there and how pleasant it was to see that.

"How was the cruise?" Carol asked.

"It was wonderful. The weather was great until we were docking back here."

"How is father?" Carol asked.

"Oh, he is fine."

"What about his stomach?"

"Oh yes, he must have gotten a hold of some bad seafood. He will be all right."

The waiter arrived with her drink and she sipped it and asked, "How are things on your job, Reggie?"

"Things have slowed down for the holidays."

"That must be a relief considering the pace of things in advertising."

"I guess so. I have to get used to it all."

"You two are full of surprises," Mrs. McKay said looking from Carol to Reggie with a forced smile. "It took your father and I a couple of days to digest the announcement of your engagement. It seemed so sudden. However, if you have found love enough to hold you together, we are happy for you. You will probably have some rocky times in your lives as a couple, but if you love each other enough you will be able to withstand it. Your father and I will stand with you. How do your mother and brother feel about it Reggie?"

"I haven't had a chance to discuss it with them yet. I plan to tell them when I go home for Christmas."

"Oh, are you going home for Christmas?"

Before Reggie had a chance to answer, Carol jumped in and said,

"Reggie and I discussed your invitation and decided I would spend Christmas with you and dad and he would go home to his family and spend New Year's with us."

"I guess that's okay," Mrs. McKay said in a solemn tone.

"Well, what kind of wedding are we talking about?" Mrs. McKay asked.

"Mother, Reggie and I were thinking about a small ceremony in February maybe Saturday, February 22nd."

"My my, that's pretty soon for even a small wedding. What do you call a small wedding?"

"Three or four bridesmaids and no more than twenty or thirty guests," Carol answered.

"I think that's workable. The numbers seem right and if we begin planning now, I guess we could probably get it together within your preferred time. We will have to get out the invitations the first week in January. Your father thought it might be more convenient for your friends and Reggie's family to have it in New York. He knows someone at the Riverside Church which is a beautiful cathedral and both the wedding and reception could be held there."

"Oh mother, that sounds wonderful. Reggie, I will show you the church. I know you will like it and your family will only have to travel to New York instead of going on to Ridgefield."

"That's a great idea." Reggie said enthusiastically. He figured he could now present the whole idea to his mother, including planning Doug's and her trip to New York. He could also call Harry and give him the date. He was sure Harry's family would also come.

Reggie and Carol rode in the taxi with Mrs. McKay up to Grand Central for her trip home. After bidding her good-bye, they hugged each other in the station and declared they were well on their way. Carol said, "This is going to take a lot of work. I think I will have to scale back on doing all the things I would usually do for Christmas."

"There will be many more Christmases. We will make up for this one next year," Reggie said feeling Carol had relieved him of the pressure to outdo the engagement ring. "Oh, by the way the president of our agency is having a Christmas party for staff and their guests some time next week. How about coming along with me?"

"Sure, when is it?" Carol asked as if it were a foregone conclusion that she would go with him.

"As soon as I find out the exact date and time I'll let you know. I understand it's going to be in his conference room and sort of like an open house. Staff will come and have champagne and help themselves to the buffet and be greeted by the president, mingle for a moment then go. I don't imagine we would need to be there more than an hour."

"That's fine. We only have individual office parties at my company. Oh Reggie, I am going to need your list of people you want to invite to the wedding. We will also need to tell the caterer the number of guests."

"Let me see. Right now, I can only think of eight or ten at the most. Now that should help keep it a small wedding. I'll give it some more thought and write down addresses for all I can think of. Speaking of numbers, you told your mother you were thinking about three or four bridesmaids. Do you know now which it will be? I need to decide on groomsmen."

"I'm leaning toward three, but father might want one of his nieces to be in it."

"Well, the sooner I know the better."

"Okay"

As the subway pulled out of Times Square on their way home, Carol looked at Reggie with a forced smile hovering over her face and said, "We haven't talked about where we will live after we are married. Please tell me you don't expect us to move to Riverdale. Manhattan is so much more convenient. You could move into my apartment. Say you will."

"I think I can buy that. I'll have to give notice now if I am going to break my lease. You got your wish. Is there anything else I can do to please my bride?"

"Not at the moment," Carol said with a look of mischief in her eyes. She said good bye to him as the train pulled into her station. Reggie leaned back and rested his head on the window of the train and closed his eyes. A major hurdle was behind him he was thinking, one down and two to go.

The president's party happened on Thursday from three to six. Carol arrived at four dressed in a navy blue suit looking like she just posed for the cover of Vogue Magazine. Reggie felt like he had just been crowned "man of the year." They walked into the conference room and were greeted by the piercing eyes of Jeff and Harriett. Reggie pretended he did not see them. He guided Carol to the president and introduced himself and then Carol. The president, with a perfunctory smile that never changed while shaking their hands, thanked them for coming and wished them a happy holiday then looked over Reggie's shoulder as if he were looking for someone he was expecting.

A waiter approached Reggie and Carol and offered them champagne. As they began to sip, Gordon, steady on his feet but glassy in his eyes looking like he arrived at three and never disappointed the waiter when offered a glass of champagne, walker up to them. His wife, an unpretentious woman in a plain black dress, minimum make up and her hair in a pony tail, trailed behind him.

"Reggie, my man, Merry Christmas. How have you been and who is this beautiful woman standing next to you?" he asked.

"Carol, I want you to meet my boss, Gordon, the top account executive in the agency," Reggie said joyfully, glad for Gordon's rescue from the president.

"Well, for now he has another boss, but I will accept the compliment. Oh, yes, Reggie and Carol meet my wife, Helen."

"I am finally glad to meet you, Reggie. Gordon has spoken of you often. I hope you are adjusting to this place," she said sarcastically. "Carol is that an engagement ring you are wearing? Could I see it? It's beautiful. Have you set a date?"

"We are looking at February 22nd if we can get everything together by then."

"Congratulations."

"You son of a gun you move fast don't you. Congratulations," Gordon, whose glassy eyes now seemed a bit perplexed with the news, said.

"Merry Christmas you guys, Gordon, Helen, Reggie," Henry said as he approached the group.

"Henry, I want you to meet Carol McKay." Reggie responded.

"Hello Miss McKay and a Merry Christmas to you," Henry greeted her with a handshake.

"If you ladies don't mind, could I borrow Gordon and Reggie for a minute to take care of some business?" Henry asked.

"You have my approval," Helen said sarcastically. As they walked away, she seemed to relish the moment and appeared to engage Carol in animated conversation.

"I just wanted to thanks you Gordon for lending us Reggie to work on the affirmative action plan. I've been talking to the president about the plan and he wants us to get ahead of the Labor Department's approval and develop a summer intern program in management for minority juniors in college. I told him that you had direct experience in this area, Reggie. So I want you to begin working on that after the holidays. Gordon, depending on how long it takes for us to put such a plan into action, and what kind of response we get back from the Department of Labor on the affirmative action plan, we may need to keep Reggie a little longer than we anticipated, if you don't mind," Henry said.

"Well, you may also want the approval of Carol McKay. She is going to become Mrs. Reggie Morton on February 22nd ," Gordon said trying to muster up a smile.

"No kidding," Henry said as his countenance changed in a blink from sober to shock. In a tone more appropriate for condolences than congratulations, he said congratulations and shook Reggie's hand. "Gordon I really appreciate your cooperation in this matter. Reggie, we will talk further after New Year," he said as he dashed away.

Noticing that Helen and Carol seemed to be really hitting it off and feeling the effects of two glasses of champagne, Reggie asked Gordon to excuse him. He took a deep breath and started to walk over to Jeff and Harriett. When Harriett noticed, she turned her back to him and walked over to the buffet table.

"Hey man, how have you been?" Reggie asked Jeff.

"I'm hanging in there. What about yourself?"

"Things are about to pick up with the affirmative action plan. The president wants to develop a summer intern program in management for minority college juniors," Reggie answered.

"What about your personal life? I see you brought your old lady here today to meet the president. That's mighty brave of you. Giving you a job is one thing. Watching you mess around with their women is another. A lot of liberal whites often have lines that they are not interested in having Blacks cross." Jeff warned.

"I know we will face problems but we have discussed that and are ready to deal with whatever comes up," Reggie said.

"What does that mean?" Jeff asked.

"We are getting married in February," Reggie said before he realized what he had done.

"What!" Jeff said. "What did your mother say when you told her?"

"I haven't told her yet. I am going to tell her when I go home for Christmas," Reggie answered.

"With Carol at you side?" Jeff asked anxious to hear the answer to that question.

"No, I'm going home alone," Reggie said as he began to feel anxious and the loss of the champagne effect.

"At least you are using your head in that situation," Jeff said, shaking his head in disbelief.

"I would like for you to be in my wedding." Those words also just slipped out of his mouth.

Jeff stood in silence with a "you got to be kidding look" on his face.

"Think about it before you answer. You are one of the few friends I have in New York," Reggie said in a humble tone.

The statement and tone disarmed Jeff a bit and he said, "Let me think about it. What is the date?"

"Hello you two. What are you so serious about at this Christmas party?" Carol asked in a very kind, unassuming tone as she walked up behind Reggie and looked at Jeff.

"Oh Carol, this is Jeff. He works in the creative department. We were just talking about the affirmative action plan." Reggie answered from a dry tongue almost choking.

Carol extended her hand and with a very friendly smile said, "I'm glad to meet you."

"Likewise," Jeff said with a half smile.

"Are you working with Reggie on the affirmative action plan?" Carol asked.

"No, we work together on the Texas Oil account. I'm just following up on the status of the plan," Jeff answered cordially, in deference to Reggie.

"I was telling Reggie what a great opportunity it is to be chosen to develop such an important policy for the agency," Carol said.

"It certainly could be," Jeff responded in a somewhat sarcastic tone.

"Would you like to check out the buffet?" Reggie asked Carol.

"Yes. It was nice meeting you Jeff. I look forward to seeing you again."

"Okay Jeff, I'll check you out before I leave for Christmas." Reggie said as he wasted no time walking to the buffet. As he and Carol approached the table, Harriett noticed them and walked swiftly out of the room as if she were late for an appointment. Both Carol and Reggie took note but made no comment. As they sampled the various dishes, Reggie looked across the room and saw Rick pointing in his direction, his face contorted with what seemed like anger and whispering to the person standing next to him. That bastard, is he still glowing in the knowledge of how he stole my idea or is he plotting something more sinister this time, Reggie wondered.

"Have you had enough, baby?" Reggie asked Carol.

"If you have," she answered. "Let me say good-bye to Helen."

Reggie looked for Gordon and noticed that he was talking to the president. It seemed that he was having trouble getting some point across. The president looked away and accidentally made eye contact with Reggie and, seemingly embarrassed, quickly turned back to Gordon. He put his hand on Gordon's shoulder and began to say something as if he were trying to comfort a child.

"Let's go. That was easy enough. It didn't seem at all like I had pictured it. You know advertising has the reputation of being a cutthroat business. I didn't get that impression today. So I guess the thought of Santa Claus putting ashes into their stockings can transform them into civil human beings," Carol said as they walked out of the room

"I'm glad we convinced you today. One down and millions and millions to go," Reggie said in jest. However, he couldn't get the picture out of his mind of Rick pointing at him and Gordon's conversations with the president and the president looking at him in embarrassment. Unable to figure out what might be going on, he wondered if he was being a bit too sensitive. He turned to Carol, looking as if he had found a safe refuge to escape his thought and said. "You look fantastic. Thanks for coming with me."

"Thanks for inviting me. I really enjoyed meeting Helen and Gordon. The guy from creative seemed nice, too. I forget his name," Carol said.

"You mean Jeff."

"Yes, Jeff. We will have to get together with him sometime."

"I might ask him to be in our wedding," Reggie said as if he were testing the idea.

"I didn't get the impression that you knew him that well. But that would be great if you decide," Carol said enthusiastically.

"Oh yes we have been working together every since I started here." Reggie responded without looking directly at Carol.

As they walked toward the subway Carol said, "It looks like I won't see you again until New Year. You are leaving Wednesday and I won't get back from Ridgefield until Wednesday. I promised mother I would come up this weekend and stay over a few days helping her get ready for Christmas and preparing for the wedding. She insisted on a Christmas celebration especially since she already invited Aunt Melba and Uncle Jack for dinner."

"I'll be counting the days until New Year. Wish your folks a Merry Christmas for me." Reggie wanted to kiss Carol, but settled for a loving hug just before boarding the subway. When the train pulled into Carol's station, she kissed him on the cheek.

"Wish your family a Merry Christmas for me and I will see you New Year. Don't forget to call me and let me know your mother's reaction to the news about the wedding. I am anxious to know." She then waved at him as the train pulled out of the station.

"I will," Reggie said as he threw her a kiss.

CHAPTER 18

Reggie looked out the window as the plane began its descent into Memphis. He recognized the expressway leading to the airport and the neatly kept single family homes lining the streets. He exhaled and rested his head on the back of his seat. The overcast sky and chilly temperature resembled past Christmases. He began to imagine walking into the house and inhaling the smell of a cake fresh out of the oven, shopping for the perfect tree and decorating it with all those ornaments his mother had preserved for years, and stacking those boxes wrapped in red, green and white paper and colorful ribbons under the tree. After the pilot brought down the plane in a smooth landing and he exited behind the slow moving passengers, Reggie walked into the terminal and was greeted by the velvet voice of Bing Crosby meandering through the terminal singing, "A White Christmas." He felt like he was about to cross over into toy land where you can never return again. The mood helped him endure the long wait for his bag to come rolling off the conveyer belt and the sluggish, but friendly clerk at the car rental counter.

After his drive to Smoky Mountain, Reggie pulled his car into the driveway where his father's old Mercury used to sit. It was a sobering moment. He took a deep breath and thought of the challenge he was facing to make this Christmas a happy one for his mother.

He walked into the house as quietly as possible trying to provoke a surprise. He was indeed greeted by the aroma of that cake coming from the oven. The box of decorations sat in the middle of the living room floor. He walked into the kitchen and grabbed his mother from behind.

"Oh son, I am so glad to see you!" his mother blurted out with tears rolling down her cheeks.

"Merry Christmas, mom. I am really glad to be home. I see you are keeping up the tradition. Is that going to be my favorite pineapple coconut cake?"

"It sure is. I won't be baking as many cakes as I usually do, but I had to do this one and a sweet potato pie. If I feel up to it I might whip up a chocolate one. You know how much Doug and Doug Junior like Chocolate and you know Doris can't boil water unless it's for some man to bathe."

"Well, I'm home and I've learned a few things about cooking since I've been living alone. I can help you with the turkey, the stuffing and I can peel the oranges and grate the coconut for the ambrosia."

"With your help, I think we can have our usual dinner. Thank the Lord you are here. What am I thinking? Let me get you some breakfast. It won't take me long to fix a "ho cake," some eggs, grits and bacon. You just get settled. Maybe this will be a decent Christmas, glory to you, Heavenly Father."

Reggie and his mother drove around town the next few days doing last minute shopping. He found a shiny blue bicycle for Doug Junior. They decorated the artificial tree, which had become the trend in town, and put up the outside lights around the roof. Mrs. Morton's spirits seemed to be in tune with the season and that made Reggie feel good so far.

Doug and his family arrived at the house around noon Christmas Day. Doris was bearing one gift box. Reggie and Mrs. Morton had waited for them to open the gifts. Doug hugged Reggie and his mother and continued to repeat, Merry Christmas, Merry Christmas. Doris took off her coat and placed the box under the tree without saying anything. Doug looked sober, but it appeared the prolonged use of alcohol had caused him to age faster than he should have. Reggie told Doug Junior that Santa Claus had dropped something off for him at their house and it was in the bedroom. He ran into the bedroom and returned shouting, "Uncle, Uncle, It's just what I wanted! Can I go out now and ride it!"

"Ask your parents."

"Mom, Dad, may I, may I?"

"Yes, but be careful," Doris said.

Reggie then took charge as if he were Santa and began to pass out gifts. He started with Doris who responded with a look of awe and great appreciation as she pulled out the scarf. Doug seemed embarrassed. He described the sweater as "cool" and thanked Reggie for thinking of his family. Reggie then reached under the tree and pulled out the box with the dress for his mother.

When she opened it, for a moment, she was speechless as she stared at it. She walked over to Reggie and hugged him and said, "You didn't have to do all this. Son, I really love it." While she stood there admiring it, Reggie brought out the other two boxes and handed them to her. "What is this?" she asked as she tore into the boxes. When she saw the shoes and purse, tears began to roll down her face. "Lord, what a blessing," she said, looking at Reggie as if he were an angel that had descended to earth that Christmas morning.

"Well, now that Mr. Rockefeller has emptied his sleigh, here is a little something from the pauper of Main Street" Doug said to his mother in an overly, loud jovial tone with eyes that seem to become glassy. It was a box of toiletries.

"Thanks son, you can bet I will use them," she said in a quiet humble tone.

Mrs. Morton reached under the tree and took out a gift for Reggie. It was a pair of leather gloves. He hugged her and told her he needed a pair.

"Well, make sure you don't lose them. They are some good ones." She then handed Doug a large box and said, "this is for you and Doris." Doug opened it and found a set of towels. He kissed his mother and handed the box to Doris. "That other box under the tree is for Doug Junior. He's too happy with his bike now. I will give it to him later."

Reggie felt he had taken a huge step toward making this the Christmas his mother had hoped for.

"All right, you all can clean up all this mess while I finish dinner. Reggie why don't you pull out that last bottle of wine Mama made before she died and give Doris and Doug some?"

"Great idea. Don't you need some help?" Reggie asked.

"No son, you'll just be in my way.

With glasses of wine in their hands, Doug led Doris and Reggie out into the cloudy day to watch Doug Junior testing his new bike. After Doug Junior seemed to have exhausted his enthusiasm, Doug and Reggie decided they wanted to see if they still had what it takes to conquered a few hills on a bike. Doris and Doug Junior cheered them on and laughed heartily when Doug couldn't climb the second hill. Reggie felt like time had stood still and the joys that he and Doug felt on Christmas Day when they were growing up had returned.

"Reggie, you all come on in, It's ready," Mrs. Morton called out.

The look of the table added to Reggie's nostalgia-the Virginia ham, the turkey with cornbread stuffing, chitterlings, collard greens, candied yams, macaroni and cheese and mashed rutabagas.

"All right let's bow our heads and thank the Lord," Mrs. Morton said. "Lord, thank you for all your wonderful blessings. Especially for bringing my children home to celebrate your coming to earth to save us all from sin. Thank you for our health and help us to lead a life worthy of your grace. We ask that you continue to guide us as we travel this journey before us." Doug junior opened his eyes and looked at the food until he saw his father doing the same. He quickly closed his again.

"Now we thank you for the blessing of this food. May it be nourishment to our bodies. These and other blessings we ask for in your name dear Lord. Amen"

"Amen!" They all said in unison.

"Reggie will you carve the turkey?" Mrs. Morton asked.

"Yes. What kind of meat do you want Doug Junior white or dark?" Reggie asked.

"White," he answered and Reggie smiled as he began to carve.

"That phone always rings at the wrong time. Would you get it Doug?" Mrs. Morton asked.

"Merry Christmas. Morton's residence," Doug greeted the caller.

"Merry Christmas is this Douglas?"

"Yes, it is," he answered.

"I'm Carol McKay. How are you?"

"I'm fine," Doug said wondering who is this sweet voice causing mischievous thoughts to chase through his mind.

"Is Reggie there?" She asked.

"Yes, I'll get him for you," Doug said, beginning to grin.

"Reggie it's for you," Doug said, almost snickering.

"Could you tell whoever it is that I will call them back?" Reggie responded with a frown on his face.

"I think you would want to take this one," Doug said as he patted Reggie on the shoulder while trying to contain his grin.

Reggie bounced out of his seat and walked to the phone and said impatiently, "Hello."

"Hello, what's wrong on this Christmas morning? You sound annoyed."

"Oh hello baby. I'm sorry," Reggie said as he lowered his voice. "Things are little hectic around here. You know Christmas day- opening gifts, feasting, etc. But I'm all right. How are things with you?"

"We are having a quiet Christmas, a little exhausted from the wedding planning. What was your folk's reaction when you told them about the wedding?" Carol asked anxiously.

"It's been so hectic I haven't had a chance to tell them yet. Mom had delayed a lot of her Christmas planning until I arrived. So it's been a whirlwind since I got here. I plan on doing it tomorrow when things have calmed down. I'll call and give you a report," Reggie said nervously.

Feeling disappointed and a bit curious, Carol said in a subdued tone, "I understand. I look forward to your call. Wish your family a Merry Christmas for me and take care of yourself. I'll keep my fingers crossed for you tomorrow."

"Thanks baby. I'll definitely get back to you tomorrow and wish your family a happy Christmas for me. I love you."

"Who was that Reggie?" Mrs. Morton asked in an impatient, intolerant manner.

"That was my friend Carol McKay from New York," Reggie said looking down at his empty plate. Doug looked over at him and with a sheepish grim and said, "Right on, bro."

"Is that the friend you went to visit on Martha's Vineyard for Thanksgiving?" Mrs. Morton asked with a frown on her face.

"Yes, she is the one," Reggie said.

"Well, well, baby brother what's going on? Martha's Vineyard?" Doug asked, still smiling.

"Are you getting serious about that white woman?" Mrs. Morton asked.

Reggie began to lose his appetite as a lump rose in his throat. There was no way he could hold on to the news of the wedding until tomorrow after this conversation. He looked over at Doug as if he wanted to choke him. Doug held up his hands as if he was being subjected to a police search and twisted his head as if to say what did I do.

"Mom we have been dating since I moved to New York. She is really a nice girl. I am sure you will agree with me when you meet her," Reggie said trying to contain his anger so that it would not be reflected in his voice.

"I'll take your word for it. I don't need to meet her. I'll wait to meet the nice girl who's going to make you a good wife," Mrs. Morton said as if to bring that conversation to closure.

With a trimmer in his voice and beads of perspiration forming on his forehead, Reggie said, "Mom we are going to get married."

"Boy, don't play with me like that," she responded.

"I'm serious mom. The wedding is planned for February 22nd in New York," Reggie said, looking directly at his mother.

"Oh. Lord help me. This boy has lost his mind. I've been praying, ever since he got ambushed by that ill-informed white and wanna-be-white family in Chicago that it would not come to this. Lord, Lord, help me," she said looking up toward the ceiling shaking her head from side to side. "Oh my Savior this is not what I prayed for after that Brown decision," she said with her eyes closed and an untouched plate of food in front of her.

"Mom, I assure you that Carol and her family are nothing like those people in Chicago." As soon as the words escaped his lips, the image of Carol's father and uncle flashed before him. He quickly realized they indeed were not like the Chicago friends. They actually harbored real prejudice feelings.

His dishonesty made him more nervous so he tried to shift the conversation in a more appealing direction. "Carol really loves me for me and that makes me love her. That kind of feeling is what I've been told is what to look for in a mate. She just happens to be white. Didn't the justices say in their decision in the Brown case that separate was not equal and that segregated schools cause a feeling inferiority in Black kids? Carol and I are a symbol of bringing the races together."

"Son, we have a long way to go and you are not responsible for taking us all the way. The prejudice Black people have been subjected to is like a corn on your toe. You can cut off the head, but then you realize it is deep in your skin and you have to keep digging to get rid of it. That kind of prejudice will not crumble with one blow. You have to whittle it away. You have made a great contribution already. You think I don't know how much you went through at Davis University. You had to endure a lot to graduate from that school and I am sure that job you have now will put you through some of the same things. You can't do it all, son. You are a glutton for punishment marrying a white woman. There will be no end to battles you will have to fight if that happens. Why don't you wait until you find a nice Black woman who will give you a chance for a happy marriage?" She said with frustration, sadness and fury in her face. She pushed her plate away from her and buried her face into her cupped hands while shaking her head.

Reggie was agitated and saddened. This was not when or how he wished to broach the subject. God knows he didn't want to spoil Christmas dinner for his mother with this news. But he realized he had to finish the discussion still engaged to Carol.

"Mom don't you remember Mona, the nice Black woman who stole my heart and jilted me? This is the first time I have been in love since then." He didn't think it was wise to tell her about the white woman who did the same thing to him. "Carol and I are prepared to take our knocks about being a mixed-race couple." He realized again that he was not being honest.

"Reggie, you and that woman have no idea what you're in for," she said, throwing her hands in the air.

"I'm going to need your support if I am ever going to be able to deal with whatever we are in for," Reggie said in a calm voice.

"Son, you know I love you and I will always be at your side whatever you do. I just wish you had sense enough to avoid known dangers. We are all going to be in for a rough ride ahead with you having a white wife," she said with sadness in her eyes.

Doug sat chewing on what was happening at the table as well as what was on his plate. The news seemed as delicious to him as the food. Doris kept her head bowed as she ate and occasionally snickered while Doug Junior asked his father if Uncle Reggie was going back to New York and getting married.

"Hey Chess cat, I need you to be in the wedding. Do you think you can handle that?" Reggie asked Doug with defiance in his voice and eyes.

"I will be there with bells on. I wouldn't miss it for nothing," Doug said.

"Do you understand what I meant when I asked if you could handle it?"

"Yes, I think I do and my answer is still yes." Doug said without a smile.

"I will make arrangements for you all to travel to New York. The wedding will be there" Reggie said, hoping that announcement would bring that discussion to closure.

"What kind of arrangements are you thinking about? Lord knows I don't want to fly," Mrs. Morton said with tears in her eyes.

"I'll get you there any way you want to travel mom- by bus, train or plane. Don't you worry. I am sure once you meet Carol you will change your mind about us making it. I love you mom."

"I love you too," Mrs. Morton said with tears rolling down her cheeks.

Reggie was glad the subject had been aired, but he was shaken. He had no appetite but forced himself to eat as if he were famished so as not to offend his mother further. He now became consumed with the thought of how to tailor the story for Carol. It occurred to him that he was now in a mode of delivering half-truths to justify his relationship with Carol. He wondered how much of that he would continue to need to do after he was married.

"Hey baby, mission accomplished," Reggie said surprising Carol with a call back on Christmas night.

"Oh Reggie, I was worried about you after our earlier conversation. What was their reaction?" She asked.

"Mom was shocked, but she is on board. My brother is excited about being in the wedding."

"Well, I'm glad we have gotten beyond the parents. When are you arriving back in New York?" Carol asked with exuberance in her voice.

"Baby I am not going to be able to make it back for New Year's Eve. I need to spend more time with mom to help her make it through the entire holiday without pop. It seems she really needs that. I hope you won't mind. Please explain to your parents and wish them a Happy New Year for me. I'll call you after I make my reservation." He felt that spending more time with his mother could help to ameliorate the blow he had inflicted on her even though he was anxious to escape the situation.

"I understand. This has to be a difficult holiday for her-the first after losing her husband. Please give her my regards. I'll look forward to your call."

Over the next few days, Reggie drove his mother around to visit neighbors and friends in keeping with the usual tradition; however, they never shared with anyone Reggie's upcoming marriage. His mother was hoping maybe the Lord would guide him to his senses.

Mrs. Morton walked to the car with Reggie. She was holding back tears as she said, "I'm going to keep you in my prayers, asking God to guide you. I love you and pray that you will find the happiness you deserve."

"As long as I have your prayers I know I will be all right. I love you too and thank God that you are my mom," Reggie said as he kissed her good-bye.

Carol was waiting at the terminal when Reggie entered. She rushed up to him and locked him in a hug. "I'm so glad you are back. How did you leave your mother?"

"Baby, you don't know how glad I am to see you. Mom is coming along okay. It really made a difference having her children and grandchild share the holiday with her. She is looking forward to coming to the wedding."

"I'm looking forward to meeting her. Mother and I have made substantial progress in planning the wedding. We have the church reserved, the caterer for the reception and the invitations have been ordered."

"Doug is really excited about coming to New York. I have now asked two groomsmen and a best man."

"I guess we are moving forward as planned," Carol said, holding Reggie's arm tightly.

CHAPTER 19

"Happy New Year Reggie. How was your holiday? How did you leave your mother?" Henry asked as he barged into Reggie's office without knocking.

"Happy New Year, Henry. Everything went fine. Mother is hanging in there. She had a really wonderful holiday. And yours?"

"It was the usual. The kids had a great time and Christmas is really for them, you know. You remember we spoke about the Management Intern program for minority students. Well, the president is nudging me to get that together so we can start recruiting for this summer. I would like for you to get started on that right away."

"I had already planned to get right on it," Reggie said in an upbeat tone.

"Why don't you map out the different phases for the program- places where the interns will be assigned, the length of each assignment, some colleges where we can recruit, etc, etc. You need to make contact with some account executives to get their approval to take on an intern. Let's try to get the plan to the president in a couple of weeks."

"Fine Henry, I'll get right on it." As soon as Henry let the door hit him in the back, Reggie leaned back in his chair and pounded his chest a couple of time in a gesture of satisfaction. He began to fantasize what this project could mean for him. He could put some teeth into this affirmative action plan, especially since the president seemed to be choosing to be proactive without the government's approval of the plan. If he could institutionalize a management training program, it might take the sting out of his reputation back home for marrying a white woman and his mother could walk with her head held high.

As if he had been injected with a shot of a narcotic that made him feel lifted into the air, Reggie dove into developing an outline of a plan. He identified different segments of the agency's operations for intern participation- creative, traffic, marketing, research, and of course, accounts management. He identified individuals who might be appropriate for mentoring minority students. He jotted down minority colleges for on-campus recruiting and fraternities on those campuses to promote the agency. He then set out to bring the outline to life. All of those he approached for mentoring assignments immediately agreed, expressing excitement about an opportunity to extend a hand to an underprivileged minority as long as the intern was smart enough to benefit from the experience. Atlanta, Howard and Fisk, Black colleges and universities, were identified for on campus recruiting.

Between executing the project and planning for the wedding, Reggie began to feel that he was swept up in a whirlwind spinning into a fantasyland where dreams actually come true. The demands of each left him no time to ponder any pot holes that may lie ahead. He had planned a honeymoon in Jamaica where he imagined white sandy beaches, clear warm ocean waters, calypso music and exotic cocktails. When he shared his management intern program with Jeff, he gave his skeptical approval and at the same time agreed to be a groomsman in the wedding, aware of his responsibility to a "brother." Everything seemed to be falling in place. Arrangements had been complete for his mother and brother to fly to New York and stay in the Abby Hotel in the heart of midtown Manhattan. Doris and Doug Junior would not attend-too costly. Reggie chose the Waldorf Astoria hotel for Harry, his best man, and his family. He didn't want to add to his mother's stress if she thought she was sleeping that close to them. She still saw them as the misguided, uninformed Chicago carpetbaggers who whittled away the roots of her son's native culture and had resulted in this Black-white wedding.

A couple of weeks after getting the assignment, Reggie received Henry's enthusiastic approval of the proposal. Without any changes, he hurried it off to the president. Reggie breathed a sigh of relief, sure that he would be able to give his mother some good news to take back home after the wedding. He walked back into his office and the phone was ringing.

"Hello Reggie, how's your day going? You do remember we are supposed to meet mother at the Riverside Church at six to meet the minister and go over the plans. She is taking us to dinner after to discuss the final plans and map out what each of us has left to do," Carol said.

"Things are going well here. Henry just sent my proposal to the president for the management intern program without any changes. How about that?" Reggie said almost giddy.

"Reggie that's wonderful! The president won't forget your good work. It will probably bode well for your future there."

"I'm counting on it," Reggie said with a feeling of caution and hope. "I remembered and I will meet you all at the church."

Just after five o'clock, Reggie walked over to Broadway and Fifth streets, basking in the fading sun and whipping winds. The thought-life is good- kept swirling in his mind. He shelved himself into the packed Number One train, along with the rush-hour crowd, exactly at five-thirty. He was pinned in the middle of the crowd with no ability to hold onto a rail. The car felt more like summer than winter. However, he was unperturbed. He had scored one at work and was headed for the final planning of his marriage to the love he thought he would never find.

At the 116th Street station, he pushed his way through the crowd, got off the train and walked up the stairs back into the howling winds charging up from the Hudson River. As he casually looked around to see where he was, there standing to his left was Barnard College. For a moment his heart seemed to sink deep into his chest. This is the campus his first love walked around and found the white boy who took her away from him. How ironic, he thought, that he would have this encounter at this moment. He walked the next four blocks to the Riverside Church feeling vindicated, but a bit sad and wondering how life turned out for Mona. He wished he knew what her mixed race marriage was like. He had heard no rumors about a break-up, so he assumed it was working. The thought made him feel confident and he began to whistle "Because God Made You Mine" as he approached the church.

"Reggie over here," Carol beckoned as he entered the narthex of the church.

This Gothic cathedral with its long aisles, medieval style chandeliers, a chancel adorned with intricate carvings and the classical stained glass windows jarred Reggie. Such elegance, but mighty big for a small wedding, he thought. It suddenly reminded him that he needed to brief his mother and brother on as many details as he could remember so they would not encounter surprises that could embarrass them or him.

"Good evening," Reggie said cordially, hoping his facial expression would not convey his thoughts.

"Reggie, this is Rev. Whitfield and he will be performing the ceremony," Carol said as she introduced them.

Reggie stiffened at bit to portray confidence as he shook the minister's hand and said, "My pleasure."

Rev. Whitfield walked them through the church's various facilities used for weddings. As they headed down the center aisle toward the altar, the Reverend pointed out the pews for friends of the bride and the ones for the groom.

Reggie, wanting to impress the minister and indicate to Mrs. McKay and Carol that he was listening and involved in the discussion asked, "Wouldn't it better to seat everyone on the same side? I only have about ten people coming and the church is so large."

The minister paused. Carol continued to look toward the chancre and Mrs. McKay gave Reggie what looked like a condescending smile and without saying a word turned to the minister and said, "That's fine, bride left and groom right."

Rev. Whitfield paused for a second giving Mrs. McKay time to answer Reggie's question. When there was no response, he proceeded to walk them through the ceremony.

"Let's take another look at the facility for the reception," Mrs. McKay said. The reverend directed them to the large room on the same level of the nave with high ceilings and a stage.

"Ideal," Mrs. McKay said looking at Carol who nodded her head in agreement. "It can easily accommodate the head table and the musical group."

After reaching agreement on all the details, Mrs. McKay and Carol thanked the reverend. He shook each of their hands, but he also placed one hand on Reggie's shoulder and smiled at him. Reggie had remained silent after his question seemed to have landed on deaf ears. He couldn't figure whether it was a dumb questions or an absurd suggestion or whether anything he had to say counted.

"Are you all hungry now? I am, Mrs. McKay said. "Why don't we walk around the corner to the West End Restaurant and have a bite? It's a good restaurant and the location is good for each of us for getting home. " Mrs. McKay asked seeming a bit nervous.

"It sounds good to me. What about you Reggie?" Carol asked.

"Fine, fine," Reggie said wondering if Mona and her friends hung out there and if she met her husband there. There were indeed a lot of college- age students in this spacious, rustic restaurant with a long bar and high- backed booths. Every now and then you would hear a loud burst of laughter coming from a group of students. Reggie looked around every time it happened, wondering what life was like then and now for Mona. He hoped she was as happy as he was now and he wished he could tell her.

After they had placed their orders with the waiter, Mrs. McKay pulled out her list of things to be done leading up to the wedding. She carefully went over the responsibility of each person and set a date for each person to check in with her regarding status.

"Have you made arrangements for your family and the family of your best man- hotels, transportation, etc?" Mrs. McKay asked looking directly at Reggie and then quickly dropping her eyes to her note pad.

"I've made the arrangements," he responded.

"Well, I think we are pretty much set. Now we can enjoy our meal," she said more relaxed than she had been all evening.

Reggie thought now that she was more relaxed she would get around to addressing his question. However, throughout the meal the whole conversation centered around Carol talking about the appropriateness of the church for the wedding and how happy she was that her father had arranged to have it there and Mrs. McKay talking about how great the wedding pictures would be.

Reggie breathed a sigh of relief when the check was paid and they walked out of the restaurant and hailed a cab for Mrs. McKay and Carol. They both gave him a fast, perfunctory hug and jumped into the taxi. Reggie took the subway. During the long ride to his station, he tried to figure out what had occurred. He thought maybe he was being overly sensitive about it, after all wedding planning is a female thing and they probably resent males interfering with their expertise. Still, he couldn't shake the feeing that he probably looked stupid. But couldn't someone have, at least, acknowledged he said something, he wondered.

Reggie found a note on his desk from Henry the next day saying the president approved the plan and that he should go ahead and began making arrangement for on-campus recruiting. Reggie wasted no time solidifying a plan. His confidence about the project continued to rise when the account executives he identified to accompany him on recruiting trips expressed great enthusiasm. Henry also accepted Atlanta University's invitation to address a class on advertising.

A week before the wedding, everything was in place and ready for implementation as soon as Reggie returned from his honeymoon. Henry congratulated Reggie for an outstanding job done in record time. He told him to take as much time as he needed for the wedding. Reggie gladly accepted his offer. It would give him time before the wedding to spend with his family. They were due to arrive in a few days. It was their first trip to New York and he wanted to be available to do the things they wanted to do and see. He also wanted time to prepare them for what they were about to experience, especially getting to know Carol.

Reggie rushed over and hugged his mother and brother as they entered the terminal. They both looked razzed. It was their first flight and the plane had encountered some mild turbulence.

"Son, I hope you have planned for me to go somewhere where I can relax my nerves. They are shot. I have been praying for the last hour telling the Lord I know he will watch over me, but I didn't mean to tempt him by getting on this plane."

"Was it a bad flight? The weather seems good for flying."

"Well, I would hate to be flying in bad weather."

"Well, you have the whole day to relax. There is nothing planned until this evening. Carol is meeting us for dinner."

Doug pretended he was unaffected but it was hard to wash the stress off his face. "Well, we are finally going to meet Carol McKay. Right on, little brother. I can't wait. I always thought you would end up with a white chick when you went off to that college where they were all around you, and very few sisters in sight," Doug said, smiling.

"Yes, you are finally going to meet her and, by the way, I didn't plan on marrying a white woman. When I fell in love, it just happened to be with a white woman. You had better watch your mouth around her. You hear me," Reggie said without cracking a smile.

"If you are embarrassed by me you shouldn't have asked me to be in the wedding. I would have been okay with that. What are you trying to do make us act like a white family?" Doug asked with hurt in his eyes.

"If you mean acting like civilized people is acting white then yes I am."
Reggie said haughtily.

"You know what Reggie," Doug said with his nostrils expanding and his glassy eyes widening, "Lincoln freed the slaves from working without a paycheck but now that the white man has given you a paycheck, you have become an intellectual slave and it would take another revolution to free you."

Reggie looked at Doug, shook his head and said, "I doubt you really know the meaning of what you just said."

"All right you two, people are looking at you. Cut out this fussing. We are a family and just as good as any white family. Doug, this is your brother's wedding and we are standing beside him, okay?" Mrs. Morton said pointing her finger at Doug.

Doug walked ahead to the baggage claim area and collected the bags while Reggie hailed a taxi. The taxi ride through Queens and Manhattan seemed to have energized Mrs. Morton. Her face lit up in childish surprise as she encountered the number of cars on one way streets, the congestion of people on the sidewalks and the seemingly unending tall buildings. Her face was almost stuck to the window as she kept mumbling, "umh umh, its just like what I've seen on television." Doug sat in his seat as if he were being chauffeured. As he encountered the Manhattan skyline he nodded his head, his anger obviously quelled, saying, "This is my kind of town."

After checking them into the hotel, Reggie offered to give them a walking tour of the area. He felt a moment of pride, and with the enthusiasm of a tour guide, took them along the glamorous Great White Way and pointed out the plays that were on stage at the various theaters. They walked through the fancy shops on Fifth Avenue, toured Radio City, Saint Patrick's Cathedral and Rockefeller Center. After walking them back to the hotel and before each headed for their rooms, Reggie reminded them that they were meeting Carol for dinner at seven and they should meet in the lobby around a quarter to seven. He had taken a room in the hotel to be near them.

The dinner reservations had been made for the Cattlemen Club. Besides being conveniently located near the hotel, Reggie wanted to impress his folks with a hearty steak dinner. They arrived at the restaurant about ten minutes before the hour. Tensions were high. Mrs. Morton's fingers kept thumbing her purse as she sized up the place. Doug paced the limited space in the reception area and Reggie kept folding and unfolding his arms and looking at his watch. There was no conversation going on between them.

Promptly at seven Carol walked through the door looking cool as a cucumber and as self-assured as she would be combing her hair. She didn't wait to be introduced. She walked right up to Mrs. Morton and reached for her hand and said, "I have looked forward to this moment for a long time. I am really glad to finally meet you. I hope you had a pleasant trip and that you are comfortable in your quarters at the hotel."

"I'm equally glad to meet you. Our flight was a little rough, but the Lord brought us here safely and that's what counts," Mrs. Morton said seemingly a bit disarmed by Carol's approach.

"Indeed, indeed," Carol said as she approached Doug. "You are obviously Doug. You are, without a doubt, brothers. I would be able to tell if I met you on the street. How are you? What do you think of our city so far?"

"Well, first of all, I am glad to meet you and discover that you are more beautiful than I imagined. I should have known because baby brother has always hooked up with beautiful women. Second, I am loving New York. The pace of life seems to fit my style. Maybe I should have come to New York before I got hitched. I might have been as lucky as baby brother." Doug said as he shifted his weight from foot to foot and continued to extend and retrieve his hands as if he were directing a band. Reggie tried to smile as Doug was talking, but you could see the fear in his eyes.

"Your table is ready Mr. Morton," the waiter said then led them to a table near a wall which gave them an expansive view of the restaurant. Each was given a menu which they all began to peruse until the waiter asked for their order of drinks. Mrs. Morton ordered iced tea, Doug-a scotch on the rocks-which heightened Reggie's nervousness. Carol ordered white wine and Reggie a scotch and ginger ale. As soon as the waiter left, Carol asked Mrs. Morton, if there was any shopping she wanted to do while in New York. She then rattled off the great stores –Saks, B Altman, Lord and Taylor and Macy's.

Mrs. Morton immediately responded. "Yes, Reggie took us through all those stores except Macy's. I need to buy some stockings and gloves before the wedding. Which one would you suggest?"

"Oh there is one other I forgot to mention that you might want to go to. It's on Fifth Avenue. It's called Korvetts. You might want to try them. It's not far from your hotel."

Mrs. Morton remembered that Reggie had pointed that one out and said it was a discount store. She thought Carol made that recommendation because she had decided she was a penny pincher which she felt embarrassed by although it was true; but it was not something she wanted to reveal to Carol at this time. Remembering she wanted to be as cordial as possible for Reggie's sake, she thanked Carol for the suggestion and assured her she would go to Korvetts.

"Mother and father are coming into town tomorrow and would like to take you all to dinner if it's convenient," Carol said as her eyes shifted from Reggie to Mrs. Morton.

"That sounds fine," Reggie answered. The drinks arrived and dinner orders were taken. Reggie recommended the steaks and they were ordered except for Carol. She ordered trout.

"Here's to a happy road ahead for Carol and Reggie," Doug said as he raised his glass and the others joined in. He then took a deep sip of his drink as Reggie watched closely.

"Doug, you must come back to visit us when things are not so hectic. You could bring your wife and son. There is so much to show you that time won't permit this time."

"Oh, I plan to come back. Once I got a whiff of the city I knew I had to take in a lot more of it," he said as he leaned back in his chair holding his drink in his hand like a man in charge.

"How old is your son?"

"He's six going on ten. He's really smart for his age," Doug said as his face lit up. Reggie took note and breathed a sigh of relief. At least we might make it through the night, he was thinking. The food arrived and everyone's attention turned to their plates. Reggie, Doug and Carol picked up their utensils and started to dig into their food.

"Wait a minute you'll. You suddenly forgot how I trained you. Now let me say grace before we eat," Mrs. Morton said as she bowed her head. Reggie cringed. Carol, for the first time, seemed to have her cool brushed. Her shaking hands slowly laid down her knife and fork as she bowed her head and closed her eyes.

"We thank you Lord for the food we are about to receive. May it be nourishment to our bodies. Please wash away all the impurities it may have. And Lord thank you for bringing me and my son here safely. These and other blessings we ask in your name. Amen."

Doug echoed, "Amen! Amen!" Reggie looked down at his plate and Carol raised her head without looking across the table at Mrs. Morton.

"What's your denomination Carol?" Mrs. Morton asked seeming to have become more confident in her environment.

"My denomination?" Carol repeated with a quizzical look on her face.

"Your church," Mrs. Morton clarified.

"My church" Carol said, again seeming confused.

"Yes, the church where the wedding will be held," Mrs. Morton said with a bit of impatience in her voice.

"Oh, the Riverside Church is interdenominational, interracial and international. However, it is not my church. Father chose it because it would be convenient for most of the guests to get to," Carol said seeming to regain some of her cool.

"Oh, I see. So what is your denomination?" Mrs. Morton asked again feeling more confidence as she spoke.

"Actually, I don't belong to a church. I grew up in the Episcopal Church, but I haven't been active for many years," Carol answered in a friendly, but confident tone.

"Well, honey, how prepared are you to meet God?" Mrs. Morton asked, this time leaning back in her chair.

Carol looked up at Mrs. Morton, like a teacher trying to encourage a low achieving student to keep trying, and through a forced smile said, "I'm a good person."

Reggie was squirming in his seat. "Hey mom, what do you think of that steak? Is it cooked to your satisfaction?" Reggie asked desperate to change the subject.

"I haven't had a chance to taste it yet," she answered looking down at her plate.

"I guarantee you it tastes better hot than cold."

"Okay son, okay," she answered with a "did I do something wrong" look on her face and, with a shaking hand, cut into her steak.

Carol had embraced silence as she forked through her fish. Doug was practically halfway through his steak. Reggie had only managed to slice his. Tension hung over the table.

Carol, reminded of her goal to project a positive impression, decided that she couldn't afford to be seen as defeated or intolerant. Therefore it would be in keeping with her goal to melt away some of the tension, said with a forced smile, "I think you all will enjoy the restaurant chosen for the rehearsal dinner. It serves Jamaican cuisine. The food can be spicy. It's one of Reggie's and my favorites."

"That's right down my alley. Do you think we might run into Harry Belafonte?" Doug asked while chewing vigorously on his food.

"I doubt it, but I think you will enjoy the food." Carol answered feeling a bit of disappointment that it was Doug and not Mrs. Morton who responded.

Reggie felt the pressure to take control of the conversation and divert it to something he thought would be less incendiary. So, he announced the agency's approval of his proposal for a management intern program for minority students. You could see the sparkle return to Mrs. Morton's eyes.

"Son, that's wonderful. Thank the Lord. I know Rev. Bailey will want to announce that in church. Everybody will be so proud of the work you are doing for our community."

"Do you think you could put in a good word for your brother to get into that program?" Doug asked in jest but feeling serious.

"You have to be a business major in your junior year in college." Reggie answered with a slight bit of "put down" in his voice.

"Okay, brother I get your message. Congratulations, I'll make sure Doug Junior knows about his uncle's successes," Doug said with a bit of sarcasm in his voice.

Carol sat with a forced smile on her face without commenting. As soon as the waiter collected the plates from the table, Reggie asked for the check without offering dessert or coffee.

As they gathered in front of the restaurant, Carol folded her arms and pulled the collar of her coat up to cover her ears as if she needed some quick shelter from the cold temperature. She then announced that she would take a taxi. She gave Mrs. Morton and Doug a hug and said, "I am really glad we had this time together before things got hectic. I'll see you all tomorrow. She kissed Reggie on the cheek and hailed a taxi. Doug and Mrs. Morton through a happy smile reciprocated telling her how happy they were to meet her and they looked forward to dinner with her parents.

Reggie breathed a sigh of relief. He concluded that things could have gone much worse and that he really did need to brief his family on his impressions of Carol's family, especially her father, before they met for dinner. He was disappointed that Carol didn't want to come up to his room for a few minutes. He would love to have heard some of her comments about the evening. Maybe she could have convinced him that things weren't as bad as he thought.

"Son, I hope I didn't embarrass you too much."

"Mom, don't worry. Everything is okay," Reggie said trying to hide the frustration he was feeling.

"Carol is very pretty and has nice manners. She would do well to ask the Lord into her life. Both of you need to get back into the church."

"Mom, everybody doesn't see their relationship with God the way you do. Some people think of their relationship as very personal and see no need to become missionaries."

"Yes, but the Lord requires me to spread the word to those who need to seek Him. I won't be saved and he won't spare the rod if I don't do his work."

"Yes, mom but there is a place and time for that and maybe now is neither," Reggie said while looking at his mother with affection and frustration. "I am sure the McKays think of themselves as good Christians as you do, so discussing the different faiths would only result in a debate. Would you want that the first time you met my in-laws?" Reggie pleaded.

"Son, I don't want to do anything that would embarrass you. If this is the marriage you want, I want you to be happy and as content as you can be because I love you," Mrs. Morton said, looking at Reggie with affection, but feeling embarrassed.

"I love you too mom and I know you have my interest at heart. By the way, I've been intending to mention that Carol's father might seem a little southern in his views, but she assures me he is not prejudiced. Her Uncle Jacks seems the same. When you see him, you might think he is Black, but he is Cape Verdean- a mixture of Portuguese and African. He doesn't identify with Black people and it is important to remember that."

"Well, I guess Carol's family is like any other. We all have our good and bad sheep," Mrs. Morton said casually.

Reggie wished Doug and mom a good night's rest and headed for his room. His night was restless. He wanted to help Carol understand his mother. He wanted to explain that religion was all that Black people of his mother's generation had to cling to in the midst of the humiliation of segregation-the inability to stop lynchings, exploitation on the job, and injustice in the execution of the law. However, he felt embarrassed to talk about the struggles of Black people in the presence of white people. He wanted to be seen as someone who rose above those problems even though his college years had immersed him in them. He did not, however, want to alienate his family that had made sacrifices that led to his achieving what he had so far.

After about four hours of uninterrupted sleep, Reggie rolled out of the bed, cleaned up and traveled down to the coffee shop to meet Mrs. Morton and Doug for breakfast. After eating breakfast he would take them shopping for Mrs. Morton's stockings and gloves and then to the rental for Doug's fitting for his tuxedo.

Mrs. Morton was waiting for him in the coffee shop with a look of gloom. It seems she had gone to Doug's room during the night to see if her cosmetic bag was among his things. When he opened the door, she noticed his glassy eyes and slurred speech. He told her to wait while he checked, but would not let her in the room. When he went to look she peeped in and saw a white woman in his bed. "My Lord what am I going to do with that boy- his drinking and whoring with a white woman. His soul is damned. My Lord! My Lord! Help me," she said looking toward the coffee shop ceiling in a helpless manner.

"Mom I wouldn't worry about him. He must have left the hotel looking for a bar and wandered down to Forty-Second Street into the seedy section and was lured by a prostitute. This is probably no different from what he does at home except this time it is with a white woman he didn't know. He knows how to take care of himself and as long as he is okay this morning, there is nothing to worry about," Reggie said trying to console his mother, but he felt like choking Doug. He wished he had never asked him to be in the wedding. He's turning out to be nothing but trouble.

"Good morning, everybody," Doug said projecting a chipper mood. "I'm really hungry. Are pancakes on the menu?"

Mrs. Morton did not respond. Reggie realized he needed to suppress his feelings in order to calm his mother. "I'm pretty sure the menu has whatever your hearts desire." Reggie said in as cool a tone as he could muster.

After breakfast, the three of them went shopping for Mrs. Morton's stockings and gloves and for Doug's fitting. Mrs.

Morton seemed to have put Doug's escapade behind her. She had her two sons with her, without arguing, while shopping on Fifth Avenue and walking the crowded streets of New York among people who looked liked they stepped out of a fashion magazine.

Upon returning to the hotel, Reggie reminded them that they were supposed to meet the McKays for dinner at seven and that the restaurant was in Greenwich Village and they needed to get a taxi around six thirty. He wanted to give them the experience of riding the subway, but was certain the McKays would arrive in a cab or limousine and he figured getting out of a cab would be more impressive than walking from the subway. The restaurant chosen by Mrs. McKay was Horn of Plenty. Some of its food reflects the southern cuisine. She thought that would make the Mortons feel more at home.

Just as Reggie predicted, the McKays arrived in a limousine, just as the Mortons were stepping out of their taxi. Reggie felt proud. He walked over to the McKays while his mother and brother stood back.

"Good evening," Reggie said as he hugged Mrs. McKay and Carol and extended his hand to Mr. McKay. "Come, I want you to meet my mother and brother, Doug. Mom this is Mr. and Mrs. McKay and of course you met Carol."

Mrs. McKay immediately extended her hand to Mrs. Morton and in a nervous overly joyous manner said, "It's really a pleasure to finally meet you. Reggie has told us so much about you. How are you enjoying your trip to New York?"

The greeting eased Mrs. Morton's perceived discomfort about the meeting. "Well, it's a pleasure meeting you. I'm really enjoying my visit to New York. Back home people consider

New York the capital of the world. They all envied my trip here. I've got a lot to tell them when I get back," she said, smiling and shaking Mrs. McKay's hand.

"Oh Doug, how are you? Is Reggie showing you how much fun New York can be?" Mrs. McKay asked as she shook his hand.

"Good to meet you. He's a little slow as a tour guide, but I am finding my own way," Doug answered as if he were speaking to an old friend.

Mrs. McKay stood back and said, "This is my husband."

Mr. McKay extended his hand to Mrs. Morton in a very business like manner and said, "I'm glad to meet you."

Mrs. Morton shook his hand and said, "Likewise."

He then reached for Doug's hand and said, "Nice to meet you."

Carol and Reggie were standing holding hands with looks of satisfaction plastered all over their faces.

"Come, let's go inside. It's cold out here." Mrs. McKay said.

Mr. McKay announced his party and they were led to a table next to a window overlooking the street where you could see a bustling crowd eager to escape the cold wind charging in off the river. Some climbed the steps to one hundred year old attached brownstone houses.

"You are in Greenwich Village, a section of the city that is known for a more bohemian flair. Writers, artists, entertainers gravitate to this section of town," Carol offered, looking and smiling directly at Mrs. Morton and then at Doug.

"Yes, I've heard a lot about Greenwich Village. So this is it. It looks like a scene from a movie about New York," Doug said with a bit of excitement in his voice and amazement in his eyes.

Mrs. McKay, like a skilled hostess, took charge of the seating arrangements. She placed Mrs. Morton next to her, Carol next to Mrs. Morton, Reggie next Carol, Mr. McKay next to Reggie and Doug Next to Mr. McKay. Beaming with a look of mission accomplished, she took her seat and joined the rest of the group burying their heads in the menu.

"Would you like to order drinks?" the waiter asked.

"Yes!" Mr. McKay bolted.

"What would you like, sir?"

"I'll take a double scotch on the rocks."

"And you sir?" the waiter asked Doug.

"I'll have the same."

"Well, I thought you people only drank bourbon," Mr. McKay said to Doug in a casual but serious tone.

"Well, I thought you people only drank martinis," Doug shot back as if to say, "gotcha."

Reggie's heart beat sped up. Before the waiter could ask for his order and in a forceful but what he hoped was an unemotional tone said, "I will take a gin and tonic." Doug picked up his implication and looked puzzled. Mr. McKay cast his eyes back to the menu. No one else seemed to notice the exchanges. Carol and Mrs. McKay ordered white wine.

Mrs. Morton seemed to be in another world when the waiter asked for her order. She did not respond. She was distracted by two men standing at the top of the steps of one of the brownstones giving each other a good-bye kiss on the lips. Oh, my Lord, she was thinking, this place is another Sodom and Gomorrah and I am probably sitting in the seat of sinners. Help me dear Lord. She prayed silently.

"Ma'am," the waiter said. "Would you like something to drink?"

"Yes, I will take a glass of iced tea if you have it," she said in as polite a tone as she could, but her eyes conveyed disgust. She felt like getting up and walking out, but the reality was that she had no idea how to get back to the hotel and she really did not want to embarrass Reggie.

Mrs. McKay sensed what had happened and immediately thought some damage control was needed. "Did you find what you were looking for at Korvettes?" She asked.

"Oh no, oh yes. We went to Lord and Taylor," she said trying to pull herself together.

"That's a great store," Mrs. McKay said a bit embarrassed that she had asked about the discount store.

The drinks arrived and Doug raised his glass and said, "To the bride and groom. May they live happily ever after."

Mr. McKay raised his glass along with all the others and grunted, "Umh."

"Are you ready to order?" the waiter asked.

"Yes, I'll have the shrimp," Mrs. McKay said.

"I'll have the same," Carol followed.

Mrs. Morton spotted fried chicken on the menu and ordered it. Mr. McKay smiled without saying a word.

Reggie ordered steak and the other men followed with the same. As the waiter was leaving, a burst of loud laughter thrust from a table across the room. Everyone at the table looked over to see where it was coming from. There were four effeminate men gesturing with their hands as they engaged in very jovial conversation. Carol and Mrs. McKay turned their heads back to the table trying to convey that it was nothing unusual. Doug snickered. Mr. McKay looked disgusted. Mrs. Morton frowned as if she had come in contact with an awful smell. After noticing Doug's and his mother's responses, Reggie became very irritated. He bit his bottom lip and balled up his left fist which was hidden under the table. He picked up his drink and took a gulp. As he laid down the glass, the waiter returned with a basket of the restaurant's famous warm corn bread and butter. Mrs. McKay reached for the basket, took out a slice and passed the basket on to Mrs. Morton.

"What in the world is this? Corn bread?" Mrs. Morton asked looking as if she had discovered a long lost relative.

"Take a bite and tell me if it is as good as yours," Mr. McKay said with a hint of sarcasm.

"Well, my Lord it is really good, but not quite as good as mine." Mrs. Morton said looking at Mr. McKay with a half smile. At that point, everyone laughed and Reggie exhaled.

Feeling a buzz from his double scotch and the thought that he was partially responsible for the group's laughter, Mr. McKay decided to push forward. Leaning over the table and looking at Mrs. Morton, he said in a serious but somewhat condescending tone. "You must really be proud of how far your son has come."

"Yes, he's coming along very well in helping Black people break into the business world. All the folks back home are proud of the work he is doing in that area," she said biting her tongue in an effort to keep things cordial.

"You must be proud of Carol. She is such a gracious young lady," Mrs. Morton said as gracious as she could.

"I love my daughter." Mr. McKay replied. The food arrived and he turned his focus to his steak, feeling a bit disappointed that his fishing did not get any reaction from Mrs. Morton about the marriage. The table went quiet as they all dived into their food. Mrs. Morton hesitated, ready to offer grace, but realized how awkward that would be at the moment. So she closed her eyes and meditated her own grace.

The waiter returned to clear the table and take orders for desserts. There was a tray of different desserts stationed on a trolley in the middle of the room. Among them were pecan and sweet potato pies, cheese, coconut and chocolate cakes. Doug had been eyeing them throughout the meal. He immediately looked up at the waiter and said. "I'll try the cheese cake."

"Why don't you try the sweet potato pie, Mrs. Morton and you can tell us how it measures up to yours. I'll bet you can whip up a pie that causes your neighbors to come calling," Mr. McKay said hoping to get another laugh. This time everybody only smiled.

"I think I will take you up on that suggestion," Mrs. Morton responded.

Mrs. McKay and Carol refused dessert. Mr. McKay ordered chocolate cake and Reggie order coconut. When the waiter arrived to bring the check, Mrs. Morton said, "Young man you can tell your chef that he is doing a really great job."

"Thank you ma'am," the waiter said and everyone broke out in a pleasant smile.

"It was a pleasure meeting you ma'am." Mr. McKay said as the limousine rolled up in front of the restaurant. Mrs. McKay and Carol hugged Mrs. Morton and Doug and Carol hugged and kissed Reggie.

"We look forward to seeing you tomorrow," Mrs. McKay said leaning out the window as the limousine pulled off. As soon as she closed the window, she said, "We cannot return to the Village for the rehearsal dinner. Mrs. Morton will probably have a stroke if she encounters another gay person. Honey do we know anybody with connection to the Plaza? Maybe we can get space in the Oak Room with this short notice."

"This is really late, but I'll see what I can do."

"We need to move fast because we have to notify everybody of the change and cancel the reservation at the Jamaican," Mrs. McKay said with fear and tension in her voice.

"Why don't we stop at Carol's and I will make a call," Mr. McKay said.

The cold wind hurling up from the Hudson River made Reggie grasp for his breath. The force seemed to wipe away some of the tension that had gripped him during the evening. It was enough to dissolve his need to make mention of anything that had embarrassed him.

"I'm not sure what to make of Mr. McKay, but they seem like decent people, son."

"Thanks mom, they really are good people, especially Mrs. McKay and her sister. Carol says her father takes a little while to get used to anything that's a change, but he is a good person," Reggie said feeling some vindication.

"They're nothing like those carpetbaggers in Chicago that wanted you to forget where you came from. Well, it looks like they had some effect, but I thank the Lord for giving you that work in affirmative action. That's one answer to my prayers," Mrs. Morton said.

"Mom, my friends from Chicago are coming to the wedding and Harry is my best man."

"I thought your brother was your best man." Mrs. Morton said frowning.

"I was Harry's best man and I thought it would be appropriate to ask him to be mine," Reggie said apologetically.

"If my memory serves me right, Harry was an only child. He probably didn't have anyone else to ask. You did. Lord, what is this world coming to?" She said, looking like she was searching for a way out of a labyrinth.

Doug sat quietly looking out the window over the river to the night lights of New Jersey seemingly unflustered by the conversation between Reggie and his mother as the taxi rolled up the West Side Highway.

The phone was ringing as Reggie entered his room. He rushed to answer it thinking it was probably Carol.

"Hey fellow are you still engaged or have you come to your senses?" Gordon asked in a very jovial tone.

"I'm afraid I am still out of my mind because the wedding is still on," Reggie said jokingly.

"Well, I have rounded up a few of your colleagues and we want to give you a proper send-off tomorrow after the rehearsal dinner. It's better known as a bachelor party, but we won't mention it in Carol's presence. You need to notify your brother and your best man."

"Oh Gordon thanks man, I'll alert Doug and Harry." As soon as he hung up the phone rang again.

"Hello honey, how are you holding up?" Carol asked.

"I'm doing fine. I miss spending time with you." Reggie answered.

"Just think in two days we will be alone under the warm sun on the sandy beaches of Montego Bay with steel bands serenading us while we sip on exotic tropical drinks," Carol whispered into the phone.

"I can't wait," Reggie said.

"The reason I'm calling is we are changing the location for the rehearsal dinner. Instead of the Jamaican restaurant we are going to the Oak Room in the Plaza. Father just arranged it," Carol said with a bit of strain in her voice.

"What happened?" Reggie asked quizzically.

"Well, the truth is mother felt that your mother was not comfortable in the Village atmosphere and we didn't want to put her through that again."

"Well, I am sure she will be impressed with the Oak Room. I know I will. Thank your mother and father for me," Reggie said without acknowledging their perception of his mother. He was grateful for the change, but embarrassed. As he lay in bed tossing and turning trying to go to sleep, the lyrics of one stanza of the Negro National Anthem seem to chase him.

"God of our weary years, God of our silent tears, Thou who hast brought us thus far on the way; Thou who hast by Thy might led us in to the light; Keep us forever in the path, We pray lest our feet stray from the places our God, where we met thee; Lest, our hearts drunk with the wine of the world, we forget Thee; Shadowed beneath Thy hand may we forever stand, True to our God, true to our native land."

CHAPTER 20

As the taxi came to a stop in front of the Plaza, the smartly dressed concierge in his dark blue uniform and high top hat opened the door. Mrs. Morton stepped out reaching for her hair defending against a charging gust of wind. "Thank you sir," she said and nodded then began a hasty rush up the red carpet to the entrance which she was certain was warm. She was stunned by the wind and impressed with the royal service she had received. Doug followed, walking as if he were a recognized celebrity getting well- deserved recognition. Reggie paid the taxi and walked nervously behind Doug. Although he was impressed with the Plaza's style of service, he was hoping his mother and brother would not embarrass him by seeming overwhelmed by the grandeur. They were directed to the Oak Room and walked into this masculine aura with oak panel walls, barrel-vaulted ceilings and carved niches with murals.

"Does this place really serve the spicy foods Carol mentioned?" Mrs. Morton whispered into Reggie's ear.

"No, I don't think so. There was some problem with the reservations at the Jamaican restaurant and the dinner was moved here," Reggie said proudly while patting his mother on the shoulder. "This is one of New York's finest. I am sure it was not easy to get it at the last minute."

"Umm," Mrs. Morton replied as she braced her shoulder as if she were preparing to put on her best behavior.

"Good evening, Mrs. Morton, how are you doing?" Mr. McKay greeted her with the air of a feudal lord permitting a serf to enter the castle. "I hope the accommodations are acceptable to you," he said sarcastically with a grin on his face.

"I'm fine and everything looks just fine to me," Mrs. Morton replied, sounding humble. Before Mr. McKay could get another word in, Reggie approached with the Sanders family.

"Mr. McKay, Mrs. McKay, Carol, I want you to meet my best man, Harry and his wife, Linda and his parents, Mr. and Mrs. Sanders. Mom, you remember everyone don't you," Reggie proudly announced.

While Mrs. McKay and Carol were exchanging very friendly greetings, Mr. McKay looked puzzled. They are all white, he noted. However, he wasn't sure about Mr. Sanders. He thought he could possibly be one of those Blacks who try to pass for white. Maybe my little girl won't have to get involved in all that Black stuff if this is what Reggie's circle of friends looks like. Before he could absorb the thought, Gordon, his wife and Jeff walked up. Behind them were Madeline, Carol's maid of honor, Rose and Jenny.

After being introduced to all of them and observing that Blacks were indeed a minority in that crowd, Mr. McKay became more relaxed and began to mingle with the guests as if he were enjoying himself. He took the initiative to introduce everyone to his sister, his nieces, his sister-in-law and brother –in- law. Jack seemed uncomfortable in this slightly mixed racial group. He was unusually silent, completely different from his constant sarcastic racial innuendo remarks to Reggie at Thanksgiving. As soon as Jacqueline was introduced to Doug, she corralled him off into a corner the same way she approached Reggie at Thanksgiving dinner. Doug relished every moment. After her reintroductions to the Sanders, Mrs. Morton, still clinging to her resentment of them for what she decided was their misguided advice to her son about abandoning his Black heritage which in the end, she declared, led to this wedding, greeted them graciously. However, she wasted no time stepping away from them and shaking hands with Jeff, hugging him and engaging him in a conversation.

As Mrs. McKay began directing people to their particular seats along the long table in this private room, Mrs. Morton held her breath until she learned she would be nowhere near the Sanders. She was seated next to Jeff, a comfortable accommodation, she concluded. To the chagrin of her mother and aunt, Jacqueline, who was supposed to sit next to Uncle Jack, negotiated a change with her sister who was seated next to Doug. Doug had a big smile plastered on his face to the chagrin of his mother.

The unpretentious meal of a garden salad, filet mignon, baked potato, green beans with almonds and apple pie a la mode was served. Mrs. Morton looked at Reggie with a slight smile showing her approval, even though it was not the spicy food she was expecting. Reggie winked at her.

As the waiters cleared the table, Harry rose and lifted his glass of champagne and said, "To Reggie and Carol, May the love that has guided you to this moment guide you throughout your lives."

Madeline followed Harry raising her glass and said, "To Carol and Reggie, may your sunshine days outnumber your cloudy days two to one."

Mr. McKay then rose and began. "I only have one child and she is precious to me and, of course, I want nothing else but happiness in her life. Fathers tend to have a hard time letting go of their daughters, especially if she is his only one. So Reggie I am permitting you to share my daughter and you had better make her happy," he said while managing a smile that made the guests think he was joking, but he wasn't. Reggie felt the sting.

As the crowd began to disperse, Mr. Sanders cornered Reggie, shook his hand and said, "You have done well, young man. You are on the right track. Stick with it."

Reggie hugged him and said, "Thanks for your guidance and the opportunities you gave me."

Mrs. Sanders walked up, hugged Reggie and said, "I am so proud of you."

"Thanks for all the things you did for me. I will always remember them," Reggie responded with tears welling in his eyes.

Gordon left his wife chatting with Carol and rushed over, took Reggie by the arm and said, "Let's go." Reggie walked over and reminded his mother that Carol would drop her off at the hotel. Gordon, Reggie, Doug, Jeff and Harry grabbed a taxi and headed for the Americana Hotel where Gordon had rented a suite for the bachelor party. All the guys from the Texas Oil account were there except Rick. They greeted them as they entered the room. Reggie was surprised and happy to see everybody. He began to relax as the liquor began to flow and soon he was feeling no pain.

Dave Brubeck's "Take Five" was playing in the background when there was a knock on the door. Gordon raced over and opened it. A Black strip dancer stepped in shedding her coat and revealing an almost naked body. There were woos all over the room. In rhythm with the music, she made her way over to where Reggie was sitting. The adrenaline in his system seemed to overtake the liquor effect and he began to entertain sober thoughts. He decided he needed to be sober enough to pretend he was amused and turned on by this Black woman. But he also needed to appear drunk enough to convey that the liquor had dulled his ability to go all the way. As she stripped down to the minimum and began to gyrate in front of him, he began to pop his fingers and move his hips like he was dancing on the floor. She straddled his lap and he rolled his head back and closed his eyes while continuing to pop his fingers.

Everybody in the room kept screaming, "Yea! yea! Reggie go get it. It's your last chance," as they pointed toward the bedroom. Doug was getting a big kick out of it all. He figured Reggie was in a situation he didn't know how to get out of and that made Doug feel a bit superior, since he knew exactly what he would do to that woman. Jeff was standing there wishing she was sitting on his lap with no thought of what might have been on Reggie's mind. Gordon asked Jeff to pull the woman up off Reggie's lap and he would pull Reggie out of the chair and they would carry them both into the bedroom and close the door.

As soon as the door closed, Reggie fell on the bed and pulled the dancer down next to him and embraced her and then pretended to fall asleep. The dancer had been contracted for an hour so she lay with him until he pretended to wake up and kissed her on the cheek. He escorted her out to the cheering of everybody in the room.

The telephone rang promptly at nine the next morning and bolted Reggie out of a night of fatigue and alcohol induced sleep. Through a high testosterone morning voice, he growled out, "hello."

"Man, are you still sleeping? It's time to hit the floor. This is the day to put a hook in that fish that was floating around in the sea that I told you you were bound to catch. You remember that day when we were freshmen and you were so depressed about losing your girlfriend Mona? Well, come on let's get started. You are becoming a new man in two hours with your fickle past behind you. Okay, I'll be there at ten. Why don't you all meet me in front of the hotel?" Harry said in an upbeat and jovial tone.

"Okay, I'm up now. We will meet you downstairs, buddy." Reggie dashed into the shower feeling rushed, anxious, apprehensive and joyful. When he came out he went looking for the ring and couldn't find it. He began to shake and then remembered he had already given it to Harry. He took a deep breath, dressed and headed down to the lobby where Mrs. Morton and Doug were waiting. Mrs. Morton was looking like a stately lady dressed in her Christmas gifts from Reggie and covered in a full-length fur coat she had borrowed from one of her friends and wearing a Jacqueline Kennedy pill box hat gently placed on her head so as not to disturb her hairdo. Doug's overcoat was opened all the way down the front revealing his tuxedo that made him look like he had been liberated from his past. Reggie felt a great moment of pride forgetting those moments of embarrassment over the past couple of days.

"You all look like new money this morning," Reggie said with a big smile covering his face.

"Well, we don't want to embarrass you, son. You are looking handsome yourself."

The limousine rolled up and Harry rolled down his window and greeted them while the chauffeur opened the door.

"How are you all doing this morning? Mrs. Morton how are you enjoying your trip to New York?" Harry asked.

"New York is quite an interesting place. It's more crowded than I would like and it seems everybody is in a hurry. I guess it takes some time to get used to, but it does seem a lot like what you see in the movies and that makes it a nice place to visit." she answered, leaning back in the leather covered comfortable seat with her hands folded over her purse and looking out the window.

"I have never been here before in the winter and I was a little surprised how cold it gets. Of course it's not like Chicago."

"If it gets any colder than this in Chicago, I don't think I want to visit Chicago in the winter."

"Well, I hope that means you will visit us in the summer or spring."

"Well, maybe one day," Mrs. Morton said as the driver dodged some of the uptown traffic by taking the route through Central Park. "This is quite a big park right in the middle of this crowded city. I guess it is good for the people to have some place to go outside of those tall buildings. My Lord, they have horses and buggies riding through the park."

Reggie sat in silence. He was happy to see Harry trying to engage his mother and her seemingly comfort with him. He began to wonder if he had everything ready for a quick stop over at the hotel on their way to the airport after the reception. He went through a check list in his mind and concluded he was ready. The limousine pulled up in front of the church a half hour before the eleven o'clock ceremony. Mrs. Morton stared at the startling façade.

"This is the church the Rockefeller family built," Harry said.

"You don't say." Mrs. Morton replied. "It's a beautiful structure," she said and concluded it was in keeping with everything else the McKays had been doing.

Doug joined Jeff as they assumed their positions to greet and usher guests to the appropriate seats while Harry rushed Reggie to the waiting area for the groom. Jeff ushered Mrs. Morton to her seat in the pews on the right side of the aisle. The organ began to play Ave Maria as the guests arrived. Doug and Jeff politely ushered them to their seats. On the groom's side there were a total of six people. Mrs. Morton was the only Black. On the bride's side there was fifty, one Black, Phyllis, the McKays' Jamaican housekeeper. Those were numbers reflecting the image Reggie was anticipating, but a picture he wanted to avoid.

The organ stopped and a plus sized white woman walked out into the middle of the chancel. The organ started up again and the woman began to sing, "Because God Made You Mine." At the end of the song, Reggie and Harry walked out and took their places in front of the chancel and the organ began to play Mendelssohn's wedding march and down the aisle came Jeff and Jenny who was counting the minutes until this was over so she could distance herself from this Black American. Doug and Rose followed looking like a happy couple.

After assuming their positions, Madeline marched slowly down the aisle and took her position. The organ paused then began to play "Here Comes the Bride." Reggie looked down the long aisle. There she was in a puffed sleeve hand embroidered floor length gown and a head piece pulled away from her face. Reggie thought she looked like something descending from above. He began to feel that the day was really his to relish. Mr. McKay's body was as erect as a Buckingham Place guard. He projected the image of a soldier marching in a victory parade; however, his eyes revealed some lasting apprehension. He backed away to his seat, like someone in total control, after answering the call of who is giving away this bride. Standing there before Rev. Whitfield who was dressed in his colorful robe and with the sun illuminating the stained glass windows and Carol holding his hand, Reggie felt he truly understood the meaning of happiness.

"Ladies and gentlemen would you join me in a prayer for this lovely couple." With all heads bowed and eyes closed, he asked the Lord to bless the union of these two people that their lives might be a testament to the glory of our Lord Jesus Christ. He raised his head and, for a moment, looked at the wedding party. It occurred to him that their make up would probably be something Martin Luther King would praise-a black groom, and a white bride; a white maid of honor and best man, two Black groomsmen and one black and one white bridesmaids. "Ladies and gentlemen, the bride and groom have decided to write their own vows. We will now hear from them."

Reggie looked into Carol's beaming eyes and said, "Carol, I will love you when the sun goes down. I will love you when each day begins. I will love you during those moments of pain. I will love you during those moments of joy. Carol, I will love you when we grow old and I will love you when we say good-bye to this world. I surrender to you my heart this day."

"Reggie, you have brought joy into my life like no other. You have brought sunlight into rainy days. You have added that missing link to fulfill my life. I hope my love for you will fulfill your life as yours has fulfilled mine."

"Reggie will you place the ring on Carol's finger and repeat after me? With this ring I thee wed." Reggie slipped the ring on Carol's finger and looked into her eyes and repeated the words.

"Carol will you now place the ring on Reggie's finger and repeat after me? With this ring I thee wed."

"With this ring, I thee wed," Carol said with a smile on her face.

"By the power vested in my by the state of New York, I now pronounce you husband and wife. You may kiss the bride. Ladies and gentlemen I present to you, Reggie Morton and Carol McKay, husband and wife." Carol had decided to keep her last name much to the chagrin of Reggie.

The guest stood up and clapped as the wedding party marched out of the nave while the organ played "What the World Needs Now is Love." They quickly formed the receiving line in the hall around the corner from the nave where the reception was being held. A quartet of Black jazz musicians with a soloist was already playing when they entered. The guests began to roll in, extending their hands and offering the traditional best wishes. The McKays stood at the head of the line and Mrs. Morton at the end. As the last guest was shaking Mrs. Morton's hand, the photographer summoned the wedding party to form and the usual photos were taken.

Harry then took charge and ushered the wedding party and the parents to the head table. The garden salad, Cornish hens stuffed with fruits, roasted sweet potatoes and creamed Brussels sprouts were served while the quartet played soft music in the background. Following the lunch, the bride and groom were led to the cake for the cutting. The room seemed more jovial than curious about the mixed marriage. The music stopped and the quartet's leader took the microphone and invited Mr. and Mrs. Morton to the dance floor for their first dance as husband and wife. The quartet began to play and the soloist belted out, "I'll be with you in apple blossom time. I'll be with you to change your name to mine........" When Reggie beckoned others to join them, Harry reached for Mrs. Morton's hand and led her to the floor. It was a transitional moment for her. She no longer felt isolated and the reception became a fun party for her. Doug led Rose to the floor and held her closer than usual for a casual dance. Jeff teased Jenny by bowing before her and asking her to dance. She said yes to avoid drawing attention to her feelings that this was not for her.

The floor filled up and the music played on and it seemed everybody was having a great time. After many efforts to get to his daughter, Mr. McKay finally got his dance and they swayed across the floor with her head resting on his chest. Reggie danced with his mother as the time drew near for his and Carol's departure.

Mrs. Morton said, "Son this has been quite an impressive wedding. I pray that the choice you have made will make you happy. Carol seems like a nice girl. I pray you will be able to make it. Grandma would have had a hard time accepting this considering all those lash marks she saw every time grandfather took off his shirt. Mama probably would also have a hard time too every time she thought about how they were cheated by sharecropper landlords. I pray every night that the Lord will continue to remind me that we are all God's children. Now don't you forget to keep the Lord in your life. You will always be in my prayers. I love you, son."

"I love you too mom and I'm happy you were here with me for this occasion. With your prayers, I feel Carol and I will make it. I won't forget to pray."

The crowd gathered for release of the garter which was caught by Jeff who held if proudly. Jacqueline caught the bouquet and immediately passed it on to her sister as the crowd broke out in loud laughter.

The guests braced for the cold weather and gathered on the steps of the church and threw rice as Reggie and Carol rushed for their car and headed for her apartment then the hotel and them the airport.

Back in the reception hall, Mrs. McKay hugged her husband and said, "Honey, this was really beautiful. You have been wonderful all throughout. I am so proud of you. Our daughter is really happy and that is what matters."

"I hope you are right," Mr. McKay said in a melancholy tone as he held his wife.

"I want to thank you for all your hospitality during our trip. I really enjoyed meeting you all and I think you have a lovely daughter. I will be praying for their happy marriage," Mrs. Morton said while extending her hand to Mr. and Mrs. McKay.

"It was really a pleasure having you here and of course we know you are proud of Reggie. He is a man of strength over many obstacles. We are happy for him too and wish him and Carol the best as they go forward. You have done a wonderful job raising your sons. I wish his father could have been with us today. I think he would have been proud," Mrs. McKay said, holding Mrs. Morton's hand.

"I wish you a safe trip back home. You must come again to visit us. Next time we will take you to Harlem to a nice restaurant where you can have some good down home cooked food," Mr. McKay said through a forced smile.

"Thank you," Mrs. Morton responded. Just as she and Doug were about to depart for their car, Harry walked up with his parents and wife and offered to take Mrs. Morton and Doug to dinner that evening. "Thank you so much," Mrs. Morton responded. "But we are going back home this evening."

"You promised to come to visit us in Chicago when Reggie graduated and we haven't seen you there yet. When can we expect you to keep your promise?" Mrs. Sanders asked reaching for Mrs. Morton's hand.

"Well, it's hard to say. Things are so different since I lost my husband, but you never know," Mrs. Morton said as she pulled her hand out of Mrs. Sanders'

Doug went chasing around the room giving Jacqueline an affectionate hug and Rose a perfunctory hug and shaking Jeff and Gordon's hands before joining his mother in the car for the ride back to the hotel and their later ride to the airport.

CHAPTER 21

British West Indies Airline was having a most usual experience. They were leaving on time. Reggie and Carol therefore wasted no time after the limousine chauffeur dropped them off at the terminal. The plane was loading when they finally arrived at check-in. They took their place in line with a herd of travelers carrying boxes, shopping bags, and array of other items that were permitted for carry-on. Although the temperature was in the thirties outside, there were some obvious tourists dressed in Bermuda shorts. Carol and Reggie took their two- across seats and exhaled. Reggie looked over at Carol who had taken the window seat and said, "You are the angel sent down from heaven to make me happy. I want you to know that you have succeeded and have more than earned your wings. I am one happy man today."

"You are worthy of any happiness that I am able to pass on. You are the one I want to be with for the rest of my life," Carol said as she leaned over and kissed Reggie on the cheek. Reggie grabbed her hand and leaned his head back against the seat and closed his eyes. Carol stared at him with a look of unyielding admiration. When the stewardess came around after the plane had taken-off and asked for orders for drinks, Reggie asked if they could have two glasses of champagne. The light tan complexion stewardess said, "Newlyweds?" Carol raised her ring finger and, with a smile, said, "Yes."

"Congratulations, Of course you can. Hold on to that thought. I'll be right back," the stewardess said in jest.

By the time dinner was served, Reggie and Carol had downed two glasses of champagne and were feeling the effects. After dinner and the start of the movie, the champagne and the stress of the day began to take their toll and they both fell asleep.

"Hello lovebirds," the stewardess said as she shook Reggie on the shoulder. "We are getting close to landing and you need to complete these immigration forms."

"Thank you, thank you," Reggie said opening his puffy eyes. He kissed Carol on the cheek and said, "Honey we will be landing soon and need to complete these forms." Carol yawned and nodded her head.

"Ladies and gentlemen, we are on our final approach to Montego Bay. The weather there is a balmy seventy-eight degrees. I want to thank you for choosing British West Indies Airlines and wish you a happy visit to the island." the pilot announced.

"Seventy-eight balmy degrees, that sounds like heaven after leaving those freezing thirties. I can't wait," Reggie said.

"And the sandy beaches and bright sunshine, steel band music and interesting rum drinks," Carol reminded him.

"Baby, this sounds like the next best thing to heaven and having you there with me. I must have done something right."

"Ladies and gentlemen would you fasten your seatbelts and pull your seats back to the upright position. We are entering the final approach to Montego Bay," the voice over the public address system announced. The landing was smooth. After waiting impatiently for the crowd in front of them to exit, Reggie finally stepped out onto the tarmac into the smell of the salty ocean air and the feel of light summer breezes sweeping across the land. After enduring about an hour of Caribbean style, no rush service, Carol and Reggie walked out of the terminal into a cadre of taxi drivers aggressively peddling their services. One accosted Reggie with a "hey, cool brother need a ride?" Reggie slapped his hand in a high five and they were off to the Holiday Inn.

"Are you newlyweds?" the driver asked checking them out in the rear view mirror where they were holding hands.

"Yes, we are," Reggie answered looking into Carol's face and gripping her hand.

"Well maan (man) you have come to a great place for a honeymoon. Our beaches are famous, our mountains are beautiful and we can whip up some food you won't forget. Where are you from?" He asked in his heavy West Indian accent.

"New York," Reggie answered.

"I have cousins there. I'm going to visit them one day, maybe during the Labor Day West Indian festival. They say it's wild."

"It is and you should really plan to be there at that time," Carol said.

"Have you gone to it?"

"Yes, one of my friends took me there on a couple of occasions. The costumes are amazingly creative and beautiful and the steel bands are great."

"Maan, that really cool," he said with sparkles in his eyes.

"Make sure you take a trip to Negril. That's where you will find the best white sandy beaches the tourist love."

"How is the beach around the hotel?" Reggie asked.

"Oh, its fine, maan. You can walk right out of your room onto the beach, so it's nice for a midnight swim. You know what I mean," the driver answered with a mischievous grin on his face.

"Yes, I get it," Reggie said as Carol gave him a sly look.

"Well, here we are maan-the luxurious Holiday Inn," the driver said as he wasted no time jumping out of the car and rushing around and opening the door. He then lifted their bags from the trunk and carried them to the reception desk.

"Thank you," Reggie said as he paid the fare and tipped him.

"Thank you maan," he said while heartily shaking Reggie's hand.

The hotel lobby was spacious and painted in a light yellow tone with tropical plants placed in strategic locations.

"Good evening and welcome to the Holiday Inn," a light tan complexion receptionist greeted them.

"Thank you. I'm Reggie Morton and this is my wife Carol. We have a reservation under my name."

"Yes, Mr. Morton if you will sign in, your suite is ready and a bellhop will escort you to it. These are your keys. Enjoy your stay."

Carol looked awed as she stepped into the suite with a pale rose colored couch and love seat. There were sliding doors that led to the terrace facing the ocean. She walked out onto it. The cool, salty air brushed across the terrace and sent her hair flowing. Reggie walked up behind her and wrapped his arms around her waist.

"Oh Reggie this is wonderful."

"Not as wonderful as you," he said, looking out to the ocean that glistened with the reflection of the moon.

They walked into the bedroom painted a soft blue. The bed spread's design was colorful flowers. Resting on the dresser were a basket of fruit and a bottle of champagne chilling in a silver bucket with two glasses beside it.

"They have done us well," Carol said.

"Yes, the dream comes true," Reggie said.

"Well, I'm going to get comfortable so I can enjoy this," Reggie said through a mischievous smile.

Carol unpacked and laid out her carefully chosen wedding night lingerie. When Reggie emerged covered with the white terry cloth bathrobe supplied by the hotel looking fresh and bearing the smell of soap, Carol asked, "Should I eat you or the fruit?"

"Me baby, me baby," he said.

"Well, hold that thought until I return," she said as she disappeared into the bathroom.

Reggie pulled out a pair of pajamas, laid the top aside and slid into the bottom leaving his upper body exposed. He popped the cork on the champagne and poured two glasses, lowered the lights and pulled the drapes together and adjusted the fan on the air conditioner. He placed the champagne on the night stand next to his side of the bed and crawled in and pulled the sheet up to his waist. Carol emerged in a scant night gown and said, "What's going on here? Are you planning to take advantage of me?"

"You bet," Reggie said, "But you're going to enjoy it" as he pulled her into the bed and handed her a glass of champagne. He raised his glass and said, "Here's to the start of a life fulfilled."

"I can drink to that," Carol said as she took a sip and rested her head on Reggie's naked chest.

Halfway through the bottle of champagne, Reggie leaned down and planted a savage kiss on Carol's lips. She wrapped her arm around his head and pulled him close. Reggie stripped her gown off and began to kiss her plump breasts. Carol closed her eyes and rubbed his head. Reggie made his way back up to her lips and filled her mouth with his savagely prowling tongue. Carol reached for his pajama bottom and shoved it down to his knees. He kicked it off completely. At that moment, they joined together as one, both breathing heavily while rolling over and over until the moment of climax when Carol called out, "My Mandingo, my Mandingo." Reggie followed with, "Oh baby, oh baby." They lay in silence as their breathing subsided. Reggie held Carol in his arms as she closed her eyes and dozed off to sleep.

As Reggie lay there holding Carol while the feeling of passion ebbed away, it seemed the word Mandingo, which had been hiding in the back of his brain, pushed forward. He didn't immediately recognize its meaning and dismissed it as some innocuous passionate response of Carol's. But like the burst of light from a turned-on light bulb, it hit him. Mandingos are the strong, virile, brave African warriors. Reggie's mouth went dry. Surely she doesn't see me as one of those nappy headed, scantily dressed, spear carrying savages.

His heart began to race and his mood shifted to hurt. He slowly released Carol from his embrace and she rolled over away from him. He turned off the dimmed light and turned on his side with his back to Carol. When he was certain she was sleep, he carefully slid out of the bed and went and sat on the terrace staring at the waves slapping the shore. I graduated from Davis University. I am a Davis man. I am an account executive in a prestigious advertising agency and I rented an apartment in Riverdale, New York. I'm no damn Mandingo, he kept telling himself. His heartbeat finally began to slow down and his eyes began to get heavy. Sleep beckoned him and he eased back in bed.

"Wake-up. Morning has broken, I just lifted the Do Not Disturb sign from the door and that means its time for us to breathe in some Jamaican culture. Phyllis said we must climb the rocks of Dunn's River Falls and spend some time on the Negril beaches. I noticed they have tours leaving from the hotel.

Why don't we give it a try today? Before we know it, these few days will be over and we will be back in our nine to fives. So, come on get up and let's get started," Carol said as she stood over the bed snuggled in her bathrobe with her head wrapped in a terry cloth turban. She leaned over and kissed Reggie on the cheek.

Reggie was awake, but struggling to get his bearings together. He felt a streak of sadness, but wasn't sure the source of it until Carol kissed him and Mandingo flashed through his mind. He turned his head, stretched and wiped his eyes as if he were moving toward full alertness; but he really was trying to decide how to cope with his feelings. The answer struck him. He didn't want his honeymoon spoiled by maybe a misunderstanding. He looked up at Carol and said, with a grin on his face. "Let's grab every minute and squeeze out every second." Uttering those words increased his heartbeat and lifted him away from his sadness. He rolled out of the bed telling himself that he was going to make this honeymoon an epic of fond memories.

"What time are the tours?"

"There is one starting at eleven. That should give us time for breakfast."

Reggie emerged from the shower whistling Johnny Mathis' "Wonderful, Wonderful" trying to project a happy person. Carol recognized the tune and began to sing the words. They embraced as he whistled and she sang.

Climbing the slippery rocks of Dunn's River Falls along with the tour guide and other tourist; reaching out to hold on to each other to keep from falling; and the tour guide using tourist cameras to snap shots was a totally engulfing experience, full of laughs. Then spending a couple of hours on the beach in Negril brought to life the stories they had been told about its beauty.

Back at the hotel, they had dinner at the restaurant sitting at a table with an unobstructed view of the ocean while breathing in the warm tropical breezes. A steel band serenaded the guests with classical tunes. A young man fashionably dressed approached their table peddling marijuana which they refused. Carol and Reggie chose Jamaican Appleton rum and coke as their drink for the evening and were not bashful in ordering them. After a meal of Jerked Snapple, fried plantains, rice and peas and green beans with pineapple and mango chutney, they moved back to their suite feeling light on their feet. They stood on their terrace listening to the steel band and dancing in the privacy of their suite.

This time Carol was first to bed having stepped into her seductive night gown with her hair flowing freely around her shoulder. She positioned herself in the bed to add to her appeal. Reggie emerged from the bathroom only in his briefs and crawled in the bed beside Carol and took her in his arms and kissed her passionately. Carol swung her arms around his shoulders and pulled him close. Ordinarily, at this point, Reggie would be highly stimulated, but this time nothing happened. Carol landed a passionate kiss on him and pulled him tightly. But there was still no excitement. Reggie rolled over utterly embarrassed and pulled the sheet over his lower body.

"What's wrong?" Carol asked as she stroked his head.

"Too much liquor," Reggie claimed. "I'll be all right after a few hours of sleep."

"Okay," Carol said as she rested her head on his chest and stroked his face with her hand. Carol finally fell asleep and

Reggie eased himself away from her. He lay there trying to erase Mandingo from his mind.

Carol rose the next morning more subdued than the previous day. Reggie lay on his side with his head buried in his arm.

"What would you like to do today?" Carol asked as she sat up in the bed.

In an effort to uplift their spirits, Reggie turned over on his back and said with contrived enthusiasm in his voice, "Let's start by checking out the waters here and cooling out on the beach. Maybe we could try some snorkeling and check out animal life under the water. How about that? This evening we can try that restaurant Phyllis told you about. What's it called, Day O Plantation and Bar?"

"That's it. Well, I guess you had a good night's rest and are raring to go. Your suggestions sound pretty good to me. Let me start by making myself pretty," Carol said.

"Baby, you don't need to do anything more. You are already pretty," Reggie said slapping her on the butt as she jumped out of the bed.

"Well, how about prettier?" she said, dashing into the bathroom.

Reggie got up repeating his vow to make this honeymoon an epic of fond memories. He tried to whistle. He paced the floor and slammed his fist into his hand. Two nights of bad memories, the second worst than the first. How do I get this back on track, he thought. When he heard Carol opening the door to the bathroom he was finally able to whistle. All day long he was able to keep up a happy front. They swam, snorkeled, stretched- out under an umbrella on the beach with tropical drinks at their beck and call. The Day O Plantation and Bar, in the middle of a beautiful garden, provided a romantic atmosphere where they held hands and kissed across the table. However, at bed time Reggie and Carol felt anxious. Reggie took the lead with his passionate kiss. When the erection didn't come, he pulled Carol closer and massaged her body with his hands. The erection kept coming and then fading. Eventually, it lasted long enough for him to penetrate. His love making then became more vigorous which thrilled Carol but left her feeling a bit inadequate.

Their last day was filled with a tour of the local area, souvenir shopping and one last swim in the warm waters of the Caribbean Sea. They went to bed that night with their backs to each other.

CHAPTER 22

The telephone rang as Reggie sat at his clean desk thinking nothing has changed, thank God. Maybe I can use my time to focus on wrapping up things here as quickly as possible so I can return to the Texas Oil account. Hopefully, the Department of Labor's decision, if not already made, would soon be forthcoming. The only thing left on the intern program was recruiting which should be completed within the next month, he concluded.

"Hello, Reggie Morton here."

"Hello Reggie Morton, welcome back. You sound like the honeymoon keeps going," Sandra said.

"You could say that."

"Well, I'm sorry to be the distracter from your dip into dreamland. Henry would like to meet with you at eleven. Is that convenient for you?"

"Thanks, that's fine."

"Okay, we'll see you then."

Reggie hung up the phone and pulled out a pad to begin mapping out his strategy for bringing things to closure. He thought he should come up with the list of colleges for recruiting. He decided Howard University first, followed by Atlanta University and then Fisk. He then called them and they agreed on the best time to come.

When eleven o'clock rolled around, Reggie strolled into Henry's office with an air of confidence, holding his list of colleges in hand. Henry stood up and extended his hand and said.

"Congratulations again, Sandra tells me everything went well."

"Yes, everything was fantastic," Reggie said.

"Did you have good weather in Jamaica?"

"Oh, yes, warm temperature, warm ocean waters and cool breezes in the evening. I couldn't have asked for more."

"How is your wife?"

"Carol is doing fine."

"Oh, yes, it's Carol," Henry said looking away from Reggie and dropping his head then sat back down and began to thumb through some papers on his desk. He lifted his head and said. "I have an interesting development in the intern program. One of the vice presidents has recommended a candidate that I will be having lunch with today. I will bring him by on our way to lunch to meet you. He is in his junior year at Harvard."

"Oh, good, I look forward to meeting him. I've developed a list of Black colleges and universities to go to and have contacted them about an appropriate time to visit. They are all excited about the possibility. Here's my list," Reggie said proudly.

"Well, why don't we hold off until I see what this guy is like? Since this is our first year, we need to start off slowly with one candidate and if things go well, we could expand. I wouldn't want those colleges to get excited and we don't choose one of their students. It could be bad for public relations. Wouldn't you agree?" Henry asked looking at Reggie and then down at his desk.

"How should I follow-up with these schools that I have already contacted?" Reggie asked, feeling anger and frustration churning in him."

"Tell them we had a budget problem and that we will be back in touch with them in the fall. I am certain they are very familiar with budget problems."

"Sure," Reggie said, thinking how embarrassed he would be calling those colleges and lying to them, but feeling he needed to be viewed as a team player. "By the way, have we heard from the Department of Labor?" Reggie asked, hoping the Department would have come back with some recommended changes that would be a bit of revenge for the agency's embarrassing back- stepping on the intern program.

"Oh, yes, I almost forget to tell you. The letter came in last week and you will be glad to hear they approved the plan. So congratulations, you must have done a great job. There was nothing they wanted to change."

"Really," Reggie said hoping his stunned reaction was not apparent on his face. He immediately remembered Jeff's predictions that this would be the case. He wondered if there was any way the folks back home could ever find out what was in the agreement and how he would explain it if they did.

"We can talk later about implementing the plan. There is no rush. It will take a long time before the Department of Labor checks on us. Anyway, we are taking a big step with the intern program. They will love it," Henry said with a genuine smile.

"Okay," Reggie said as he stood up and walked out of the office. He walked into his office and closed the door in an effort to hide his disappointment from public view. Before he could muster up one grain of self-pity, there was a knock on the door. He wanted to let it go unanswered, but the door opened and in walked Jeff without an invitation.

"Well, hello my brother how is married life? Are you still hanging onto Cloud Nine or have your feet hit the ground?"

"Hey Jeff, thanks again for joining the wedding party. I really appreciated it."

"No problem, I didn't mind helping a brother. Well, welcome back to this place."

"Thanks for stopping by."

"Oh, by the way I heard a rumor you might be interesting in."

"Yeah, what is it."

"Gordon is supposed to be leaving to accept a Senior VP job at another agency and they are planning to give the Texas Oil account to your buddy, Rick and you will be offered the position of Rick's assistant when you are released from human resources."

"Where did you hear that rumor?" Reggie asked, feeling like a rock had landed in his stomach.

"Let's just say it's a rumor from someone you can usually rely on for information. However, I would just suggest you watch your back," Jeff said, noticing the change in Reggie's face and not wanting to push him closer to an edge. "By the way, when do you think you will be finished here? How are things going with the affirmative action plan and the intern program?"

Reggie's anger overwhelmed him and he blurted out, "You were right about the affirmative action plan. The Department of Labor approved it lock, stock and barrel. As for the intern program, Henry has identified a potential candidate and will be meeting with him today."

"Where did you find this guy?"

"I didn't. He was recommended by some vice president, probably some Harvard alumni."

"Is the guy from Harvard?"

"Yes," Reggie said as he dropped his head and looked at the floor.

"Why don't you check out some dudes from one of those Black colleges down south?

"The plan is to delay recruiting at them until maybe this fall semester. The agency wants to start the program with just one to test it before expanding," Reggie answered still looking at the floor.

Sensing Reggie's discomfort, Jeff said, "Well, man as long as this guy is Black that's a beginning for the agency. Anyway, you gave them an option –one I don't think they will ever take. They probably think those guys from Black colleges are a little too militant. As for the Department of Labor, maybe they will fool us and do some serious monitoring. In the meantime, hang in there, man."

"Thanks man," Reggie said as Jeff walked out.

Reggie paced the floor, slapping his fist into his hand. What the hell am I worried about. Maybe all this means is, I will be out of the affirmative action mess faster than I expected. But mom sees this as my redemption for abandoning my roots. She would be hurt and ashamed if she couldn't counter criticism of my marriage with my commitment to helping other Blacks gain opportunities. But am I supposed to be the great Black hope? I paid a great price making it through all that prejudice at Davis University. But what the hell will I do if the rumor is true and I am forced to work with that scheming thief, Rick. It would take a hell of a lot to get past the memory of him stealing my idea and selling it as his own. Reggie's torturous pondering was interrupted by another knock on the door.

"Reggie I want you to meet Carlton Barkley. He is they guy we are considering for the intern program. Carlton this is Reggie Morton. He is our point person for our affirmative action program," Henry said with a proud look on his face.

"Nice to meet you Mr. Barkley," Reggie said through a forced smile as he extended his hand to this tall, light skinned, straight haired Black man. He reminded Reggie of Mr. Sanders.

"Same here," Mr. Barkley said, giving Reggie a very firm handshake and with a stern, unemotional expression on his face.

"Here is my card. If I can answer any questions for you don't hesitate to contact me," Reggie said trying to exude some above the fray professional behavior.

"Thank you," Mr. Barkley responded still with a stern face.

"Well, Reggie we are off to lunch," Henry said, leading Carlton by the arm into the hall.

Reggie sat at his desk trying to think of a convincing way to inform the Black colleges that he had to back away from his commitment. He picked up a pen and fumbled a piece of paper, but couldn't focus. His mind was stalled on how he thought he had been used to cover up the agency's lack of commitment to providing opportunities to Blacks and other minorities. And the thought of having to work under Rick was frightening. He bolted from his chair and walked out of his office and down the elevator and into the Chicago like cold winds that almost took his breath away. He wasn't certain where he was going, but he was sure he didn't want to linger in that weather. A taxi stopped at the red light and he jumped in.

"Where to sir?' the driver asked.

Without much thought he said, "Harlem, Sylvia's Restaurant, Lenox and 127th street."

The white driver looked askance at him in the rearview mirror, bit his bottom lip and gripped the steering wheel.

Reggie sat looking out the window, wondering what he was doing heading up to Harlem. However, he noticed that some of the tension he was feeling began to ebb. He paid the driver who blurted out, "Is this all you're giving me for a tip?" Befuddled, Reggie reached into his pocked and pulled out another dollar, handed it to the driver and then walked into the restaurant thinking he shouldn't have given him any tip since he seemed so reluctant to drive up to Harlem.

Sylvia's was crowded with mostly Black customers who were engaged in jovial chatter. Reggie was led to a table by a friendly young Black man who handed him a menu. No one paid any attention to him as he sat looking over the menu, contrary to how things usually were when he was in a restaurant with Carol. That thought gave him a small bit of comfort. The waiter came to take his order. He was ready. He ordered barbecued ribs, collard greens, potato salad and sweet ice tea. As he devoured the meal, he felt like he had traveled back in time and was sitting around his mother's table on the Fourth of July. After that meal, he was full, but when the waiter came and asked if he were interested in dessert, he ordered coconut cake, not that he really had room for it, but it would delay his return to the office and that troubled environment.

When Reggie stepped out of the taxi in front of his office building, he spotted Gordon. Reggie waved and got his attention. Gordon looked nervous and began to walk rapidly as if he were late for something.

"Hey Reggie, what's up? When did you get back? How was the honeymoon?" he asked with a quiver in his voice.

"This is my first day back. The honeymoon was excellent," Reggie said.

"You look well, marriage must be agreeing with you. Look, we must have lunch. I'm on my way to a meeting. I'll call you for lunch," Gordon said as he trailed away in haste.

Reggie stood with the wind slashing his face as he watched Gordon disappear into the crowded street. He felt Gordon's obvious nervousness could indicate that something was amiss and that Jeff's rumor just might be true.

CHAPTER 23

"Hello baby, I'm home," Reggie called out as he walked into the two bedroom apartment that Carol had charmed her building's superintendent into letting her know was available. She wanted to be able to accommodate some of the things Reggie might be attached to when he moved in, without feeling overcrowded.

"Hey honey. I picked up some Chinese food," Carol said as she kissed him on the cheek. "How was your day?"

Reggie wrapped his arms around her, held her close and in a whisper said, "I'm glad to be away from that place and in my castle holding you in my arms."

"What happened?" Carol asked pushing away from his embrace and looking him in the eye.

"It seemed like it was, 'let's punch a hole in Reggie's bubble day'." Reggie said in a kind of sarcastic, but angry tone.

"How could they manage that?" Carol asked with a slight smirk on her face.

"First, Henry asked me to lie to the Black colleges I had contacted about recruiting on their campuses. He squashed my plan and told me to tell them we didn't have the money to recruit this year. Instead, he had identified one guy from Harvard who some vice president had recommended. He said they wanted to start out with just one student and see how the whole thing worked out."

"Is the guy from Harvard Black?" Carol asked with a quizzical look on her face.

"Yes, he is," Reggie said with a bit of irritation in his voice.

"Then what's the problem? The goal was to bring minorities into the program and you have a minority. It makes sense to start out small and refine the program before expanding. Don't you think? Listen, they asked you to develop a program and you did. Its naïve to think that everything you recommend will be implemented. That's not how companies work. So give it your best shot and move on, honey," Carol said standing before Reggie and holding his hand like a proud teacher who had just taught her student an important lesson of life.

Reggie pulled his hand out of hers, sat down in the Lazy-Boy chair, leaned back and said. "That's only part of today's story. The Department of Labor approved the affirmative action plan lock, stock and barrel-no requirement for more specifics."

"Well, congratulations, at least they accepted your recommendations without questioning," Carol said as she walked into the kitchen and began pulling food out of bags.

"The plan was crap. It was full of vague statements about what the agency stood for but very little of what they would actually do to improve opportunities for minorities and women," Reggie said with anger in his voice."

"Well, didn't you write it?" Carol asked in an accusatory tone.

"What I wrote suffered a major overhaul at Henry's hand," Reggie snapped back.

"Like I said, you can't expect all your recommendations to be adopted. Remember you are only making recommendations. That's how companies work. Your job is to give them options and theirs is to make the decision," Carol said, seeming to become impatient with Reggie's thinking. "You must not be paranoid about every decision made by your agency. There are many factors involved in their decisions."

"Paranoid!" Reggie shouted as he sat up in the chair.

"Honey, I didn't mean any harm," Carol said as she walked out of the kitchen and over to Reggie and affectionately patted his head.

Reggie leaned back in the chair reached for Carol's hand and said, "The story doesn't end there. Jeff told me he heard a rumor that Gordon was leaving and Rick would get the Texas Oil account and I would be made his assistant."

"I can imagine that would be disappointing to you since you have been working on the account before they loaned you to Human Resources. Was Rick working on the account before you and does he have more experience as an account executive than you?" Carol asked in a quiet, caring tone resembling a mother trying to teach a child the facts of life.

"Rick is the scoundrel who stole my idea about advertising to the Black community and sold it to Texas Oil as his own. He worked under me when I was managing the account," Reggie said in a burst of anger.

"I can see why you would not want to work under him. But I understand there is a lot of that kind of behavior in the advertising industry. You have no idea what went into that decision, or if the rumor is really true. You need to wait and find out if it really is true before you start worrying about how to react to it. If it is true, see what explanation they will give you and what they intend to do to make it up to you. There could be a great opportunity coming your way, honey," Carol said while kissing Reggie on the cheek.

"Time will tell." Reggie said feeling unfulfilled.

"Come, let's eat before this fried rice gets cold. I got you chicken and broccoli in dark sauce, your favorite," Carol said pulling Reggie out of the chair and leading him to the dining table where the paper containers, a plastic fork and chop sticks were lined up. Oh, not again, Reggie was thinking as he looked at the boxes of food. They sat silently at the table with the sound of Walter Cronkite's deep, reassuring voice in the background bringing the news report to an end. Carol with her chop sticks and Reggie with his fork cleaned out the paper containers. After dinner, Carol snuggled up to Reggie on the couch while they watched the comedy, "Laugh In," which was funny enough to distract them for an hour.

"Honey, are you still worried about working with Rick?" Carol asked as she slipped into bed next to him laying there with his hands behind his head and staring at the ceiling.

"Not at the moment," he responded.

"Well, what's wrong? You seem to be in another world." Carol asked resting on her elbows and looking down at Reggie.

"I'm just thinking what will the people back home think of me if they ever find out about that do- nothing affirmative action plan." Reggie answered without looking at Carol.

"What could they think? You gave it your best shot and the government declared it well done."

"They could accuse me of selling out and that would be hard for mom to take."

"Who would you have sold out?" Carol asked looking puzzled.

"The whole race," Reggie said quietly.

"Come on Reggie, you are only one person. You are not the Messiah for Black people. Don't be paranoid."

"There is that word again," Reggie snapped looking directly at Carol.

"Oh honey, I didn't mean any harm. I love you," Carol said as she leaned down and began kissing Reggie passionately. Reggie returned the kiss but it took a while for him to muster a more physical response and when he did his voltage of passion remained at a low level. He engaged her as if he were following the instruction of a "How To" book. Carol eventually rolled over on her side with her back to Reggie and lay there thinking the last place she expected trouble in this marriage was in the bedroom. Reggie lay there now praying that his reading of Gordon's body language was wrong.

"Wake-up honey," Carol said as she tapped Reggie on the shoulder. "It's your turn in the bathroom. My flight is at nine-thirty so as usual I'm rushing. I'm supposed to meet my boss at the airport at eight-thirty. I don't have time for breakfast. I'll get something on the plane. I'll call you tonight from Seattle," Carol said trying to catch her breath as she rushed around the room dressing and throwing last minute things into her suitcase.

"When are you due in San Francisco?"

"We will arrive there Thursday evening and fly back to New York Saturday." Carol then gave Reggie a hasty kiss before he went into the bathroom. Halfway through his shower, Carol knocked on the door and said "I'm leaving. I love you."

"I love you too, baby. Have a successful trip."

CHAPTER 24

A light dusting of snow covering the ground greeted Reggie on this second work day after his honeymoon. The tattered landscape visible the day before hid itself under the falling snow giving the illusion of being in a wonderland where all is well. Reggie took a deep breath and wondered if it were a sign. He arrived at his office, shook his hat and coat to remove the snow, and then sat down to take a few moments of relaxation before facing whatever was in store for him. Just as he was about to lean back and prop his feet up on his desk, there was a light knock on the door followed by an uninvited entry.

"Hey fellow, how is married life treating you? Keep the honeymoon going as long as you can, because the day will come when you will have no doubt that it is over. So milk it dry while you can," Gordon said through a forced, nervous smile.

"So far so good," Reggie said anxious to hear what was on Gordon's mind.

"Well, my man I'm moving on, got a great offer from another agency. My last day is Friday. When I found out I had the job, I spoke to Henry about his plans for you. He said with the affirmative action plan approved and the first intern identified, it would be okay to move you back to the Texas Oil account, unless you wanted to remain with the affirmative action program. That program is new and could produce some great opportunities for whoever works with it. I know this is probably a surprise and you probably need some time to think about it and discuss it with your wife. Do you think you might know by the end of the week?" Gordon asked with his hand shaking and as he crossed then uncrossed his legs.

"Well, congratulations, I'm really going to miss having you around, but when opportunity knocks you have to grab. You have to promise to keep in touch. I don't need time to think. I want to return to the account. What's the deal?" Reggie asked, hoping Carol was onto something when she said the agency might have something positive in store for him.

Gordon began shifting in his seat as if he had a back problem. When he started to speak, he stuttered then took a sip of his coffee. "Okay, that's good," Gordon said sheepishly. "What we have worked out is to have you and Rick jointly manage the account. You have a good relationship with the creative team and that's a plus for the account. Rick has been working with the client recently and we don't want to interfere with that. So we thought those relationships could continue. I spoke with Rick and he totally bought into it. He's looking forward to working with you. You guys will make a great team for the time being. Of course as you become more familiar with the business, you will get your own account and so will Rick. But for now the agency needs you all for this account. You have great potential and I know you are going to do well in this business. I'll keep in touch and always be available to advise you." Gordon leaned back in his chair and exhaled.

"Don't you think I have more experience working with the client than Rick?" Reggie asked trying to manage his anger. He didn't want to let it all out on Gordon because he liked him and believed that he had spoken up for him and probably lost the battle.

"It's about even I would say and his is more recent than yours. Clients are sensitive about things like that. You are going to be all right and at least you are back into what you came to the agency to do. The way you handled the affirmation action plan and the Intern program made a good impression on the president and Henry. So don't worry, things are going to work out for you."

"Okay, Gordon, if you say so. I'm going to hold you to that," Reggie said while still harboring some doubts and resentment. When Gordon left, Reggie closed his door and sat at his desk. His mind drifted back to the advice his class was given when he graduated from high school-"If you can take it you can make it." He bit his bottom lip and said, "maybe." He felt a nature call and started to go to the bathroom. When he opened his door there stood an immediate test of whether he could take it.

"Good morning Reggie congratulations on your wedding. How are things going for you? Blissfully I hope." Rick said through a nervous smile. "I understand you have decided to return to the Texas Oil account. I think we will make a good team. I'm looking forward to us working together. Do you know when Henry has agreed to release you? I just spoke to Gordon and he would like to meet with both of us to bring us up to date on things. Are you available this afternoon around two?" He asked as if he were rushing through a speech he dreaded giving.

"I haven't had a chance to speak to Henry, but I can make a two o'clock meeting," Reggie answered without the display of any emotion. Rick extended his hand for a shake and Reggie reciprocated.

"Okay, I will see you at two," Rick said as he wasted no time turning around and heading down the hall.

Reggie sat back down in silence, wondering how much crow he would have to eat to make this work. Maybe, he thought, the agency was testing him to see if this Black man has what it takes to make it in this very competitive business. He wondered what was the definition of an even playing field in this business and, if one existed, was there a different threshold for Blacks? He tried to think back to see if he had displayed any behavior that was considered typically Black that may have turned off someone. He wondered if the whole scenario was dictated by Texas Oil. He wished he could talk to someone who would understand what he was experiencing; but there was only Jeff who would probably see things more bleakly than he did and he didn't want to hear that kind of thinking at the moment. He pounded his fist on the desk then remembered he was on his way to the bathroom.

Promptly at two, Reggie walked into Gordon's office. Rick was already there speaking in a whisper tone which he ceased as soon as he saw Reggie. Reggie felt like a heavy meal had parked in his stomach. Gordon had cleared the walls of his art and the pictures on his desk and book case. Rick had placed pieces of his art on the walls and there were boxes around the floor which Reggie concluded belonged to Rick. Reggie hadn't given any thought to the office assignments until then. Rick was inheriting the big office and obviously he would return to his smaller office which would immediately define the relationship between them. Things were unfolding exactly as the rumor Jeff had relayed. There wasn't really an agenda for the meeting. It appeared Gordon just wanted to get the two together. He said as soon as possible Rick should brief Reggie on the last meeting with the representatives from Texas Oil. He then tried to ease the tension in the room that he detected by joking about "mooning" everybody at the end of the going away party that was scheduled for Friday. Reggie forced a smile and Rick let out over reacting nervous laughter.

On his way back to his office, Reggie passed the reception desk where Harriett was sitting. When he realized where he was and saw Harriett, his first reaction was an embarrassing awakening. He had forgotten that when he returned to his old office he would have to see Harriett on a regular basis. He quickly regrouped and said, "Hello." She did not say a word. She just looked at him with a gotcha kind of smile as if basking in his obvious misery and then turned her head back to her desk.

.

When Carol called that evening, Reggie put up a front that things were working out at the office. He told her that Gordon had looked out for him and he was satisfied with the new arrangement. He didn't want to hear Carol utter that word, "paranoid" again. He shifted the conversation to how things were going in Seattle. Carol was enthusiastic about how well the meeting with the company had gone and she felt sure they would get the contract they were pitching. Reggie congratulated her in an upbeat tone.

"I'll see you Saturday baby and we will celebrate. Until then, I love you."

"I love you, too. Have a good night's rest," Carol said.

Reggie hung up the phone and began pacing the floor. He walked to the window and starred at the pedestrians trampling through the slush that had devoured the newly fallen snow and uncovered the dark dirt that had been hidden under the morning wonderland. Feeling the stress of the day crumbling down on him, Reggie crawled into his empty bed and drifted off to sleep.

He woke up feeling tired. He looked at the clock and realized he had been asleep only about an hour. He lay there being bombarded with a replay of the events of the day and thoughts of what might still be coming. He tossed and turned and kept looking at the clock. At some point he must have fallen asleep because when the alarm clock went off, he realized he was coming out of sleep.

After depositing his hat and coat in his office, Reggie decided to check with Barbara about some things he wanted her to order for his old office. After giving her his list, he asked where Gordon and Rick were. Barbara informed him that Gordon would not be back until Friday for the farewell party and that Rick had gone to Houston to meet with the people at Texas Oil, but he would be back tomorrow. Reggie felt blood had been drained from his face. Rick had made no mention of his planned trip. At that moment, Reggie remembered the Christmas party where Rick was huddled with someone and pointing at him in anger and Gordon's conversation with the president who seemed embarrassed when making eye contact with him. He wondered if this whole thing started then.

Rick returned the next day, but made no attempt to contact Reggie. Over the next couple of days, Reggie made several trips to the compound to transfer things to his office. Rick's door was always closed and he was always on the phone. At Gordon's party, he came to the conference room where the party was being held after it had been going on for about an hour. He avoided any contact with Reggie.

Jeff walked up behind Reggie and said, "Hey fellow what's up? What are you drinking?"

"Hey Jeff," Reggie said. He immediately felt like spilling his gut about everything. "This is a scotch and ginger ale."

"Getting a good start to your weekend, huh?" Jeff said in an inquisitive tone hoping it would give Reggie the license to talk about what was obvious to Jeff.

"I think I need more than this drink to escape this place. I'm having a hard time figuring out what Rick's up to. He seems to have forgotten we have equal responsibility for the Texas Oil account."

"Hey man, let me give you some advice about what you are up against. I've observed these bastards enough to know what they and I do mean they are up to. Rick's probably got his marching orders, not that he needed any. He is such a snake. He would be trying to sock it to you even if he was not being used to do the dirty work of the agency and I would venture to say the president. Trust me, when they found out the Department of Labor bought into that worthless piece of paper that was the end of their commitment to affirmative action and the Intern program. Now they don't know what to do with you because, I am sure, Texas Oil has made it known they would prefer to have someone other than you handling their account. They would never fire you, but Rick's job is to make you so uncomfortable that you will leave on your own. Gordon was your rabbi and he is gone. If I were you I would update my resume and contact a headhunter to find you another job."

Reggie felt Jeff was telling the truth, but hearing it felt like Muhammad Ali had landed one right in the middle of his face. His mouth went dry and he could feel sweat rolling down his back. He took a sip of his drink, trying to moisten his tongue so he could utter words without stuttering. "Thanks, man, I need to digest all this and get myself together. Do you know any headhunters?" Reggie asked, dropping his head.

"What are you up to after work? Want to stop for a drink?" Jeff asked as he patted Reggie on his shoulder. Just as Reggie was ready to say, yes, he raised his head and there standing next to him was Harriett with a look that could have stabbed him if her eyes were swords.

"Are you ready to go?" Harriett asked Jeff in a hostile tone.

"Yes, yes I'm ready. Reggie are you coming along?"

"No man, I have to get home. Thanks for the invitation."

"Okay, I'll see you around," Jeff said. He and Harriett started walking toward the door when Rick swept by them and dashed out the room.

Reggie stood nursing his drink. He wanted to have a last word with Gordon hoping for some explanation that would counter Jeff's account, but Gordon was bombarded with well wishers. So Reggie rested his drink on a table and walked out of the room. When he walked into his empty apartment, he headed straight for the bar and mixed himself a drink. He sat down in the dark without television or radio and began to down his drink. His mind couldn't focus. He tried to block out everything Jeff had said. He tried to come up with a strategy to out- do Rick. He wondered if he should contact Gordon and ask his advice, but none of those thoughts would stick. He began to pace the floor and, without prior thought, picked-up the telephone and dialed his mother.

"Hello mom this is your baby calling. How are thing going down there?" He asked, trying to hide the weight of his depression.

"Oh Reggie, it's so good to hear your voice. How are you doing son? You have been on my mind. I have been praying that the Lord will take care of you. I dreamed the devil was trying to torment you. Are you all right?"

"I'm hanging in there, mom. There are always hard things to cope with, but your prayers must be working because I am doing fine. Keep praying for me, but I am okay now. How are thing going with you?"

"Well, son I don't want you to worry, but the devil is at work here. My knees are sore from all the time I spend on them seeking the Lord's help. It seems Doug and Doris had one of their fights and she ran off leaving Doug Junior behind. Doug says she is with some man she had been messing around with. Anyway, Doug Junior is here with me. He's good company, but I have been feeling poorly lately, just the results of getting old. But I know my Lord will take care of me, so don't you start worrying about me or what's going on with Doug and Doris. Those two will probably never amount to anything. Thank God I'm here for Doug Junior."

"Mom are you sure you are okay? Do you need anything? Do you need any money?"

"No son, I'm going to be all right. The Lord watches over me. Don't you worry. How is Carol?"

"Carol is fine. She has been on the west coast this week on business. She is due back tomorrow."

"Well, give her my regards."

"Okay, mom, now you let me know if you need anything."

"I will son. I love you and the Lord loves you and He will watch over you. Don't forget to pray and ask for His guidance."

"I love you too mom." Reggie said clinging to his mother's reassurance of her love. He laid down the phone feeling some relief, but new concerns about the state of things back home which drove him searching for another distraction. He decided he would get up early the next morning, go shopping and prepare a home cooked meal, for a change, and surprise Carol.

"What is this I smell?" Carol asked as she entered the apartment.

"Hello baby, it's your chef preparing a meal for his favorite customer," Reggie said as he embraced Carol and kissed her on the cheek. "Welcome home, baby I really missed you."

Through sagging eyes illuminating her fatigue, Carol said, in an attempt to project an upbeat mood, "It's really great to be home. I've been thinking all week about the moment I would be back in your arms. How have they been treating you at work?"

"I'll catch you up on all that after you have praised my hot meal. Why don't you get settled? By then I'll have everything ready. Here, take this glass of wine to get you started."

"Are you trying to get me drunk again so you can take advantage of me?"

"Maybe," Reggie said with mischief in his eyes as he juggled the pots and pans nursing his various dishes

"Well, what do we have here?" Carol asked flaunting her blue jeans and one of Reggie's shirts unbuttoned down to her navel.

"Have a seat at the table. You will know soon enough."

"La, La, La!," Reggie said as he unveiled the pork chops, mashed potatoes, green beans, and hot store bought rolls.

"Oh Reggie, that looks great! I wouldn't trade you in for anything," Carol said feeling the impact of the wine adding to her fatigue.

"Well, that's why I prepared this meal. I wanted to make sure I could hold on to you." Reggie said joking.

After tasting everything and extending her great appreciation for his efforts, Carol asked, "Now tell me what has been going on at the office."

"Well, I have been hung out to dry," Reggie said with a forced smile.

"What does that mean?" Carol asked through a curious smile.

"Well, the agency has used me and now they have shoved me to the sideline."

"Yes," Carol said looking for more details.

Reggie went into the details of what had occurred since Gordon's departure. He ended by saying, "I think they have given Rick the responsibility of forcing me out, now that they have a stamp of approval from the government to do nothing about improving opportunities for minorities."

"Are you sure you have all the facts about what's going on? There could be a lot of reasons and it's possible none could have anything to do with your race." Carol asked with a bit of irritation in her voice.

Her words hit Reggie like a fast moving, ten pound stone. His hands began to shake as he responded, "I never said it was about my race."

"No, but be honest, it's what you were thinking. If you are going to make it in this world you're going to have to change your way of thinking," Carol said this time with obvious irritation.

That response was like the stone had made a U turn. "Carol you don't really know what you are talking about. Prejudice does exist in the society we live in. Where is your memory of the mission of Martin Luther King?"

With a bit of anger in her voice, Carol snapped back. "I followed Dr. King and supported him all the way. I'm not naïve, but things have changed in the country."

"Okay, okay Carol," Reggie said as he raised his hands in a surrender mode. However, he had been wounded. They sat in silence as they finished the meal. Carol felt fatigue closing in on her and announced. "If you don't mind I'm going to turn in. I'm exhausted."

"Go ahead, I'll clean up," Reggie said feeling he again had been put out to dry.

CHAPTER 25

Reggie sat leaning back in his chair bouncing a pencil against the desk trying to think of a strategy to deal with this situation when the door swung opened.

"Morning Reggie, how are you doing? Let me apologize for not getting with you sooner. With your moving between offices and the president pushing for a meeting with the folks at Texas Oil in Houston, there wasn't much time left for us to sit down. Nothing significant has happened that we need to discuss. First of all, with this new responsibility, I think you need a better office. I have secured a larger space for you near the creative team. It will be convenient for you in working with those guys. Barbara has set it up and you can move in today," Rick said looking everywhere in the room except into Reggie's eyes.

Reggie was trying to overcome the surprise of Rick's abrupt entry and what appeared to be an effort to correct a bad start to their relationship. He had successfully disarmed any thoughts Reggie had about confronting him about his seemingly negligent behavior. "Thanks man, that's thoughtful of you. We should establish some kind of schedule for getting together to keep up with what's happening on the account," Reggie said.

"Definitely, why don't you get settled and I will have Barbara set up something."

"Okay, I look forward to that," Reggie said feeling maybe Carol was right about things may not be the way he had perceived them. He thought about calling Carol that evening and sharing with her his conversation with Rick and taking her out to dinner when she returned from Washington and Atlanta Friday night. He walked over to Barbara's desk and said, "I understand you have set up a new office for me."

"Yes, I have. You know it's on the seventh floor. I'll take you down to it," Barbara said without making eye contact with Reggie. She nervously started searching for something on her desk and finally picked up a set of keys. "Here they are," she said as she walked a bit hastily ahead of Reggie toward the elevator. Her behavior was contrary to how the two usually related. Reggie thought she must be having a bad day, so he refrained from asking her if everything was okay. When they arrived at the office, she opened the door and said. "I hope you like it. It's certainly larger than your old office. Let me know if you need anything," She said as she wasted no time heading out.

Reggie stood in the middle of the office taking it all in. It was larger, but not much. The window space was no more than what he had before. There was a new couch. Not bad, he thought. The one thing he relished the most was he wouldn't have to pass by Harriett every time he walked through the reception area. He paced the floor and checked out the view from his window which was no different from his old office. He then organized his personal belongings as he waited for the call from Barbara to set up that schedule of meetings with Rick.

The rest of Monday passed by, then Tuesday and Wednesday with no sight of Rick or a call from Barbara. Reggie dialed Rick's number and Barbara answered. She told him that Rick was not in and that she would give him the message to call back. Her tone of voice was more formal than usual and she sounded ill at ease. He hung up the phone and decided to take Gordon up on his offer to be at his disposal whenever he needed him.

"Well, what's it like in your new world Mr. Senior Vice President?"

"Hey Reggie, good to hear from you man, how is life at Benton, Barnes and Fowler?" Gordon asked in a tone of true excitement.

"Well, I hate that my first call to you is about trouble, but you said I could call any time."

"No problem, what going on?" Gordon's voice became quiet and concern.

"I've been moved to the seventh floor in what Rick called a better office in keeping with my new responsibility. But I think I have just been shoved out of his sight so he could be comfortable ignoring me. I haven't seen or heard from him since I've been here. I'm sitting here with nothing to do but look at the walls. Can you shed any light on what's going on here or what I should do?"

"Listen Reggie, I thought things would work out the way it was described to you. But that doesn't seem to be happening. Rick is a snake and can't be trusted. You are going to have to confront him and keep reminding him of everything he promises. He convinced the president that he was the man to take over my job and that he would keep the agency out of trouble in dealing with you. They wanted to leave you in personnel, but when you turned down that idea, they had to come up with a back-up plan. I was sure you had figured that Henry isn't too strong on affirmative action and taking that job would have been a dead end for you. So man, you are up against a tough situation that is going to keep you on your toes at all times. You are right; Rick thinks putting you on the seventh floor will make it easy to keep you out of his hair, but you can stay on his ass by calling and marching up to his office."

"Thanks man, you have helped to open my eyes." Reggie said feeling like a laxative he had taken was just beginning to work.

"Don't hesitate to call me whenever you need to. I'm here for you. We'll have to get together for lunch as soon as I am settled here."

"Thanks again. I'll keep in touch." Reggie hung up the phone and, for the first time in a long time, he felt like an angry Black man, betrayed and alone in a sea of deceitful whiteness surrounding him.

He stood at the window pounding his fist into his hand. He wanted to explode to someone, but there were no likely candidates. He was ashamed to give Jeff the opportunity to say, I told you so. He could only imagine Carol saying, paranoid, paranoid. He needed to get out of the place for a while and decided to go for a walk. It's not like anyone would be looking for him, he thought. He put on his overcoat and headed out. He bristled, when he was reminded that it was winter, then pulled the coat collar up around his neck and started to walk east with no destination in mind. He was hoping for some revelation that would guide him gently through the torment he was feeling. However, his mind kept returning to other testing moments. There was a flash of Carol's father harassing him about his work in affirmative action; Carol saying to people, "what he means," after he had clearly explained what he meant; the taunts from Carol's uncle during his trip to Martha's Vineyard; how he was ignored during the discussion of the wedding plans at the

Riverside Church; Carol's devastating passion call to Mandingo and her accusation of paranoia.

He felt like running to some refuge where he could hide from the world around him. He reached for the handkerchief in his pocket to whip the tears that the wind was drying on his face. He heard the loud sound of something flapping in the wind. He looked up and saw all those flags from different nations adorning the United Nations. He stood there staring at them seemingly in awe, shook his head side to side with a sad look on his face, then started to walk back to his office.

Just as he was turning the knob on the door, he heard the telephone ringing. He rushed in. His first reaction was, it's Rick apologizing and assuring him everything was going to be all right. He immediately picked-up the receiver and as calmly as possible said, "Reggie Morton here."

"Hello Reggie, this is Mrs. Walker, your mother's next door neighbor. How are you doing honey?"

"I'm fine. What's up?" Reggie answered feeling panic overtaking him.

"It's your mother. She has been taken to the hospital. I found her unconscious on the floor. I think she had a stroke. Douglas Junior is here with me. I haven't been able to find Douglas or Doris. I'm going to the hospital as soon as I get someone to take care of Junior. I wanted to let you know. I will keep you updated on her condition. You can call me.

Oh, God, how much more can I take? Reggie asked in silence. "Thanks for letting me know. Tell mom I will be there as soon as possible."

His heart began beating at a rapid pace. His hands started to shake. He felt weak in the knees. He stood over his desk, his overcoat embracing him, trying to figure out what he was to do. He finally picked up the phone and called to leave a message with Barbara for Rick that he would be out of the office for a few days due to a family emergency. However, much to his surprise, Rick answered the phone. Reggie immediately explained what had happened and said that he was leaving immediately. Rick emphasized that he should take all the time he needed and that he hoped his mother would be all right. He said he would be glad to have Barbara make plane reservations for him. Reggie thanked him and left for home. He called Carol's hotel and left a brief message and said that he would call her again as soon as possible.

As Reggie fastened his seat belt and the plane took off, he sat back in his seat and strangely felt some relief. His first thought was there was nothing he could do for the next two and a half hours and maybe the stress brought on by the initial shock of the news was beginning to stabilize. As he began to feel more relaxed, the thought crept into his mind that he had escaped the anguish of dealing with his assumed fate at the agency. At least, for a while, he would not have to make a decision about what he wanted to do and would not have to suffer the embarrassment of walking into that office and feeling everyone was whispering what a fool he was. Also, he would get a break from Carol's endless efforts to show empathy for something she could not relate to and her seemingly favorite description of him as being paranoid.

He sighed and accepted the scotch and ginger ale the stewardess handed him. After finishing the drink, his mind drifted to the situation at hand. What if his mother was permanently disabled, who would take care of her? What would happen to Doug Junior if Doug was too strung out to take care of him or what it would be like if he had to go live with his mother and some man who had no place in his life for children? Reggie rubbed his forehead and closed his eyes trying to recapture the earlier relief he felt.

Ladies and Gentlemen please fasten your seat belts and return your seats to their upright position. We will be landing in about fifteen minutes. The announcement hit Reggie like the words of a swimming coach urging a fearful beginning student to jump in the water for the first time. His heartbeat revved up its pace. He began to wonder what to do after picking up the rental. He immediately decided to drive directly to the hospital.

As he approached his mother's room what sounded like a prayer meeting traveled through her door into the halls. Reggie felt a bit embarrassed and slowed his pace thinking the service might end before he arrives.

"Lord, we know nothing is impossible for you. We ask you to lay your healing hands on Sister Morton and heal her," Rev. Bailey said looking toward heaven and holding Mrs. Morton's hand

"Yes, Lord, yes, Lord," a group of ladies repeated, lifting their hands toward the sky.

"We honor you and glorify your name and ask that you look down on your faithful servants with your shower of blessings," Rev. Bailey said. "Yes, Lord, yes Lord," The ladies repeated. "In the name of Jesus Christ we ask your blessings. Amen." Rev. Bailey said.

"Amen," the ladies echoed. Reggie tipped into the room. The ladies immediately noticed him and stood away as he walked over to the bed.

"Thank the Lord," Rev. Bailey said as he reached for Reggie's hand to shake. Reggie leaned over to kiss his mother. She opened her eyes and struggled to speak. "You're home, you're home," she finally said in a whisper then closed her eyes again.

"Yes, mom I'm here. I'm here. How do you feel?" Reggie said as he kissed her forehead and held her hand in his. However, she made no further response.

"Son, it's really good to see you. The words she spoke to you were the first ones she has uttered since being admitted. That's a good sign. Now don't you worry. The Lord is in this room and he will watch over your mother. Put your trust in him," Rev. Bailey said.

"Thanks reverend and all of you for your prayers. It's comforting to know that you all are here for her. It's a real blessing. I know my mother appreciates your caring," Reggie said still holding his mother's hand.

"Son, we are going to leave you with your mother. But don't hesitate to call any of us if there is anything you need. I will drop by tomorrow to see how she is coming along."

Reggie sat next to the bed rubbing his mother's hand, glad he got the first response from her and hoping for some more communication telling him that she was going to be all right. The door opened and in walked Doug with blood-shot eyes and the smell of liquor on his breath.

"Hey bro, I didn't know you had gotten here already. When did you get in?" Doug asked seemingly shocked, but relieved. "How is she doing?" He asked nervously standing on the opposite side of the bed from Reggie.

"She opened her eyes and spoke to me a few minutes ago. Where have you been? Mrs. Walker said she had not been able to find you," Reggie asked with irritation in his voice.

"I stayed at a friend's house last night," Doug answered, a bit fidgety. At that moment, a nurse with a friendly smile walked in to check on the level of medication being given intravenously.

"Hello, are you young men Mrs. Morton's sons?" she asked.

Doug, wanting to appear useful, responded, "Yes, we are. How is she doing?"

"Well, she is stable right now. We have to wait and see how she responds as time goes on. Visiting hours will be over shortly. I recommend that you all go home and get some rest. If there are any changes in her condition, I promise to let you know immediately. Get yourself a good night's rest and come back tomorrow and she might be able to communicate with you. The doctor will be here around ten and you will have a chance to speak with him then."

Reggie kissed his mother's hand then gently placed it next to her side. Doug led the way out of the room. He told Reggie he was parked in the lot across from the hospital. Reggie informed him he had rented a car and would meet him back at the house. Reggie felt restless, irritated and sad as he drove to the house. He wanted to light into Doug for his irresponsible behavior and make him confront his responsibility to take care of his son now that their mother was not able to. He wondered if that was a lost cause and would just be throwing Doug Junior into a totally unstructured environment that could have a lifelong negative impact. He thought about finding Doris and confronting her, but wondered if that would be just as bad since she abandoned him. Maybe, he rationalized, his mother's recovery time would be short and she would be up and about and needing Doug Junior to help her readjust.

When they arrived at the house, Doug went directly to Mrs. Walker's. After about ten minutes, he stuck his head in the house and said to Reggie that Mrs. Walker had insisted that Doug Junior be left with her for the time being, considering he had to go to work and his mother's condition. He appeared to be trying to stay out of Reggie's company. So he said, "I'm going home and get some sleep. Tomorrow is a tough day at the plant. I'll call you on my lunch hour to see how mom is doing, okay?"

"I'll see you tomorrow," Reggie said, frustrated that Doug had been drinking and was probably headed for some place where he could continue to indulge and forget the welfare of his mother and son. He wondered if Mrs. Walker had offered to keep Doug Junior or whether Doug had made the request. He decided that maybe it was better for Doug to be out of his sight for now. As soon as Doug closed the door, Reggie went to the telephone and called Carol.

"Hello, baby," Reggie said.

"Oh, Reggie I have been calling this number every since I got your message. How is your mother?" Carol asked with panic in her voice.

"She is stable for now. She recognized me and spoke to me when I greeted her. I'll have a chance to talk to the doctor tomorrow, but she was resting well when visiting hours were over," Reggie said trying to play down his anxiety.

"I'm going to arrange to come down there tomorrow," Carol said.

"No, not now, if she continues to show improvement, I'll be back to New York in a few days. If things get worse, I'll call you and discuss plans," Reggie said thinking that was the best strategy for the time being. It would be easier for him to deal with the family problems without having to worry about Carol visiting his home for the first time.

"Are you holding up okay? I have no problem coming down tomorrow to be with you," Carol asked.

"I'm doing fine. I thought she would be worse off than she is. So, I'm okay."

"Call me tomorrow and give me an update okay? I love you."

"I love you, too. I will call after I talk to the doctor."

Reggie crawled into bed feeling exhausted and immediately dozed off to sleep. He was awakened by the dream that kept coming back haunting him; however, this time when he looked out over the audience and saw his mother, she was looking up with her back straight as if it were the proudest moment of her life. Reggie sat up in the bed wondering why the change. He lay back down and fell asleep. About two hours later, he was awakened again- this time by the ringing of the telephone. He rolled out of bed and made his way to answer it.

"Mr. Morton this is the hospital calling. We urge you to come now. Your mother has had another stroke and her condition does not look promising." Reggie froze and his hands began shaking. All he could say was, "Thank you, I'll be there directly."

When he arrived at her bedside, she had already been declared dead. Reggie was in a daze. The nurse tried to comfort him. He pulled away from her and walked out of the hospital into the cold night air that was scattering the salty tears rolling down his cheeks. He immediately felt the void of that unconditional love he was always so sure of. He wanted to keep walking until he crossed the border into toy land where all his troubles would fade away. His tears ceased to flow and he could feel the salt they left behind crusted on his face. He became conscious of the discomfort of the cold and headed back to the hospital to face the reality of arranging to remove his mother's body. As he walked, those resting torments surfaced: his future at the agency, the destiny of alcoholic Doug, the future of Doug Junior and revealing his white wife to this Black community. He balled his left hand into a fist, pounded it into his right hand, stomped his feet against the pavement, looked toward the sky and said, "Why me? why me?"

CHAPTER 26

As the limousine drove the family to the church, it passed Reggie's elementary school. He noticed the nation's flag bouncing against the strong unyielding pole and waving in the air. His thoughts flashed back to that morning he rushed to class to announce the Supreme Court's decision in the Brown case. He remembered how his friends teased him about thinking he would be able to go to an integrated school that fall. He recalled those romantic thoughts his mother had about the inevitable opportunities the decision would bring to his generation. He remembered how disappointed she was when he talked about the advice the wealthy white families in Chicago had given him when he visited them his first Thanksgiving in college. She scolded him, saying their advice that Blacks lacked ambition and that he should break out of that mode, showed how little they knew about Black history and how such advice would deny his Black heritage. He remembered her reaction when she discovered he planned to marry Carol. He thought about the letter he got from his grade school teacher, Miss Wright, when he graduated from college, congratulating him for succeeding as a pioneer in integrating schools. He shifted restlessly in his seat and stared out the window seemingly in a daze as the school passed out of sight. Carol reached over and squeezed his hand.

The limousine came to a halt in front of the church. Carol in her mink coat and hat walked beside Reggie as they climbed the six steps into the church followed by Doug, Doug Junior and the rest of the family. Carol sat next to Reggie, Doug next to Carol and Doug Junior next to his father on the front row. Rev. Bailey stood in the pulpit greeting the gathering and praying that God would comfort the grieving family. A member of the choir rose to sing a solo-"Soon I Will Be Done With The Troubles of the World." She had the voice suitable for the Metropolitan Opera and she put her heart in the song. You could hear "amen" coming from all directions. Reggie cringed, embarrassed. Carol sat stoically resembling Jackie Kennedy at the President's funeral.

The solo was followed by scripture readings, reading of the obituary and comments from various friends. Those flowering comments citing Mrs. Morton's life work- visiting "shut-ins" and those confined to prisons- was comforting to Reggie. Rev. Bailey then rose up to delivery the eulogy. He delivered that same sermon he gave at Mr. Morton's funeral-taunting the congregation to get ready to meet their maker. Reggie was embarrassed, irritated and restless because of the length of the sermon and the theme. It seemed every time someone called out "amen", the reverend would be motivated to keep going. Doug was jittery, probably from the lack of a drink. When the sermon finally ended, Carol let out a sigh, probably unconsciously. Reggie noticed and felt more embarrassed.

Back at the house after the burial, Carol, seeming very confident, took charge, greeting guests as they arrived and inviting them to the table overflowing with food provided by neighbors and friends. Each guest thanked her, gave her a perfunctory hand shake and immediately turned to look for either Reggie or Doug. Carol noticed. At first she seemed offended, but appeared to recoup with a look of defiance. Reggie excused himself from one of the neighbors with the objective of giving Carol some support. Just as he was about to walk over and ask her how she was doing, Rev. Bailey walked in and seemed to engage Carol in a friendly conversation. They both were smiling. He took both of her hands into his, shook them then walked over to Reggie and again extended his condolences. He then paused, scratched his head and looked as if he just thought of a good idea.

"How long are you going to be in town Brother Morton?" he asked.

"I'm not sure. There are a lot of things that need to be attended to before I leave," Reggie answered.

"If it's not asking too much, could you stop by my office before you leave? There is a matter I would like to talk to you about."

"Sure, I will give you a call and let you know when I can," Reggie answered.

"I sure would appreciate it. In the meantime just trust in the Lord and he will guide you through this time of sorrow," Rev. Bailey said as he patted Reggie on the shoulder.

"Thanks reverend." Reggie responded, wondering what could possibly be on his mind. Was there some last message his mother left with him or did she owe somebody money?

The last guest finally left with bags of the food from the tables. Reggie went searching for Carol who had escaped to the bedroom and was lying across the bed with her eyes closed.

"Hey honey how are you doing?" Reggie asked.

Carol, feeling just a bit tired, but more weary from what she saw as the guests' deliberate efforts to disregard her position as Reggie's wife and Mrs. Morton's daughter-in-law. In an effort to hide her feelings, she casually said. "Oh, I'm fine just a little tired. I hope you didn't mind me disappearing for a moment," Carol answered.

"No, no, I wanted to do the same but couldn't get away."

"Your mother was well thought of. That's a great memory for you. I wish I had more of a chance to get to know her."

"Thanks honey it did make me feel better to hear people talk about the things she did for others."

"When do you think you will wrap-up things here and we can return home?"

"I don't really know what all has to be done, maybe a couple of days, no more than a week. But you should return without me. You need to get back to work."

"You need to get back to work also."

"Rick told me to take as much time as I needed and I have a feeling he means it literally."

"They always say that but they don't really mean it," Carol said with a bit of sarcasms in her voice and looking at Reggie like she was revealing a well- known secret.

"Well whatever, I'll be back as soon as I can; but it's okay with me if you leave tomorrow. I can handle anything that comes up here. By the way, have you seen Doug?"

"He left with Doug Junior about an hour ago. He said he was dropping Doug Junior at Mrs. Walker's. He was very fidgety the whole day. He was acting like a drug addict. Do you know if he is using heroin? It's epidemic among Black men in his class."

"What class is that? Doug and I came from the same class." Those words seemed to involuntarily roll off of Reggie's lips even though he definitely saw himself as having risen above his humble beginnings.

"Oh Reggie, I didn't mean any harm, but really you are different. You know that. You have done so much to improve yourself. Your life is the same as mine and my friends. Come on now, accept your new status and stop looking back."

Carol's words gnawed at Reggie. He felt confused as to how to respond. She was speaking some truths, he was thinking, but there was more to it than she acknowledged and or understood. He cut off the discussion by saying, with his hands shaking, "Doug is strung out on alcohol."

"You know I love you," Carol said as she walked over to him, squeezed him tightly and kissed him passionately. His response was less than passionate which made Carol feel more useless in that environment.

"If you think you will be all right, I'll book a flight back tomorrow. Are you sure you will be okay?" Carol asked as she pulled away from him.

"I think so," Reggie said relieved he would no longer have to worry about her as he faced the problems with Doug and Doug Junior and whatever caused Rev. Bailey to look so puzzled when asking him to stop by.

After kissing Carol good-bye at the airport, Reggie returned to the house and began to pace the floor trying to figure out what to do. He walked into his mother's room, opened her closet and stared at the dress he bought for her to wear to his wedding then began to shed tears. He lay across her bed hugging her pillow. Her last words to him flashed across his memory. "You're home, you're home."

He dozed off to sleep. He dreamed his mother was in Doug's and his room putting up new curtains and cleaning out the closet and smiling saying, "He's a man now and this room needs some changes." He awoke remembering the dream and feeling sad. He rumbled through the box where his mother kept important papers and found her burial insurance policy. He decided he was in no mood to tackle what to do with his mother's belongings or the house. First things first, he thought, and decided to deliver the insurance papers to the funeral home. Rev. Bailey's office was on the way so he called and asked if this was a good time for him to stop by.

"Brother Morton, it's a great time. I look forward to seeing you." His tone led Reggie to believe it was not about any debt his mother had left behind.

"Come on in Brother Morton. How are you? I'm so glad you have taken the time to see me. I know these are difficult times, but the Lord doesn't give us any more than we can bear. Just trust in Him."

"I'm okay reverend. What is it that you wanted to see me about?" Reggie asked feeling a bit impatient.

"Well, son before your mother's stroke she and I had a discussion about you. She had intended to discuss this matter with you and then she had the stroke. So I am left with the task.

The Anderson Computer company has been awarded a huge contract by the U.S. Labor Department to train young people who have dropped out of school to get their high school diploma and learn the skills of operating computers. This is a new field full of opportunities for our young people. It has the potential to change the lives of many of them who have gotten off the track to a responsible life. You are probably asking what this has to do with you. Well, your mother and I thought you were the perfect person to head this program. You have experience in the business world. Your mother tells me you have set up an affirmative action program for your agency. You understand the kids in our community. I don't know of any other Black person in this area with your kind of experience for this job. So your mother and I wanted to ask if you would consider applying for it. The president of Anderson has asked me to identify candidates. I feel certain if you are interested, it's your job. The salary is very good. So I was hoping you would at least speak to the president before going back to New York. You would be making a great contribution to the Black community if you saw fit to take this job."

Reggie sat stunned. It was the last thing he could have imagined the Reverend wanted to talk about. The idea seemed absurd. How could he possibly leave New York and return home. Also there was no way Carol would leave New York, especially to move to the South. He dismissed the suggestion in his mind, but in deference to the Reverend and his mother, decided to at least go for an interview.

"Reverend I am overwhelmed by your suggestion. There are a lot of things I would have to consider, but I would be willing to meet with the president."

"Well son, I would be grateful if you would. May I call him now and set up a time. I know this is a tough time, but since you are already close by it would be easier to do it."

"Go ahead, the quicker the better, I don't know how long I am going to be in town."

"I understand."

While Rev. Bailey was making the call, Reggie was thinking how he would turn down an offer from Anderson without embarrassing the reverend.

"Are you available tomorrow morning at ten?" Rev. Bailey asked Reggie.

"That would be fine," Reggie answered. Rev. Bailey hung up the phone, smiled at Reggie, shook his hand and said, "God bless you."

Can this man be serious? Is he blind? Didn't he see who I am married to? Did he ever think what that would be like living in this area? Further more, does he really think I would give up my career in New York and return here to take some jive affirmative action job? Maybe he's just trying to fulfill a promise he made to the president of Anderson; probably trying to convince white people that he is a leader in the Black community. These thoughts helped Reggie ignore what seemed like a budding curiosity about this job. However, it also ignited thoughts of what he saw as his status at Benton, Barnes and Fowler.

Ever since getting Gordon's assessment of the situation, he had intended to call Jacob Johnson recruiting firm, the one responsible for placing him at the agency. He wanted to explore the possibility of getting another job. As soon as he arrived at the house, he made the call. Mr. Johnson was not encouraging. He suggested Reggie hold on as long as he could and see what happens because there were not a lot of opportunities crossing his desk at that time. Reggie felt depressed and began to pace the floor. He finally concluded that he needed to spend some time developing a strategy for coping with what was happening at work. Maybe, he thought, its time to open up to Jeff and get his opinion. However, he felt he would need to invite him some place away from the office so no one would walk in on them unannounced, especially at this point in time, and find these two Black men engaged in serious conversation. They would immediately conclude they were plotting something sinister. That thought added to Reggie's depression.

The empty house filled with memories of his mother added another layer. He decided he needed a double shot of scotch and, of course, there was none in the house. The quickest way to satisfy that craving, he concluded, was to take a walk down to Sam's Café, the neighborhood watering hole, a place he had not set foot in since he left home for college. It seemed the same. The Pabst Blue Ribbon beer neon sign, though not as bright as it used to be, hung above the entrance. The tin Coca Cola sign remained plastered to the door. When Reggie walked in, he was greeted by the smell of barbecue and the sound of Sam Cooke's "Change Gonna Come" flowing from the jukebox. There, behind the counter, stood the tall, stocky, deep-voiced Mr. Sam with his stained apron clinging to his pot belly.

Indeed, nothing has changed, Reggie concluded, and this was not a place where he belonged any more. As usual, the place was dimly lit to give a cozy feeling. At that time of day, the place was practically empty. There was a couple at one of the tables, three men on stools at the counter engaged in animated conversation with Mr. Sam about Ralph Albernathy's inability to replace Martin Luther King. As soon as Reggie' s eyes adjusted to the darkness, he noticed at the end of the counter away from the three men, sat Doug with a glass in his hand and looking lost, abandoned, and downright pitiful. Reggie's temper rose immediately, but he quickly regrouped and remembered he was in a public place and needed to reflect the dignity he thought the people in the community expected of someone with a college degree.

After acknowledging the condolences of Mr. Sam and the three men, Reggie headed over to Doug who was already raising his glass and saying, "Come on over here brother and let me buy you a drink. What brings you here?"

"The question is, what are you doing here this time of day? Aren't you supposed to be at work?" Reggie asked in as best a concern voice as he could muster.

"I'm on bereavement leave for a couple of days," Doug answered in a slurred voice.

"What's happening with Doug Junior?" Reggie asked.

"I told Mrs. Walker I would pick him up after school today."

"What happens after that? Do you have some dinner for him? Are you prepared to get him some breakfast and send him off to school tomorrow?"

Doug snapped back, "He's my son ain't he? I know how to take care of him."

Doug's voice had gotten a bit loud so Reggie backed off and asked. "Where is that drink you promised to buy me?"

"Sam, give the man what he wants," Doug hollered out. Reggie began to feel sorry for him. He thought about his troubled life. But he wasn't sure what he could do to help him change and, more importantly, give his son the nurturing he needed to become a responsible man. In frustration Reggie thought to himself, is that my responsibility? His drink arrived and he took a couple of sips trying to appear at ease, but he was becoming anxious feeling out of place in the bar and depressed thinking about his brother's condition. He took a gulp and finished his drink and told Doug he had some things to do at the house and he was leaving. He began to feel a buzz from the drink during his walk home. When he arrived he filled a plate full of the leftover food from the funeral then fell across the bed and dozed off. When he awoke he looked at the clock and saw it was three o'clock in the morning. He wondered if he had slept through a call from Carol, but concluded that was not possible. He undressed and got into bed. The next morning he remembered he had that appointment with Mr. Anderson. As he prepared to meet him, he felt curious, but not excited and tried to think of what he would say at the end of their discussion that would not embarrass the reverend, if indeed a job offer were made.

Reggie pulled out his "dressed to impress outfit"-Navy blue suit, white shirt and a red, blue, white striped tie. This was in keeping with the impression he wanted to project to all the people in town-an executive in the advertising industry in New York. He also wanted the Anderson firm to want him even though he didn't want them. He walked into one of the newly constructed buildings downtown and found his way to the Anderson Technology Services Company. He was greeted by a very friendly young white woman seated behind a wood paneled reception station who said, "Good morning, sir. How may I help you?'

Sir? Reggie thought, things really seemed to have changed.

"I'm Reggie Morton and I have an appointment with Mr. Anderson."

"Oh, yes, Mr. Morton. I will let him know you are here. Won't you have a seat? He will be with you shortly. May I get you some coffee or tea?"

"No, thank you." This very friendly greeting was freaking Reggie out. Am I encountering born again Klu Klux Klansmen and this is their strategy to hook me then use me for their good, he pondered jokingly with a tinge of seriousness. The thought wasn't that discomforting, he concluded, because he was in a position to say, no thank you.

"Mr. Morton, I'm John Anderson. Thank you for taking the time to stop by and see me. I know this is a difficult time for you," he said extending his hand to shake Reggie's.

"How do you do Mr. Anderson?" Reggie responded offering a firm hand shake.

"Please call me John. Won't you come with me? May I call you Reggie?"

"By all means," Reggie said feeling more and more relaxed. As he stepped into the office he immediately noticed how different it was from those at Benton, Barnes and Fowler. There was a conventional desk, chairs and a table for meetings, no barber chairs or rocking chairs or stereo systems. Mr. Anderson looked like he was not much older than he was. On the wall behind his desk his degree from Harvard was prominently displayed. Reggie was impressed and felt more at ease thinking he could easily tell someone like this "no" to his offer.

"Reggie, I'm really glad to have a chance to speak with you. Rev. Bailey speaks highly of you. I'm sorry to hear about your mother. I can imagine what that must be like. I know what it would mean to me if I lost my mother. Do you have any sisters or brothers?"

"I have a brother."

"Well, at least you have someone close to share your grief. I don't want to take up all your time. Let me tell you what we are trying to do here at Anderson."

He went into a dialogue about the contract with the government to provide classes for young minority high school drop-outs to get their diplomas and train them in computer technology; the logistics of setting up the program; the staff size; the need for an executive director to take charge and manage the program.

And then he leaned forward in his chair, his eyes glistening, his hands raised as if to emphasize a point and said, "Computer technology is the future and we need to prepare a workforce to meet the demands of this industry if we are going to continue to be a world leader. Many of our schools have failed us and that hurts our industry, so we must take steps to bridge that gap. That's why Anderson has taken on this program."

He then leaned back in his chair, clasped his hands together and looked Reggie straight in the eye and said, "Of course we have a selfish interest in growing a competent workforce, but we also want our country to grow and we can't do that and leave minority young people behind. Your education, intern experience in business and your managing experience in the very competitive business of advertising seems ideal for managing this program. What you think? Do you think a program like this one can produce results? Can you see yourself in charge of it?"

Reggie was mesmerized by what he saw as John's honesty and dedication to making a difference. However, he chose the words of his response carefully, so as not to mislead this honest man who seems to have a favorable opinion of him.

"I think you are on to something about preparing the workforce for the future to keep the country competitive. I see no reason why the program would not produce the results you are seeking, if it is run well. I want to congratulate Anderson for undertaking such a program. I can see myself managing a program like this. It seems like a great opportunity. However there are a lot of things I would have to consider before making the decision to come on board," Reggie said feeling satisfied that it had come out just the way he wanted.

"Anderson would make it worth your while financially. Of course we would discuss salary once you have indicated your willingness to come aboard; however, depending on your current salary it's possible we could double it."

"I will take that into consideration," Reggie said calmly thinking wow, this guy really wants or needs me on board. I'm going to have to be creative in turning him down.

"We are hoping to get the program underway next month and I would be grateful if we could get your answer within the next couple of weeks."

"I promise to get back to you within that time frame."

"Thanks again Reggie for coming to see me. I look forward to hearing from you."

"Well that was a vote of confidence I haven't heard for a while," Reggie whispered to himself as he left the building. On his way back home, he stopped by Rev. Bailey's office to thank him for the referral. As soon as the reverend saw him, a wide smile spread across his face. He walked from behind his desk and pointed to a chair and asked Reggie to take a seat. "Well, young man what do you think? This seems like a great opportunity for our community and for one of our great sons. Your mother dreamed this would happen one day."

"I told Mr. Anderson that his company was to be commended for taking on the program and that I thought it had a lot of potential to succeed, but there are a lot of things I need to consider before giving him an answer about taking the position," Reggie said wondering if his mother was thinking he had returned home to take this job when she uttered her last words to him. He thought her greeting might have been, Son I'm so glad to see you. But she said "You're home. You're home." The thought made him uncomfortable so he dismissed it deciding, in her condition, she probably was not aware of what she was saying.

"Well, son I hope you will give it some serious thought. Pray on it. The Lord will show you the way. I'm going to keep you and your family in my prayers."

"Thanks reverend for all your help during this time. I will be in touch," Reggie said feeling some relief that he would not have to deal face-to-face with John or the reverend for a while. Driving back home, he concluded that what needed to be done to clear up all the issues left by his mother's death would take more time than he was willing to stay away from his job, so he would head back to New York and take a week's vacation later and come back. Hopefully, irreparable harm would not be done to Doug Junior before then.

He decided to take a slow drive back through the old neighborhood and found himself on the street where all the children used to gather on the day after Christmas with their new roller skates and spend the day racing each other. The street seemed narrower than he remembered. He passed the alley where they used to play stick ball. It was all covered with tall weeds. The faded sign, Bob's Market, could still be seen painted on the wall of the store run by the Jewish couple who kept a tight record of the credit that had been extended to his family. The store was now dingy with many empty shelves and run by Chinese. Reggie began to feel nostalgia for those innocent days. He remembered his goal then was to be a lawyer when he grew up. He thought how time had changed everything and how different his life was from what he had envisioned. He felt proud that Rev. Bailey's and the rest of the community's perception of his success is what sold Anderson on him for that important job. He felt sad they had no idea the price he was paying for that perceived success. He wondered if they had modified their perception of him after meeting Carol. He shook his head and vowed to make that positive perception a reality. He would take Gordon's advice and force Rick to deal with him. As soon as he arrived home, he made reservation to fly back to New York the next day. He called Doug and informed him that he was leaving and would come back at a later date to settle all unresolved matters.

His flight arrived at LaGuardia in the early afternoon. He decided there was plenty of time to prepare dinner and surprise Carol. He went all out with flowers, candles and wine. Everything was ready around six the time he expected her. At six thirty there was no Carol. At seven thirty, eight thirty, nine thirty, there still was no Carol. Reggie wondered if she was on a business trip she forgot to mention. The telephone rang. He rushed to answer it. "Hello, hello," he said. There was a pause on the other end of the line and then an abrupt disconnect.

Reggie decided to clear the table and put away the food. While standing over the sink washing the dishes, he became angry that she had not told him about her schedule and frightened that maybe something had happened to her. He wondered if that call was from someone looking for her and did not expect to hear a man's voice. He didn't want to alarm her family by calling or calling the police to see if there had been some accident. He decided go to bed and try to fall to asleep. He lay in the bed wide awake looking at the clock every ten minutes. Just after eleven, he heard the key in the door then saw the lights in the living room.

Carol noticed the flowers on the table and rushed into the bedroom and said, "Reggie what are you doing here? When did you get in? Why didn't you tell me you were coming?"

"First of all, where have you been on a week night?" Reggie asked in as calm a voice as he could muster.

"I met the girls for dinner and we got carried away and didn't notice the time," Carol said, seeming uncomfortable with the question. "How were things after the funeral? Are you all right?"

"I'm okay. I need to go back later to clear up things. I decided all the things that needed to be done would take more time away from the job than I could afford just now. So I'm heading back to the office tomorrow."

"I think you made the right decision," Carol said seeming a bit nervous as she prepared to go to bed.

"I wanted to surprise you, so I cooked dinner," Reggie said as Carol got in the bed.

"I noticed. You are so sweet. If I had the slightest clue, I would have come straight home from work," she kissed Reggie on the cheek, turned off the light and turned her back to him.

Reggie lay next to her with his eyes opened wondering what had just happened. He felt jealous thinking maybe some man, probably white, had moved into his territory. It brought back memories of that last time he was dumped for a white man. However, the thought didn't cause as much anguish as he thought it might.

CHAPTER 27

Reggie returned to work feeling tired from the lack of sleep and probably the stress of the past week. He called Barbara to let her know he was in and asked if he could speak to Rick.

"Welcome back. Are you okay? Did you get the flowers?"

"I'm doing okay and the flowers were beautiful. Thanks."

"Rick is in a meeting. I will have him call you when he gets out."

The day passed and there was no call from Rick. Another day and another day passed and still no returned call. Each time Reggie called Barbara would say, "I gave him your message." Reggie decided he would call the president and see if he could get an appointment to discuss his situation with him. After all, there was no other place to go. The president's secretary was very polite and said she would give him the message; however, there was no return call from the president.

By the end of the week, Reggie tried to rationalize what was happening. Maybe they were trying to make me feel so desperate that I would ask for the job in affirmative action. What in hell would I want with that puppet job? The only good thing that could come out of that would be I could continue to be seen by the folks back home as successful in New York and Rev. Bailey would not think harmful of me for not accepting that job. He felt like hitting something or someone. He snatched his coat from the hanger and stormed out of the office and headed for the bus home.

Reggie stood at the window in his living room staring out over the building's courtyard. He could see through the windows of the multiple apartments across the street that seemed stacked on top of each other. From the distance, the people seemed to be going about their business without a care in the world, eating dinner, watching television, moving about and in conversation. On the street, pedestrians were walking at a pace typical of New Yorkers- seemingly overly anxious to get to their destination. It seemed everybody else's life was in order except his.

"Hello honey, I'm home. What are you doing at the window? I hope you are not considering jumping out," Carol said, smiling.

"Well, not today," Reggie said in a serious, but forced jovial tone.

"Well, that doesn't sound too good. What was your day like?" Carol asked as she placed a box of pizza on the table and continued to move around the apartment, hanging up her coat and changing her clothes. Reggie turned from the window trying to face Carol who kept dotting in and out of his presence. "You might say my week," Reggie began but paused as Carol dotted back into the bedroom. In anger, he decided to continue talking. "I have been sitting in my office all week with nothing to do and nobody returning my calls about what I am supposed to be doing. It has been that way ever since I moved back to work on the Texas Oil account. I think they are trying to send me a message that I should move on or I should beg them for that nothing job in affirmative action. If that is what they are trying to do, I would rather move on," Reggie said definitively.

Carol returned to the living room in more comfortable clothes and said, "Slow down Reggie, has anyone said anything to you about the affirmative action job lately?"

"No"

"What makes you think that might be what's on their mind?"

"That's the only thing I could think of that would make sense considering how they have been treating me. Rick doesn't want me in his hair and they probably don't have any other place to put me and they would prefer I leave, so they won't have to worry about placing me," Reggie said with anger and sadness in his voice.

"Now Reggie don't," Carol said and then paused. She continued by saying "Let's not jump to conclusions so fast. They could indeed be trying to find another job for you. Sometimes, that takes a while."

Reggie felt added anger because he concluded that when Carol paused, she was about to again accuse him of being paranoid. "Well, why are they leaving me with nothing to do and no idea what is gong on? I can't sit there like a dummy. I'll go out of my mind"

"You have just gone through a tough time with the passing of your mother and that may have impacted how you view things right now. So why don't you cool down for a while and then see how things are turning out. There might be some things you are not able to see now. Let's not make any rash decisions," Carol said wanting to console him but feeling impatient with his constant victim attitude.

Reggie perceived Carol's impatience. He attributed it to her lack of understanding what he was experiencing. She seemed to always be measuring my behavior by her life experiences, he decided.

They ate their pizza, drank wine and watched television seated next to each other on the couch. Every now and them Carol would rub Reggie's head or shoulder. Reggie rested his feet on the coffee table and leaned back resting his head on the back of the couch. They both went in and out of sleep until they finally turned off the television and went to bed. Carol lay there feeling tension caused by a sexually dysfunctional partner and Reggie feeling the loneliness brought on by an un-empathetic wife who might be sending her love in another direction. He became furious thinking it could possibly be another Black man. That thought faded and then a more provocative scenario occurred to him. What if it really were a white man, then she must see something missing in me that I might not be able to overcome.

He began to think that there was a gap between Carol and him that seemed to be expanding as the days went by and he didn't know how to shrink it. He tried to go to sleep. He turned slowly on his side trying to keep from waking Carol. He brushed his hand over his head and it came back with hair in it. He was puzzled. He felt the nerves in his legs were on edge. He needed to move around. So he eased out of bed and walked into the living room and began to pace the floor. He felt the loss of his mother who he was certain would be praying for him if she were alive. Maybe prayers do change things, he thought. He bowed his head and closed his eyes and said, "Dear God, please help me deal with these situations and guide me in the direction I should go. Please help me, God. Please help me."

"Reggie, don't forget I have an appointment at the hair salon this morning," Carol whispered in the ear of what she perceived to be a sleepy Reggie.

"I remember," Reggie answered. "I think I will head up to Harlem and get a hair cut." After a cup of coffee, he decided to try and get to the barber shop before it got crowded. When he walked out of the subway station at 145th and Lenox Avenue, he encountered a part of Harlem's culture on a Saturday morning. Women on their way to the grocery store stopping at the truck parked on the corner with stacks of collard greens, slabs of salt pork, sweet potatoes, and sacks of peanuts; drug addicts crunched in the doorways of buildings; men peddling stolen jewelry and Jehovah Witnesses marching down the streets with their literature under their arms.

He felt anxious to get back downtown. As he walked to the shop, he was wishing he had found a shop in his neighborhood. There were elderly men in each of the three barber chairs and a young man sitting in one of the chairs for those waiting. Like a Baptist preacher at a revival, the young man was ranting about the revolution is coming and you better get ready. "There will be no mercy for the 'Oreos' (Black faces, white souls). They will be gobbled up like the white man," he warned. He was sporting an Afro and was only looking for a shape-up. Reggie nervously started turning the pages of the magazine on the seat next to him thinking he could be the object of that remark.

CHAPTER 28

After a chilly weekend with Carol where communication was at a minimum and they both avoided eye contact, Reggie felt anxious but somewhat relieved about returning to work. He stepped into the building with his shoulders braced and his head held high, projecting someone ready to tackle the day's project. As the door to the elevator was closing, Jeff jumped in. "Hey, man when did you get back?"

"Last week."

"I'll drop by your office now and catch up with you. I am really sorry to hear about your mother. How did you leave things at home?"

"As best as you could expect after a sudden death."

"How did you leave your brother?"

Reggie, feeling embarrassed, waited until they got off the elevator and then said, "He's got a lot of problems. I don't know what he's going to be like without mom to be on his back."

"Do you plan to go back and check on him?"

"Yes, I left a lot of stuff undone and need to go back when I can take more time off. As a matter of fact, I was offered a very important job just before I left and they are waiting for my answer." Those words just rolled off Reggie's lips seemingly without any prior planning. He surprised himself.

"What was the job?"

Reggie, in an effort to tone down any glamour of the job, in a casual manner, shared the details.

"Man, what are you going to do?"

"Nothing." Reggie said.

"You have got to be kidding. Man what an opportunity. With your experience and what you have gone through, you could haul a flock of young Black brothers and sisters off the streets and polish them up for good jobs. Man, you could turn their lives around and who knows you might discover another tycoon like that guy who owns Black Enterprise Magazine. And one day Ebony Magazine might do a spread on you. I would grab that opportunity in a minute. And you say, they could double your salary. You have got to be nuts to turn down an offer like that, especially when you compare it to this place. Come on man, if we don't give back to our less fortunate brothers and sisters, what are we worth? We can't afford the luxury of just going on our own. Our people have suffered too much. "

"Well, the way you put it, it is a great opportunity for someone. But what about my wife, she ain't about to leave her job and follow me down south."

"Well, brother I admit you would have a problem on your hands. If she was my wife and I was offered an opportunity like that, I would tell her come on baby or so long baby. Why do opportunities like that come along for people who don't know what the hell to do with them?" Jeff asked looking directly at Reggie and shaking his head.

"Well, what's going on here with you and Rick since you got back?" Jeff asked, leaning back in his chair seemingly trying to shed his frustration with Reggie.

With his head turned away from Jeff and reaching for his coffee, Reggie said, "I haven't been able to talk to him yet."

"And how long have you been back?" Jeff asked sarcastically.

"Yes, I know it doesn't look good for our relationship. I called the president and asked for an appointment, but I also haven't heard from him."

"And you still don't know what you are going to do about that job," Jeff said looking sternly into Reggie's eyes. "There is one way to bring this situation to a head. Why don't you offer your resignation? I guarantee you will quickly find out what they are up to. If they want to keep you on Texas Oil, they will have to come clean and set Rick straight. If they are looking to place you somewhere else, they will have to say so, or, if they want to force you to take that affirmative action job, they will have to fess up."

"Well, let me think about that," Reggie said, anxious to end the conversation. Jeff was making him feel like a selfish, ungrateful, hen- pecked lost Negro and was pushing him faster than he was ready to go to bring the situation to a head.

"I've got to go. If you need a firecracker put under your butt, stop by my office any time," Jeff said through a half grin.

"I'll remember that," Reggie said through a forced smile.

Although he was relieved Jeff was gone, he could not shake off the things he had said. He tried to paint Jeff as a Black Panther sympathizer incapable of understanding what he was going through; but it didn't work. Jeff had worked in this industry much longer than he had and survived, though not at the same level as he was. The idea haunted him that he would not take advantage of an opportunity to help people like his brother Doug turn their lives around. However, he tried to soothe his conscience by saying he could achieve some of the same results by succeeding in his current job, maybe not at the same level. He just needed to get things clarified.

As the day went on and his desk remained empty, no phone ringing and nobody asking to see him, Reggie decided he would call their bluff and drafted a letter of resignation addressed to the president with copies to Rick and Henry. He hand-delivered them just before leaving for the day. He felt relieved, but frightened. He stopped at a bar and had a couple of drinks to prepare him for explaining to Carol what he had done.

"Hey baby, it's me. Did you pick up something for dinner or should I go back to the deli?"

"No, honey, I brought some Chinese food. I'll be right out."

"Well, how was your day?" Carol asked as she kissed Reggie on the cheek.

"Come sit down and let's have our food and I will tell you all about it," Reggie said in a nervous, but jovial tone aided by his couple of drinks.

"Well, I'm down now. What brought on this happy mood?"

"I decided on a new strategy to deal with my situation. I turned in my resignation. I thought that would force them to resolve the situation between Rick and me," Reggie said leaning back in his chair and taking a bite of his chicken with mixed vegetables.

"You did what!" Carol asked raising her voice to a pitch indicative of shock and anger.

"I'm told that's the way they do things in advertising. If they think they are going to lose you, they will make your problem a priority and deal with it," Reggie said defensively as he felt the loss of the effect of his drinks.

"And who told you that? I bet it was Jeff and, of course, he sees things the same way you do," Carol said sarcastically feeling the climax of months of built-up frustration.

"What is that supposed to mean?" Reggie asked now feeling anger rising in him.

"You know what I mean," Carol said not backing down. "And why didn't you discuss it with me before you went off half cocked."

"I decided at the last minute. I got tired of sitting in my office doing nothing with people looking at me probably thinking who is that dumb fool who just doesn't get it? "

"Maybe those people would have had a point. What do you think is my role in this marriage-to satisfy your ego? We are supposed to be equal partners supporting each other. I love you and look what you do," Carol said with tears rolling down her cheeks.

"I love you too, darling," Reggie said while reaching for Carol's hand. He paused and then said, "I've heard that it takes more than love to make a marriage work." Carol was still absorbing the "I love you too," statement. She let that remark slip by.

"What happened when you gave them your resignation?" Carol asked pulling her hand away from Reggie.

"I turned it in and left. I guess I'll find out tomorrow"

"What are your plans if they accept your resignation without offering anything else?" Carol asked bursting in anger remembering her months of frustration.

"I guess I will move on. I know what I did was a gamble."

"Do you have any ideal where you can get another job comparable to what you have?" she asked, trying to control her anger.

"As a matter of fact I do," Reggie said as a quick response to keep Carol from thinking he actually was a fool. But he was not ready to discuss the job offer, especially when emotions were running high. He knew her next question was coming so he took a deep breath.

"Well, are you going to keep that from me, too?" Carol asked, sarcastically.

"While I was home, the reverend asked me to talk to people at Anderson Technology Computer Services. They offered me a job as head of their job- training program for minorities with a salary double what I am making now. I hadn't given it serious though, but I didn't want to embarrass the reverend so I promised to give them an answer within two weeks," Reggie said trying to look as apologetic as he could.

"So you are considering that job if Benton, Bowles and Fowler don't offer you something?" Carol asked with her hands shaking.

"You and I would have to discuss what options I have. I've made no decision. However, it's a tempting opportunity." Reggie said feeling defensive.

"First of all Reggie Morton, you need to overcome your past and take responsibility for life as it is today. Nobody owes you anything. You have to work hard for what you want. The rest of us do. And second," Carol said looking Reggie in the eyes without batting hers, "That would be the last straw as far as I am concerned if you decided to take that job. New York is full of all kinds of jobs. If you're not willing to confine your search here, you have pasted me out of your life. Whatever made you think I would leave my job and move to the South or that I would be compliant with a marriage where you were in one state and I in another? I love you but there are limits to what I am expected to put up with," she said with fury in her voice as she turned away and walked out of the room.

"I guess you have made your point clear," Reggie said totally sober in the face of what he considered an ultimatum. He immediately felt alone and rejected, but he couldn't hold on to it. A cloud of ambivalence swept over him. He tried to find the meaning of it. Was he relieved that the conversation had come to an end and he no longer had to argue with Carol; or was it that her words had awakened some suppressed feeling he harbored about the durability of their relationship?

He moved listlessly around the room and began to clear the table and put away the boxes of left-over food. He wasn't ready to get into bedroom and face Carol. He wasn't sure what to say or what he wanted to say. He walked back into the living room and began to gaze out the window at the bustling streets of Manhattan. He recalled the excitement he felt when he was told about the possibility of working in the most famous city in the world. He remembered that first time he ran into Carol on Park Avenue, that successful meeting he presided over with Texas Oil and the day Carol accepted his proposal. Tears welled in his eyes. He lay down on the couch and fell asleep watching television. He was awakened by the national anthem being played as the station was going off the air. He crawled into bed and lay there thinking I can't believe my future rest in the hands of Benton, Bowles and Fowler.

Reggie was scared but anxious to get to the office the next morning to see what his fate might be. He didn't have to wait long. There was a white business size envelope in the center of his desk. Seeing it made him feel like he was waiting for the results of the final exam he wasn't sure how well he had done in a course he needed to graduate. He laid his coffee and bagel on the desk, took off his coat and sat down, picked up the envelope, reached for the silver letter opener and tore into it and began to read.

Dear Mr. Morton:

I want to thank you for the great contributions you have made to the agency during the short time you have been with us. We will remain indebted to you. I want to wish you the best of luck in your future endeavors.

Again, thank you for your outstanding work for Benton, Bowles and Flower.

Sincerely yours,
Edward Fulton
President

Reggie leaned back in his chair the letter waving in his shaking hand. His heart was racing. He said out loud. "I called their bluff and they had the last laugh." The coffee and bagel sat untouched as he stared out the window realizing he was at a crossroad. He wished he was waking from a bad dream. He wanted to scream expletives at the top of his voice. His mind seemed to beg for some relief. As he fought back tears, he began to recall the moment he met Carol; the first time they made love; the pride he felt being the only Black member of his college's Student Centennial team and the only Black executive at the agency; how the white families in Chicago told him how smart he was; how his favorite college professor came to his rescue in a hostile racism infested environment. As he tried to hold on to those thoughts, another one seeped into his thinking. He couldn't recall where he heard it or who said it, but it would not go away. "Pioneers crack the shell and those that come after mold the contents into crusty breads, fruity pies and sweet cakes."

He leaned forward in his chair, rested his head in his hands, took a deep breath, picked up the telephone and dialed the number. The voice on the other end said. "Good morning, Delta Airlines. May I help you?"